A DETAILED HISTORY OF THE FAMOUS
B-24H-FO 15 42-52534
Witchcraft

790TH SQUADRON
467TH BOMBARDMENT GROUP (H)
US 8THAIR FORCE USAAF

Perry Watts

Schiffer Publishing Ltd
4880 Lower Valley Road • Atglen, PA 19310

Other Schiffer Books by the Author:
The 467th Bombardment Group (H) in World War II
ISBN: 978-0-7643-2165-8
Other Schiffer Books on Related Subjects:
Memphis Belle, Brent William Perkins
ISBN: 978-0-7643-1489-5
Clay Pigeons, Sage E. Helene
ISBN: 978-0-7643-3951-6

Library of Congress Control Number: 2015933486

Cover Designed by Justin Watkinson
Type set in Times New Roman

ISBN: 978-0-7643-4888-4
Printed in The United States of America

Published by Schiffer Publishing, Ltd.
4880 Lower Valley Road
Atglen, PA 19310
Phone: (610) 593-1777; Fax: (610) 593-2002
E-mail: Info@schifferbooks.com

Dedication

This book is dedicated to all personnel who served with the 467th Bombardment Group (H).

B-24H-15 FO 42-52534 *Witchcraft* as it was at the beginning.

467TH
BOMB GROUP

Contents

Foreword

Witchcraft is—according to some—a way of both placating the powers that be, and in turn obtaining their agreement to a plan of action that would otherwise be against the odds. "*Witchcraft*'s" achievement—in the midst of total war, where combatants' life expectancies could sometimes be extremely short—of 131 missions without loss of aircraft or abortion by technical mishap could suggest this was actually an appropriate name.

This book is my late father's second published book on the local US 8th Army Air Force's presence in our area of eastern England during the latter part of WWII. Sadly, it was also to be his last. I have the honor of completing it, in tribute to his passion for this subject and his unstinting help and assistance to both veterans and their families, and those similarly obsessed with this fascinating subject.

It is a fitting subject to finish on. Having traced the wide-ranging outlines of a typical (and yet really not typical!) 8th USAAF WWII overseas airbase in *The 467th Bombardment Group (H) in World War II*, this book focuses on perhaps the best-known feature of those bases—the B-24 Liberators that flew day after day, working for the liberation of occupied Europe. Hopefully, those who enjoyed the last book will find in this work more in the way of interviews, anecdotes, and references to "birds" missing from the former.

We move in a deductive curve from the particular to the general: *Witchcraft* was born in an industrial furnace—the white heat of America's wartime military industrial might—on a factory floor a mile long. It took wing as part of an ambitious US government aim to project concentrated and sustained strategic air power overseas for the first time—a sign of America's dawning superpower status. In so doing, this proved a strategic concept and approach that would be developed and refined in the testing Cold War decades to come. It was also the beginning of a long relationship that continues between the US Air Force and East Anglian rural communities.

I hope this book is a fitting tribute not only to those brave and painfully young aviators of the 467th to whom later generations like my own owe so very much, but also to a kind, thoughtful, and considerate man who wanted to pay appropriate tribute to those he first encountered flying in wide open Norfolk skies as a schoolboy seventy years ago.

James Watts (author's son)
Salhouse, Norfolk, England
May 2014

Preface

My name is Albert J. Shower Jr., and I am referred to as the "Son of the Colonel." I am honored to write the preface for this historic recording at the hands of Perry Watts detailing events surrounding the most famous B-24 Liberator of WWII—*Witchcraft*, assigned to the 467th Bombardment Group under the command of my father, Col. Albert J. Shower.

This book covers a detailed history of this particular aircraft from its coming off the assembly lines at the Ford aircraft plant at Willow Run, Michigan, on December 15, 1943, to the plane's final flight on September 15, 1945, to Altus, where it was finally scrapped. It is a shame this aircraft was not preserved in an aviation museum after having achieved such fame by making 130 credited combat missions without an abort.

Col. Shower was the commanding officer of the 467th Bombardment Group, to which *Witchcraft* was assigned on January 14, 1944, to the day it departed from the airfield at Rackheath, Norfolk, England, on June 10, 1945, for the United States, following the end of WWII in Europe.

It is really great that a book has finally been compiled about this unique and famous aircraft. The English people have honored us for our efforts during WWII by naming roads on the former airfield site at Rackheath as follows: "*Witchcraft* Way," "Ramirez Road," "Wendover Road," "Mahoney Green," and "Albert Shower Road."

"The Son of the Colonel," July 15, 2012

Acknowledgments

Information, photographs, and paintings from the following 467th Bombardment Group veterans and/or family members, Group enthusiasts, and friends which in some form are included in this book are greatly appreciated. It has enabled the author to compile a reasonably definitive history of that remarkable and outstanding B-24 *Witchcraft*. A great many thanks to all of them, although sadly, several of those good friends named hereunder have "folded their wings": Mike Bailey; Learned W. Barry; Janice Bates; the Reverend Martin Benians; Raymond A. Betcher, Anthony "Tony" V. Bell; Melvin L. Bland; Kevin Coolidge; Robert W. DeKerf; C.W. "Tommy" Dungar; Blackwell "Blackie" C. Dunnam; Paul V. Hatten; Max W. Hoffbauer; Col. Fred E. Holdrege; Brian J. Mahoney; Robert B. McEwen; Walter J. Mundy; John G. Oder; A. Lyle Prichard; Joe R. Ramirez; George W. Reed; William N. Scott; Louis J. Schiavo; Col. Albert J. Shower, Jay Shower, and Phyllis A. Smales; Ronald D. Spencer; Denis Sporle; Albert J. Steffen and John E. Stevens; Robert M. Stone; James E.P. Watts and Ed Wells; Andrew J. Wilkinson; and Leslie Willis.

I consider it appropriate to mention that without the kind assistance given by Col. Fred E. Holdrege—former commanding officer of the 790th Squadron, 467th Bombardment Group—and also by Ed Wells, whose father served with the 389th and 453rd Bombardment Groups, it would have been difficult to write the briefs on all the missions that *Witchcraft* flew. Fred kindly arranged for 2,093 pages of the original 467th Bombardment Group records prepared at Rackheath during 1944-45 and held at the National Archives and Records Administration (NARA), College Park, Maryland, to be sent to me way back in March 1999, but somehow, details of the first fifteen combat missions flown by the 467th Group were not found at College Park.

Fortunately, Ed Wells, who visited the Air Force Historical Research Agency (AFHRA) at Maxwell AFB, Alabama, in May 2001, to research and seek information relating to his father, by chance found the box containing records of the first fifteen combat missions flown by the 467th. (Mysterious as to how or why that one box of 467th Group records ended up at Maxwell instead of College Park!) But I certainly appreciate Ed sending me copies of all the reports relating to those first fifteen missions.

My appreciation to the talented aviation artist Mike Bailey for painting the two side-view paintings of *Witchcraft*: one depicting how it appeared prior to flying its first combat mission, and the other as it appeared following completion of its 130th credited combat missions; also for his permission to use photographs of his paintings of "*Witchcraft*."

A sincere appreciation for the kind support and thoughtfulness of Mr. Nick Hovey, chairman and owner of Tilia Properties, for perpetuating the memory of two individuals—Col. Albert Shower and Master Sgt. Joe Ramirez—as well as *Witchcraft* itself, by dedicating the name of local roads to them on the industrial site at Rackheath, which was the technical site of the 467th Bombardment Group in 1944-45.

Finally, the cooperation of Kevin Coolidge—a 467th Group veteran's son—in permitting me to use the detailed 467th Group combat maps is really appreciated. Kevin created the maps to honor his father, Myles Coolidge, a 791st Bombardment Squadron copilot in the B-24 *Bugs Bunny*/"What's Up Doc." Also appreciated are the detailed statistical records Kevin compiled relating to the combat missions flown by the 467th Group.

Perry Watts
1 July 2012
Salhouse, Norfolk
England

Introduction

Witchcraft—a rather strange word that many people shy away from, as they consider it to have some form of weird connection with sorcery, black magic, casting spells, and possibly connections with the "devil." Looking further into the description of the word *Witchcraft*: "The art or power of bringing magical preternatural power to bear, or the act or practice of attempting to do so. The act of magic or sorcery, fascinating or bewitching influence or charm." However, I would add that it is interesting that not a single flight crew member lost his life or was ever wounded while flying on the B-24 "*Witchcraft*." Very interesting words, but this book is not about sorcery or magic or such—it is about an airplane, which indeed was to become the most famous B-24 Liberator (four-engined heavy bomber) in the 8th Air Force, USAAF, during WWII.

Another important factor—as far as the author is personally concerned—relates to the fact that many of *Witchcraft's* flight crew members and ground crew members became personal and very close friends in the post-WWII years. It is with sadness I mention that most of those dear friends have "folded their wings" during recent years, but they will always be remembered by the author and his family.

Research on the building and operation of the Ford aircraft plant at Willow Run, Ypsilanti, Michigan—which played such an important and interesting part during WWII—revealed that *Witchcraft* came off the assembly lines at that plant in December 1942.

It may appear to some readers that I have written too much about the Consolidated Aircraft Company and the Ford Aircraft plant at Willow Run, Ypsilanti, but such detail is necessary, as it relates to the famous B-24 *Witchcraft*. Hence, that is the starting point of this book on the history of the plane, and hopefully, readers will also find the details about the Ford Ypsilanti factory to be of interest.

As the reader will notice, I have gone into great depth and detail and digressed somewhat on the 467th Group's Mission 10 to Hamm, Germany, in which *Witchcraft* participated—the ninth actual combat mission flown by *Witchcraft* (speaking solely on credited missions, it was the eighth credited combat mission). That particular mission to Hamm and the outcome is very interesting and resulted in quite a lot of comments by various crew members that flew on that mission that I have especially incorporated.

The author would also like to bring to the readers' attention the incorrect information that has appeared in books and articles that not only relate to *Witchcraft*, but also to the 467th Bombardment Group. It is accepted and appreciated that it is quite easy to be critical, and I am certainly not the first author to write and state that it is so easy to make a spelling mistake or an omission when writing a book or compiling some article for publication; even with proofreading prior to publication, it is still easy for a mistake to occur, and probably I will have overlooked some spelling or grammatical errors in this book. But I would refer to some of the mistakes relating to *Witchcraft* that have appeared in booklet form or local newspaper articles during the past recent years:

– *Witchcraft* "was built by Boeing at their Consolidated plant in San Diego." (I wonder what Consolidated thought of such a statement! – PW)

– *Witchcraft* was "looked after by a ground crew that became known as the 'League of Nations.' Her crew chief was Joe Ramirez, of Mexican descent. The other members of the ground crew were George Dong of Chinese/American descent; Joe Vetter of Dutch descent; Ray

Betcher of German descent; and Walter Elliott of just plain old American descent." (Not actually correct, regarding Ray Betcher and Joe Vetter—see paragraph titled "Ground Crew." I wonder what Joe would have said about this rapid demotion in rank from Master Sergeant to PFC—not in the official Group records, but unfortunately, recorded in four lines on one page in a book that I recently read. I do not think dear old Joe would have taken kindly to that comment – PW.)

There is also the matter as to how the 467th Bombardment Group acquired the title and was referred to as "The Rackheath Aggies"—a few erroneous quotes have appeared in various books or articles in the past, such as the following:

– "The Rackheath Aggies" name came about due to several of the American personnel based at Rackheath during WWII taking their clothing to be laundered by a Rackheath village resident, namely Mrs. Agatha Curtis, and hence, the American personnel based at Rackheath became known as "Aggie's Boys" and were referred to as "Rackheath Aggies" (note: "Aggie" being a slang term for the name Agatha).

– "The Rackheath Aggies" possibly came about by taking the name of a Texas football team!

– "As many of the American military prior to the war in civilian life were agricultural works—known and referred to as 'Aggi's'—hence the name 'Rackheath Aggies.'"

Extensive research as to how the name "Rackheath Aggies" came about proved that the quotes mentioned above are all quite plausible, but are indeed far from actual fact. How the name actually came about is mentioned as a footnote in the details relating to 467th Group Mission #166 on 3 February 1945 to Magdeburg, Germany (paragraph 6). The source of that interesting information is recorded in the diary of a former 467th Group copilot named Lt. William N. Scott, who served with the 789th Squadron (Lt. Robert E. Jacobsen's Crew #49).

1

Consolidated Aircraft Company

Details of How and Where B-24H-15 FO 42-52534 *Witchcraft* was built

B-24H 42-52534 was the 231st airplane out of 474 in the production batch 42-52303 to 42-52776 at the Ford Motor Company's aircraft plant at Willow Run; it came off the assembly lines on 15 December 1943.

The B-24—originally designed and built by the Consolidated Aircraft Company at their factory in San Diego, California—first flew on 29 December 1939. At that time, senior officers of the US Army Air Force were deciding what they should do regarding building up a strategic air force; they looked favorably upon the design and capabilities of the B-24 and decided it matched their requirements, but the production goal set by Consolidated to turn out one four-engined heavy bomber certainly did not. Ford Motor Company was approached in January 1941 by the Defense Department and, under the guidance of the Ford Company's Director of Production Charles Sorenson, a plan was drawn up for a factory for the production of B-24 heavy bombers. This was based on the techniques of the assembly lines used by the Ford Motor Company, but obviously on a much larger scale.

The plans drawn by renowned architect Albert Kahn for the Ford Willow Run factory were accepted, and remarkably, the building of the plant—commencing in April 1941—was completed six months later, in September 1941. At that time, the factory was the largest in the world, with a floor space of 3.5 million square feet—indeed, the main aisle in the assembly section was over one mile long. Providing housing for the some 14,000 workers initially caused some problems, as did a shortage of personnel, but such challenges were

The Ford B-24 plant at Willow Run.

Charles Sorensen

Albert Kahn

soon overcome when dormitories and residential housing were built. Workers were brought in from the South in June 1943, when the factory was employing a workforce in excess of 42,000. To counteract the manpower shortage caused by men enlisting in the military, a vast number of women were hired to work at the Willow Run plant and were paid in the region of .95 cents to $1.60 an hour—identical to the wages paid to the men. Michigan Central assisted the workers, who commuted daily from as far as Detroit, by running trains to the factory. Additionally, in 1943, a highway to Willow Run was built.

Production levels in August 1943 reached 230 B-24s a month, and steadily, month by month, the production level increased to 365 some four months later; at the end of 1944, with the factory working two nine-hour shifts a day, a total of 650 were coming off the assembly lines every month, which equates to 558 working hours to build 650 B-24s—slightly in excess of one B-24 every working hour.

A total of 8,685 B-24s were produced by Ford at the Willow Run factory prior to being closed in 1945. The first B-24 to come off the assembly lines on 1 October 1942, was named *The Spirit of Ypsilanti*, and the $300,000 cost of the plane was covered by fundraising campaigns organized by the people of Ypsilanti. The final B-24 made at Willow Run was first named *Henry Ford* as a tribute to him, but he did not want the plane to be named after him; he said that it should be named after the personnel who built it, so the name "Henry Ford" was removed and the workers wrote their names on the nose of the plane.

The basic concept was that the Ford Company would produce subassembly units supplied to the Consolidated and Douglas Aircraft Companies at Fort Worth, Texas, and Tulsa, Oklahoma, respectively. But Mr. Sorenson convinced the Defense Department that the factory would be able to build the B-24s at a faster rate and at a lower cost than any other company. However, the Willow Run plant did produce "B-24 subassembly kits" that consisted of the center wing section, nose section, aft fuselage section, and various other small assemblies. Initially, eleven small factories in Southern California—employing some 1,700 personnel, of which 90% were women—were contracted to fabricate bulkheads, electrical harnesses, plexiglas moldings, and upholstery for each B-24.

In 1940, less than 20% of the airframe components were subcontracted, but due to shortages of space, time, and manpower, new production methods were adopted; by 1943, some 100 subcontractors were involved in the production of "farmed out" components, such as tail stabilizers, bomb bay doors, and numerous other parts and accessories that were shipped to the B-24 main assembly plants, including the new Consolidated Aircraft Company factory at Fort Worth, Texas. Construction of this factory commenced in 1940; it spread over 438 acres and cost $22 million. In late-1942, the Douglas

The B-24 Assembly Line at the Ford Willow Run plant.

Aircraft Company, Tulsa, Oklahoma, was also used to turn out complete B-24s from "knock-down" kits supplied by the Willow Run factory. Also, in January 1942, the North American Aircraft Company was called on to operate an independent fabrication assembly plant in Dallas, Texas. Those plants operated around the clock with a three-shift system and employees working fifty-hour weeks.

B-24H-15 FO 42-52534 came off the assembly lines at Willow Run 15 December 1943, and after flight tests, was flown by a ferry crew to the Bechtal-McCone-Parsons modification center, Birmingham, Alabama. It was there for about three weeks, during which time combat modifications were made. On 9 January 1944, all modifications to B-24H 42-52534 were completed and the plane was ready for service with the USAAF. Within a day or so, an ATC crew collected the plane and delivered the new B-24 by way of Dallas and Amarillo, Texas, to the 467th Bombardment Group in Wendover Field, Utah, on 14 January 1944.

Finally, the old, odd piece of humor used by some when speaking about Willow Run and dubbing it "Willit Run"—well, it did run, and it ran extremely well; the production efficiency was "second to none."

2

Wendover, Utah

In late 1943, Wendover, Utah, was the main training base for the 467th Bombardment Group. At that time, it gave an appearance of sheer desolation, being surrounded by salt flats to the east and bare mountains to the west. The area was selected as an ideal site for an air base and training center mainly because of the Great Salt Lake Desert, with its smooth salt flats, coupled with such a vast area of uninhabited land; plus, an added advantage was the rail line running from the West Coast to Salt Lake City. It is interesting to note that in 1939 the population of Wendover was in the region of 100 people, and the nearest town with a population in excess of 600 was Salt Lake City, about 130 miles away.

In 1940, the US government purchased the land for the base and bombing and gunnery ranges. Construction at Wendover was commenced by the US Army Air Corps

The desolate area of the WWII base at Wendover. (Courtesy Paul Hatten)

in September1940, and continued right through to 1945, but the real building peak was reached in 1943.

The total land purchased by the US government was 1,820,000 acres. The area extended some eighty-frive miles in length and the width varied from twenty to thirty-five miles; as such, it became the largest bombing and gunnery range in the world.

The first unit assigned consisted of a detachment of one officer and ten enlisted men, who arrived on the base on 12 August 1941; a few days later, a contingent of forty men arrived, and they commenced building and setting up targets on the Bonneville Salt Flats and constructing an aerial machine gun practice range on the north side of Wendover.

By the end of December 1943, a total of thirteen USAAF Bombardment Groups had completed their training at Wendover, including three that had completed their training by the end of December 1942.

Buildings on the base at Wendover. (Courtesy Paul Hatten)

Capt. (later Col.) Fred E. Holdrege, 790th Squadron Commanding Officer.

Col. Albert J. Shower, 467th Bombardment Group Commanding Officer.

Photo of a hangar on the base at Wendover.

Enlisted men's barracks.

Lt. George W. and Mrs. Marjorie Reed outside their quarters (hut) at Wendover.

Lt. John G. and Mrs. Helen Oder outside their quarters at Wendover.

Staff Sgt. Robert B. McEwen during training at Wendover.

It was on 1 November 1943, that the 467th Bombardment Group, along with their newly appointed Commanding Officer, Lt. Col. Albert J. Shower, accomplished their 125-mile move from their base at Kearns, Utah, to their "new home" at Wendover for phase training.

An Air Transport Command crew collected B-24H-15 FO 52534 from the Bechtal-McCone-Parsons modification center, Birmingham, Alabama, and flew by way of Dallas and Amarillo, Texas, delivering it to the 467th Bombardment Group at Wendover on 14 January 1944. That same day, 52534 was assigned to the 790th Bombardment Squadron. The following day, the plane was assigned to Lt. George W. Reed and Crew #Y-15, and from that assignment date, Master Sgt. Joe R. Ramirez and his ground crew team became responsible for maintenance of the plane.

B-24H 52534 was flown by Lt. Reed and crew for the first time on 15 January 1944, on a handling flight of one hour forty-five minutes. The plane was taken on several practice flights, some of which involved rather long flight times lasting five and a half, six, six and a half, and eight hours (see the copy of copilot Lt. John G. Oder's log); most of those flights were local, except for six, including flights to and from Casper, Wyoming, and four practice flights while at Casper.

Following "phase training," B-24H-15 F0 42-52534, accompanied by a number of other 467th Group B-24s, flew out of Wendover for the last time on 12 February 1944, when it made the eight-hour flight to Herrington, Kansas; the first leg of its journey to "somewhere overseas."

Also on 12 February 1944, the ground crew and 108 flight crew members boarded troop trains at the Wendover rail depot for the first stage of transit to the port of embarkation at Camp Shanks, New Jersey.

USAAF personnel waiting to board troop trains at Wendover rail depot.

Crew Y-15 Enlisted Men at Wendover. Rear (L to R): Melvin Bland, Vernon Bundrock, and Robert W. DeKerf. Front (L to R): Henry Kubacek, Alexander McLean, and Robert W. McEwen.

HEADQUARTERS ARMY AIR BASE

SPECIAL ORDER
NO 42

Wendover Fld Utah
11 Feb 1944

R E S T R I C T E D

- E X T R A C T -

*　　*　　*　　*　　*

1. Following named O, AC, and EM, (pers indicated on List #1 which is atchd hereto and made a part of this order), Flight Echelon, 467th Bomb Gp, WP via mil ap fr this sta to AAF Herington Kansas.in the following manner: 30 Crews WP so as to arrive 12 Feb 44, 27 Crews WP so as to arrive 13 Feb 44, 1 Crew WP so as to arrive 14 Feb 44.

Upon arrival at AAF Herington Kansas the CG 15th Bomb Wg will relinquish control over pers to CG 21st Bomb Wg.

This is a temp change of sta.

Individual equipment and overseas aircraft only will accompany this orgn.

Movement will be accomplished by mil air and/or rail. If it should be impracticabl to accomplish entire movement by air, pers will continue journey by rail.

Travel by private owned conveyance is not auth.

$7.00 per diem in lieu of subs is auth O and EM while traveling by air.

TDN. 1-5250 P 433-01-02-03-04-05-07-08 A 0425-24. Auth Ltr Hq Second AF 18 Jan 44 file 370.5 G and Memo 35-15 Hq Second AF 18 Dec 43.

*　　*　　*　　*　　*

By order of LT COL CARTER:

MICHAEL J HAND
CAPT AC
Adjutant

OFFICIAL:

MICHAEL J HAND
CAPT AC
Adjutant

par 1
SO 42

-1-

Movement Order No. 42 for the Group's flight personnel to move out of Wendover to the AAF base at Herrington, Kansas.

3

The Ground Crew that maintained *Witchcraft*

The *Witchcraft* Ground Crew team—often referred to as the "League of Nations" team because of their varying ancestry—comprised the following:

19128274 Master Sgt. Joseph R. Ramirez—Crew Chief—of Mexican descent. (MOS #750 Airplane Maintenance Technician [Inspection and Maintenance])
39538285 Staff Sgt. George Y. Dong—Asst. Crew Chief—of Chinese descent. (MOS #747 Airplane and Engine Mechanic)
36559571 Sgt. Raymond A. Betcher –Aircraft Mechanic—of German/Irish/English descent. (MOS #747 Airplane and Engine Mechanic)
32796971 Cpl. Joseph J. Vetter—Aircraft Mechanic—of German/Dutch descent. (MOS #747 Airplane and Engine Mechanic)
17133803 Cpl.Walter L. Elliott—Aircraft Mechanic—American (MOS #747 Airplane and Engine Mechanic)
Note: The number shown preceding the rank is the Army Service Number and "MOS #" relates to the Military Occupational Speciality number.

The nationalities of some of the ground crew members mentioned in some articles and publications are often incorrect, with particular reference to Sgt. Ray Betcher. Quite often, Ray has erroneously been referred to as being of American or Dutch descent.

Master Sgt. Joe Ramirez and the four members of his ground crew team, along with all other members of the ground echelon and some 108 aircrew members, marched to the rail depot at Wendover, Utah, during the evening of 12 February 1944, and boarded troop trains to the port of embarkation at Camp Shanks, New Jersey. They remained at Camp Shanks for several days prior to boarding the USAT *Frederick Lykes* on 29 February 1944.

A Brief History of the *Frederick Lykes* Prior to the 467th Group Personnel Boarding it for the Atlantic Crossing from New York to the United Kingdom

After making a few crossings of the Atlantic in 1943 as a freighter carrying goods to the United Kingdom, the *Frederick Lykes* was bareback chartered to the US War Department for conversion as a troopship on 1 July 1943. In late-1945, the vessel was declared surplus and was re-delivered to the US War Shipping Administration (WSA), Norfolk, Virginia, on 13 February 1946, and that same day, was transferred by the WSA to the Lykes Brothers Steamship Company. Ownership of the vessel changed on 14 April 1965, and it was renamed SS *Harbor Hills*. In 1966, the vessel was renamed again, becoming the SS *Kings Point*, and remained in service until 1971, when it was sold as scrap and made her final voyage to a breaker's shipyard in Keelung, Taiwan.

467th Military Heritage Database
Personal Biographical Questionnaire

Please print, type or write legibly all answers to this questionnaire. Attach and identify all photos, clippings and additional information that you want returned to you. Please forward personal memories, experiences and stories on separate pages. Your stories are one of the most important parts of the 467th B.G. historical records. **All 790th Bomb Squadron members also please send a duplicate copy of your response to Fred Holdrege, 2901 Friendship Rd., Durham, NC 27705.**

Last Name: BETCHER First: RAYMOND Initial/Middle Name ALBERT
Address: 828 BEACH BUGGY LANE City LINDEN State MI Zip 48451-9695
Phones (810) 735-6326 Fax E-Mail
World War II Addresses: 19335 WALDRON AVE, ROSEVILLE, MI & 100 LINCOLN AVE, MT. CLEMENS, MI
Date of Birth 03-23-22 City DETROIT State MI Nickname RAY
Date ~~Enlisted~~ DRAFT 1/21/43 City DETROIT State MI Spouses Name DORIS (M.8-29-43)
Date Deceased (if Applicable) DORIS 07-23-91 Other Relatives OPAL (M.05-08-93)
Military Training INDUCTED CAMP CUSTER, MI BASIC ST. PETERSBURG AND CLEARWATER, FLORIDA THEN MECHANICS SCHOOL, GULFPORT AND WILLOW RUN THEN 467TH AT SALT LAKE CITY
Schools Attended AIRCRAFT MECHANIC, GULFPORT, MISSISSIPPI & B-24 SCHOOL WILLOW RUN, MICHIGAN
8th AF Group(s) 467TH Squadron(s) 790TH
Serial Number (En) 36559571 (Off) Date Assigned 467th SEPT. '43 SALT LAKE CITY
Military Rank(s) with the 467th B.G. CORPORAL TO SERGEANT Duties AIRCRAFT MECHANIC
Arrived at ETO base MARCH 1944 Arrived from WENDOVER, UT TO CAMP SHANKS, N.Y. AND LIBERTY
Details of Transport SHIP FREDERICK LYKES TO GLASGO, SCOTLAND AND TRAIN TO RACKHEATH
Assignments while at Rackheath, names of people served with or under CC M/SGT JOE R RAMIREZ ASST CC GEORGE Y DONG (S/SGT) CPL JOSEPH VETTER, CPL WALTER ELLIOTT CPL OLIVER OMUNDSON
Ground Crew: Chief ____ Assist ____ A&E Mechanic X Armorer ____ Radio ____ Radar ____
Instrument ____ Sheetmetal ____ Bombsight ____ Hydraulics ____ other ____
Flight Crew: Number & Names (pos) of Crew Members ____

Aircraft you crewed: Names & Number WITCHCRAFT 42-52534 PERILS OF PAULINE 42-95162
Please attach a list of specific missions that you flew on and describe your experiences for each, including such detail as; Shot Down, POW, Bailed Out, Wounded, KIA, MIA, Evaded, Ditched, Crashed or other details as you remember them. All will be of interest to the formulation of these data.
Base Operations: Administration ____ Clerical ____ Communications ____ Security ____ Supply ____
Photo Lab ____ Engineering ____ Intelligence ____ Medical ____ Transportation ____ Mess Hall ____
Other ____
Date Departed ETO 7/6/45 Transportation QUEEN MARY Destination NEW YORK CITY
Military Honors, Decoration & Commendations: List all including Battle Stars and Clusters and Theater Ribbons RECEIVED CERTIFICATE OF MERITORIOUS ACHIEVEMENT FROM GEN. KEPNER ON 100TH MISSION OF "WITCHCRAFT" ALL THEATER RIBBONS AND BATTLE STARS + GOOD CONDUCT AWARDED TO 467TH Please provide a short narrative of your activities after leaving the 467th B.G., including Civilian, Military Service, Schools, Business, Family, Political and Social Offices held or other achievements: AIRCRAFT MECHANICS SCHOOL, DETROIT CITY AIRPORT - RECEIVED A&E ~~ENGIN~~ CERTIFICATE 12/46 WORKED AT WAYNE UNIVERSITY IN AERO. ENGINEERING 6 YEARS THEN WAYNE ENGINEERING RESEARCH INSTITUTE 1953 TO 1955. MOVED TO TOLEDO, OH. & WORKED IN FIBERGLASS & PLASTICS TO 1959. JOINED DANA CORP. IN TOLEDO - WORKED IN RESEARCH & DEVELOPMENT TO 1970. THEN WENT TO BORG WARNER CORP. IN PONTIAC, MI AS SUPERVISOR IN DEVELOPMENT & TESTING OF AUTOMATIC TRANSMISSIONS PRIMARILY FOR TOYOTA AUTOS. RETIRED IN 1981 AND MOVED TO GAYLORD, M. WORKED IN HARDWARE STORES PART TIME FOR ANOTHER 10 YEARS. DORIS & I HAD 1. SON GARY 1944 2. JANICE 1949 3. NANCY 1958 AND 5 GRAND CHILDREN.

RAY - 1/2 GERMAN 1/4 ENGLISH 1/4 IRISH - NOT DUTCH AS IN 467th HISTORY & OTHER ARTICLES. Ray Betcher

467th Group Database – Staff Sgt. Raymond A. Betcher. (Courtesy Ray Betcher)

The converted freighter USAT *Frederick Lykes*.

Greenock Rail Station (photo by author in 2003).

On 1 March 1944, *Frederick Lykes*, accompanied by a convoy of various ships and escort vessels, hoisted anchor and commenced the voyage out of New York for the Atlantic crossing; at 0700 hours it sailed past the Statue of Liberty. All went well for the first few hours of the voyage, until the convoy was about twenty-four hours out of New York; at about 0730 hours, the propeller shaft on the *Frederick Lykes* broke and the troopship came to a standstill. Nearly 300 miles out in the Atlantic, and with the possibility of German U-Boats in the area, the convoy had no choice but to continue on its voyage, leaving one of the escort vessels (a destroyer) to provide some protection for the troopship. For some five hours or thereabouts, the destroyer circled the *Frederick Lykes* while the ship's engineers carried out the repairs, which were completed at about 1230 hours; the troopship and the destroyer got underway, and some twelve hours later rejoined the convoy.

Eventually—and with no further mishaps—the convoy sailed into the Firth of Clyde on the evening of 9 March 1944, where it berthed for the night; early the next morning, the troopship hoisted anchor and slowly made her way to the nearby docks at Port Glasgow, Greenock, Scotland.

During mid to late morning, the 467th Group personnel disembarked, marched to the nearby rail station, and boarded troop trains to a destination that was still unknown to them. The coaches were unlike any they had ever seen: two rows of seats in each compartment, with an entrance/exit door on either side of the compartment, and the seats did not adjust at all for sleeping; one had to sleep while sitting. For nearly twenty-four hours the Group personnel were on those troop trains, until about mid-morning on 11 March 1944, when the trains came to a standstill at a small country rail station (Salhouse). The personnel were then informed that was where they had to disembark, and as the trains were longer than the platforms, some of them had to jump about four feet from the carriage exit door to the ground, still unaware of the name of the place they had arrived at. The personnel

Princes Pier, Greenock, Scotland.

Salhouse Rail Station (photo by author in 2003).

then boarded the trucks that awaited them in the station yard. (None of them were aware of where they were, since in 1939, all railway station name signs were removed for security reasons, as they were regarded as a possible assistance to enemy forces in the event of the UK being invaded.) The trucks then conveyed them to their accommodation sites on the USAAF base they were told was Rackheath, in the county of Norfolk, England.

It was sheer coincidence that, as the personnel were getting off the troop trains, some of the 467th Group B-24s that they last saw at Wendover flew in to make their first landing at Rackheath, after the transitional flight from the US. In fact, eleven of the 467th Group B-24s made their first landing at Rackheath on 11 March 1944.

The ground crew—similar to all the other 467th Group ground crews with their assignments—did a wonderful job maintaining the plane that had been assigned to them. Master Sgt. Ramirez was a "stickler" for tidiness on "his plane," and indeed, the dogged, almost obsessive care given to *Witchcraft* made her great and kept the crews safe while flying her. He even insisted that all the flight panel instruments be cleaned and polished after each

Witchcraft on hardstand #32 (center right) and Joe R.'s crew "shack" (center bottom).

flight. Even the flight crews—on their return from missions—before getting out of the plane had to ensure they left it tidy and that no cigarette butts were left on the floor.

Joe "R" and his team built a shack close to hardstand 32—*Witchcraft*'s "parking space." They made the shack with wood salvaged from ammunition and bomb crates, and fitted it out with some homemade seating, unofficially obtained ("borrowed" would be the operative word) some blankets from the stores, and installed electric lighting. From a shop in Norwich, they purchased a small kerosene (paraffin) stove, which the team used for both brewing coffee and cooking food, as well as enjoying the warmth generated by the stove during cold weather spells. The team used the shack to get some warmth when they were working late at night or in the wee hours of the morning—especially on the wet and cold days—preparing and making *Witchcraft* ready for an early morning mission take-off time. The shack could not be rated as anything overly special, but it saved the ground crew having to cycle to and from their accommodation sites when they needed a proper rest or change into dry clothing.

Col. Albert J. Shower's statement in an article written by Warren Brand, staff writer for the *Whittier* (California) *Daily News* dated Monday, 25 May 1987, mentioned: "I think in any case where people and planes come back, there is luck involved, but I think Joe had an especially dedicated crew." Col. Shower twice recommended Ramirez for the Bronze Star "for outstanding achievement in maintaining his airplane."

As Joe himself stated: "I had the reputation of getting myself tangled up with officers." Referring to Joe's statement, Col. Shower made the following comment: "I think he was a bit more visible because of the airplane, and I hear he was a bit more assertive. I'm glad I never had to come up against him."

Master Sgt. Joe R. Ramirez

Indeed, as my friend, Lt. John G. Oder—copilot on Lt. George W. Reed's original Crew #Y-15—in one of the letters that he sent to me several years ago wrote the following:

> I am sending you some comments that may be helpful in your endeavor to write about *Witchcraft*, one of which was the following:
>
> One interesting thing was on Group mission #35, on May 28, 1944. It was the original crew's 15th credited mission—and I believe *Witchcraft*'s 24th—to Zeitz, Germany. The #3 engine started losing oil pressure and a crewmember in the waist reported an oil leak from the engine. The engine was feathered and we came home alone on three engines. When we arrived on the hardstand, Joe Ramirez came up to the cockpit and shouted to me "What in the hell did you do to my airplane?" I told him that I was sorry, but that "#3 engine was losing oil pressure and leaking oil. I also told him that we were over hostile territory and being shot at. It could be they hit us, we'll try to be more careful next time." I don't know why Joe blamed me for the engine failure; I guess it was because the engine was on my side (starboard) of the airplane and that as Copilot I was second in command.

The ground crew did not work on *Witchcraft* solely on the base at Rackheath, as on the return flight to base after attacking the target at Neunkirchen, Germany, on 28 December 1944, the pilot, Lt. Learned W. Barry, and Crew #55 were forced to make an emergency landing at the RAF station at Manston, Kent, in southeast England. Although the weather was far from ideal, Joe Ramirez and his ground crew team obtained a truck from the motor pool and, with a new engine on board, drove to Manston, where they fitted the replacement Pratt and Whitney. The plane was then flown to No. 3 Strategic Air Depot, Watton, Norfolk, for repairs to some of the airplane's panel work before returning to Rackheath a few days later, and was made ready to fly her next

Joe Ramirez and three members of his team working on the "Witch's" #3 engine. Ray Betcher's tool box is very prominent.

combat mission on 7 January 1945, to Rastatt, Germany.

Joe Ramirez and his ground crew team—similar to all the other 467th Group ground crew teams—did a remarkable job maintaining the Group's B-24s and, as we all should know, realize, and appreciate, all of those guys worked long hours, mostly in the open and quite often under inclement weather conditions.

Those ground crew teams were very important, and they did a remarkable job in ensuring the aircraft were maintained efficiently.

Staff Sgt. George Dong (left) and M/Sgt Joe Ramirez (right) working on #1 engine of the "Witch."

4

Transitional Flight from the United States to the United Kingdom

Following the final take-off from Wendover on 12 February 1944, *Witchcraft* was airborne for eight hours before landing in Herrington, Kansas. It was there that Lt. George Reed and Crew #Y-15, along with other 467th Group crews, had to undergo their final POM Inspector's check (**P**reparation for **O**verseas **M**ovement). The check involved flying a practice bombing mission over Kansas City on 19 February 1944, and the senior inspector, Maj. Pat Thorington—who became known as the 467th Group's adopted "Pete, the POM Inspector"—assisting the lead bombardier. The B-24 on which Maj. Thorington was flying had to abort due to some mechanical problem, but the inspectors were satisfied with the formation flying and clearance orders were given for an overseas posting.

On 27 February 1944, *Witchcraft*, flown by Lt. Reed and Crew #Y-15, flew out of the Army Air Force base at Herrington and made the seven-hour flight to Morrison Field, Palm Beach, Florida—similar to all the other crews, they were totally unaware of their destination.

During a one-day stop-over at Morrison Field, the crew changed into their summer uniforms, and other than some minor briefing, there was very little else to do there. Crewmembers were issued .45 caliber side arms and their normal backpack parachutes were exchanged for a slightly different type that had a zippered inner compartment near the back that contained a machete, fish line and hooks, high energy candy, and other small survival items. Two burlap sacks of C Rations were placed on board *Witchcraft*. The rations were packed in small olive drab colored waterproof wooden boxes; each box was labeled "breakfast, dinner, supper," and contained a small can of either bacon and cheese, bacon and eggs, or spam. The contents also included some crackers, a small package containing four cigarettes, chocolate, two pieces of chewing gum, and some sheets of toilet paper.

Crew Y-15 flew *Witchcraft* out of Morrison Field on 29 February, setting a southerly course on a compass heading that they had been instructed to fly for one hour before opening and reading the sealed orders they were given prior to take-off. Lt. Reed opened the sealed orders to read that their destination was Rackheath, England, United Kingdom, and the route would entail crossing the South Atlantic from Brazil to French West Africa, before commencing the route from West Africa to England. After flying for ten hours, they eventually completed the first leg of their route from Morrison Field, Florida, and landed at Waller Field, Trinidad, and the British West Indies.

Following a few hours rest, Lt. Reed and Y-15 took off from Waller Field on 1 March 1944, for their next stop-over at Valdecaens Field, Belem, Brazil, where they landed after flying for eight hours fifteen minutes. That second leg of the route took them just south of the equator, and for over an hour, they were flying over the 185-mile wide mouth of the mighty Amazon River.

There was another short stop-over to get some rest and refuel the B-24 before flying out of Valdecaens Field on the third leg of their route to Natal, Brazil. The crew had quite an uneventful seven hour, thirty minute flight to Natal, where they landed 52534 on 2 March 1944. But it was not a short stop-over at Natal for Crew Y-15, as next morning, Lt. Reed reported sick and was diagnosed as having a severe throat problem; he was hospitalized for six days.

The name WITCHCRAFT, painted in a semicircle, is distinctly visible behind the letters ***Witc*** of the final nose art.

Copy of a sketch of the original *Witchcraft* nose art. (Courtesy of crewmember Bob McEwen)

Correspondence over the past years from former crew members—copilot Lt. John G. Oder, tail-gunner Staff Sgt. Robert B. McEwen, and engineer Staff Sgt. Robert W. DeKerf—indicate it was during those six days at Natal that *Witchcraft* was chosen as the name for the plane by the crew's enlisted men. In the correspondence, it is emphasized that the name did not come about or have any connection whatsoever with the song "Witchcraft." Letters received from my friend Bob McEwen many years ago confirm that a rough sketch for the nose artwork was prepared from suggestions by Staff Sgt. Robert DeKerf, Staff Sgt. Robert McEwen, and Staff Sgt.Melvin Bland; also, a letter received previously from Bob DeKerf indicates the actual final nose artwork was not painted on 52534 until after arrival at Rackheath. But it is understood that Bob DeKerf painted the name *Witchcraft* in a semicircle just below the red "Fire Extinguisher" sign on the front left side. (It is difficult to determine the color of the paint used, but looking at some black and white photographs of *Witchcraft*, it was probably either white or yellow.) The "Fire Extinguisher" must have been painted on their last complete day at Natal, since the author was told by a member of the crew that the paint was not dry when they lifted off to fly the fourth leg of their route to Dakar, French West Africa. The word "*Witchcraft*" in a semicircle is still distinctly visible on some photos and is seen behind the superimposed first four letters "Witc" of the final nose artwork name *Witchcraft*. In another letter, Bob DeKerf confirmed the final *Witchcraft* nose artwork was not painted on the plane until after arrival at Rackheath, and he also mentioned that unfortunately, the name of the person who painted the artwork is unknown.

9 March 1944 was quite an eventful day, as they had decided to take off from Natal in the very early

hours and fly most of the leg across the South Atlantic in darkness. Soon after midnight, the crew got themselves ready for the flight—having filed their flight plan—when they were informed that a heavy squall line had developed on their flight path and the take-off was put on hold. Then, just about daybreak, the crew was given a weather briefing and clearance for take off for the flight to Dakar. Lt. Reed left the decision to the Crew Navigator, Lt. Charles Mintzlaff, regarding which hour would be best for commencing their flight. Charles initially said he preferred to fly during the hours of darkness and have the advantage of using the stars for navigation checks, but giving the matter further thought, he considered he could follow the plotted course by using the position of the sun and the drift of the waves in the ocean. The crew refiled their flight plan and lifted

Crew Y-15 at Dakar, FWA. Rear (R to L): Lt. C.Mintzloff (Nav), Lt. J.Kramer (Bdr), Sgt. M. Bland (R/Op), Staff Sgt. R. DeKerf (Engr/TTGr), and Sgt. H. Kubacek (Gr). Front (R to L): Lt. J. Oder (CP), Lt. G. Reed (P), Sgt. R. McEwen (T/Gr), and Sgt. A. McLean (B/TGr). (Photo taken by Sgt. V. Bundrock [Gnr])

Three of the Enlisted crew at Dakar FWA (L to R): Henry Kubacek, Bob DeKerf, and Vernon Bundrock.

Senegalese soldier at Dakar with Mel Bland (left) and Vernon Bundrock (right).

off from Natal at 0630 hours. As Lt. John Oder wrote in one of his letters to the author:

> All was going well until about 1400 hours (2:00pm), still with about a further 2 ½ hours flying time ahead of them before reaching their destination, when #3 engine developed problems—the engine RPM were fluctuating and the engine cylinder head temperatures soared to read very high, so they feathered the engine for most of the remaining flight time and restarted it just as we were making preparations to land on Eknes Field, Rufisque, Dakar, Senegal, French West Africa. The crew reached Dakar within a few seconds of Lt. Mintzlaff's estimated time of arrival and the actual flight time of 10 hours 15 minutes. As the landing gear touched the runway, there was a terrific rattling noise that startled both Lt. Reed and Lt. Oder; they realized they had landed on a steel-mat runway. When the mechanics inspected the #3 engine, it was found that the problem was a faulty engine cylinder, which had to be replaced. The repairs were completed on 12 March 1944, following which the crew took the plane up on a three-hour test flight to establish everything was satisfactory.

On 11 March 1944, the B-24 Lt. Ellwood L.Bragdon and Crew #165 from the 789th Squadron was ferrying to England for the Air Transport Command crashed when taking off from Eknes Field; four of the crew lost their lives and six were injured, with three sustaining serious injuries and three light injuries. This was the first 467th Group crew lost or injured during the transitional flight.

Lt. Reed and Crew Y-15 flew the fifth leg of the route from Eknes Field, Dakar, Senegal, to Marrakech, Morocco, on 13 March 1944. The seven hour and forty-five minute flight went well and was uneventful. However, after their arrival at Marrakech, the inclement weather conditions were not ideal for flying and they had to wait there for two complete days, until the weather showed improvement.

Eventually, on 16 March 1944, the crew started on the sixth leg of their route to Prestwick, Scotland. But when the crew was about three hours flying time from Prestwick, they received a radio message that the area was closed in by heavy fog and they were diverted to St. Mawgan, Newquay, Cornwall. After flying for a total of eight hours and thirty minutes, they touched down on the runway at St. Mawgan, Newquay, where again, the crew was delayed for two days due to inclement weather; they had to stop there until 19 March 1944, before they took off on their final leg to (USAAF Field 145) Rackheath, Norfolk—a flight of two hours and fifteen minutes. Some thirty-four out of a total of fifty-eight of the Group's original B-24s making the transitional flight had arrived before 19 March. On 19 March 1944, ten B-24s in addition to *Witchcraft* made their first landing at Rackheath.

On 20 March 1944, Lt. Reed and crew flew *Witchcraft* to 3 Strategic Air Depot at Watton, Norfolk, for some modifications; the flight is shown in copilot John Oder's flight records as taking one hour and fifteen minutes.

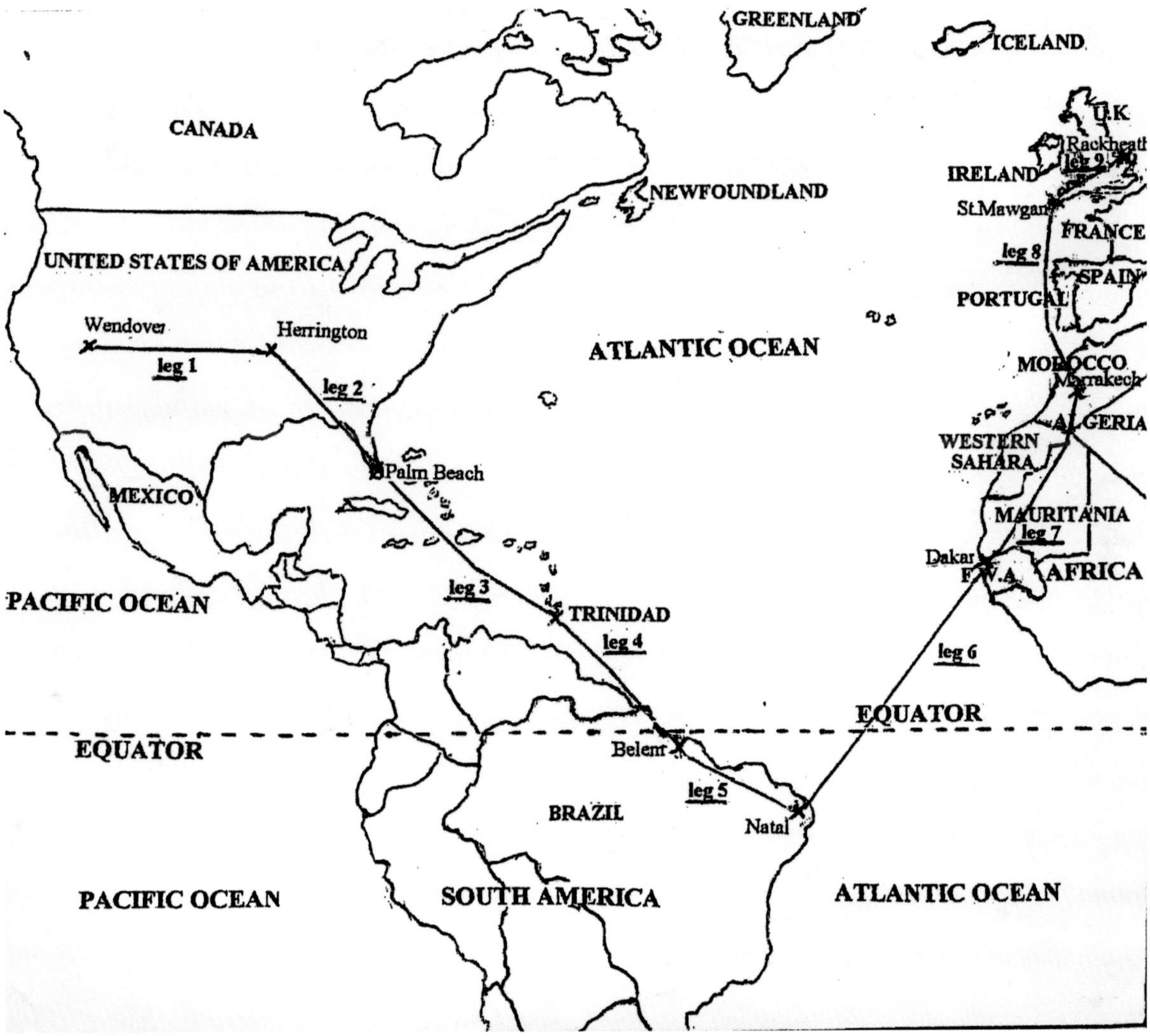

Diagram of the "nine legs" route from Wendover to Rackheath flown by *Witchcraft*.

5

Arrival at USAAF Station 145 – Rackheath, Norfolk, England

The ground echelon and 108 flight crew members arrived at the airfield at Rackheath on 11 March 1944, and were taken to accommodation sites.

The accommodation site allocated to Master Sgt. Joe Ramirez and his team was Site #8—a "Seco" building shared with other 790th Squadron maintenance personnel that was reasonably close to Rackheath Hall. Crew Y-15 was also accommodated at Site #8, along with other 790th Squadron flight crew personnel, but most of the personnel were accommodated in Nissen Huts, which initially accommodated twelve, but was later increased to sixteen. Obviously, the enlisted men's quarters were separated from the officers' accommodations.

Hardstand #32 was allocated as the permanent "parking place" for *Witchcraft* and was used solely by that particular B-24 while based at Rackheath. Also, all of the crews in the Group's four squadrons were renumbered; the numbers allocated to the 790th Squadron were 51 through 75, and Crew #Y-15 then became Crew #62.

How many days *Witchcraft* was at Watton for modifications is unknown, but it was probably there that the 790th Squadron letters "Q2" were painted on the fuselage aft of the waist gun positions. Likewise, in all probability, it was while at Watton that the large white disc was painted on the upper outer sides of both tail vertical stabilizers, containing the 467th Group letter "P" painted in dark blue and the last digit of the model number "42," along with the five-digit serial number "52534" painted in yellow immediately below the white disc. Also painted in yellow and immediately below the serial number was the letter "M" (the call letter allocated to 42-52534 to indicate it was a 790th Squadron B-24) and a yellow bar. Additionally, painted on

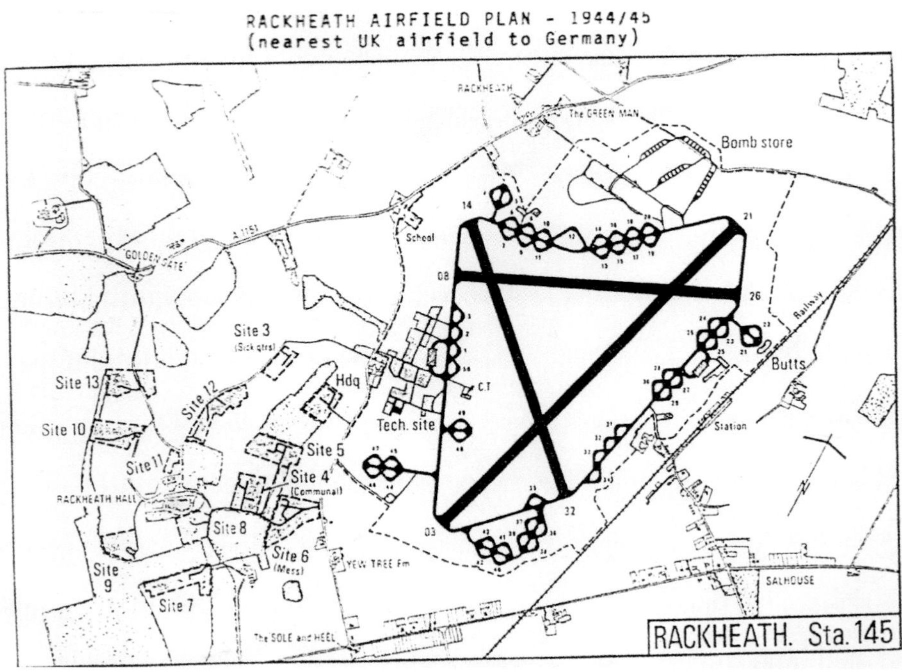

Rackheath Airfield Plan 1944-45.

the upper surface of the right wing towards the wing tip was a large white disc containing the 467th Group letter "P" in blue. The tail vertical stabilizer markings as described prevailed on *Witchcraft* and the other 467th Group B-24s until the latter part of April/early May 1944, when to assist the pilots in recognizing their own Group formations during forming-up (assembly) procedure, the paintwork on the vertical tail stabilizers was changed. For the 467th Group ships, the outer sides of the tail stabilizers were painted red and contained a broad diagonal white stripe running from the upper leading edge to the lower trailing edge of the rudder. The aircraft call letter was painted in red in the center of the diagonal white band ("M" for *Witchcraft*), and immediately below the letter was a horizontal bar, again in red. On the upper inner sides of the vertical tail stabilizers, the six digits "252534," relating to *Witchcraft*, were painted. In yellow, on the inner side of the port (left) stabilizer, the "2" was applied to the rudder and the digits "52534" were on the fixed part of the stabilizer; on the starboard (right) stabilizer, the digits "25253" were applied to the fixed part of the stabilizer and the digit "4" was applied to the rudder.

It was also during the mid to latter part of April 1944 that the 467th Group, in line with other Bombardment Groups in the Second Air Division of the USAAF 8th Air Force, started to use a gaudily painted, war-weary B-24D—53 CO 42-40370, named "Pete the POM Inspector"—as an assembly ship to assist the 467th Group crews when forming up over the North Norfolk coast and North Sea area.

Lt. John Oder's flight record indicates that on 31 March 1944, Lt. George Reed and Crew #62 flew *Witchcraft* on a practice mission lasting two hours and fifteen minutes. They next flew the "Witch" on a forty-five-minute engine check test on 1 April 1944; five days later, on 6 April 1944, Lt. Reed and Crew #62 flew *Witchcraft* on a four hour and thirty-minute combat practice mission.

The right stabilizer on *Witchcraft* as painted until the latter part of April/early May 1944.

The left stabilizer on *Witchcraft* as it appeared in late April/early May 1944 onwards.

Two photos of the first assembly ship used by the 467th: B-24D-53 CO 42-40370 Pete *The POM Inspector*. The top photo shows the original tail stabilizer markings, and the other shows as it was from May 1944 onwards, with the stabilizer painted red with the broad white diagonal stripe.

The first assembly ship nose art on the 467th's first assembly ship.

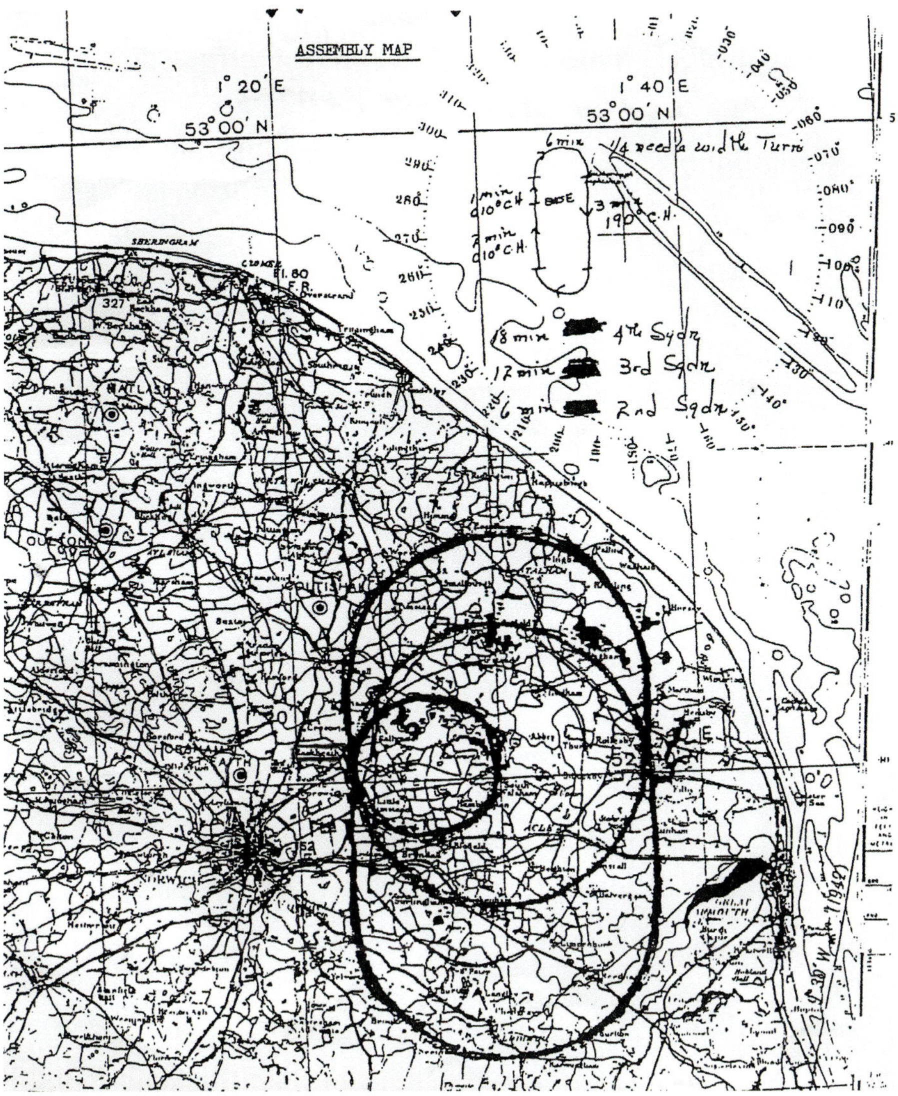

The assembly pattern used by 467th Group crews immediately after take-off.

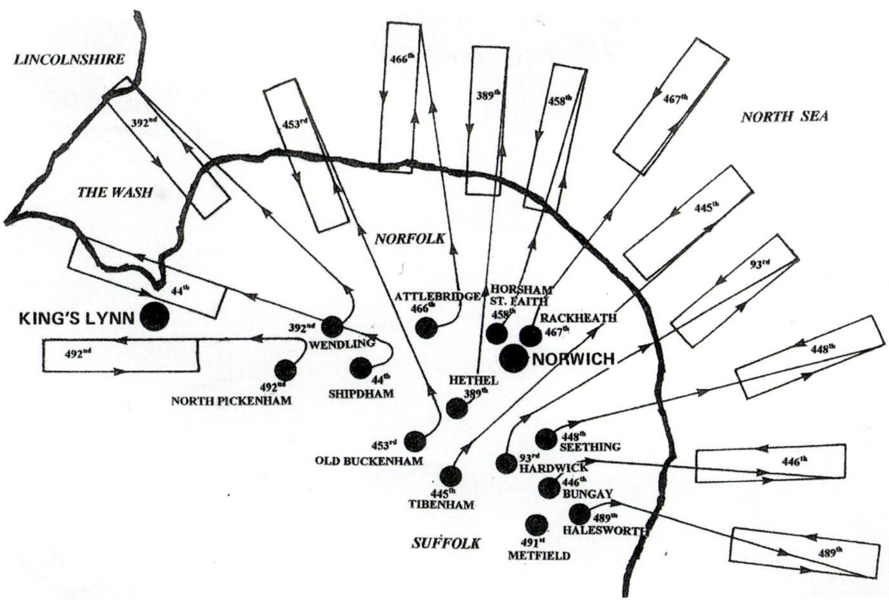

A sketch of the assembly areas allocated to USAAF Groups based in Norfolk and Suffolk.

A painting by the author of the rather "colorful" 467th Group Assembly Ship "370."

Details Relating to the Home of the 467th Bombardment Group While in England During WWII

The class "A" airfield at Rackheath was built to Air Ministry Directorate-General of Works (AMDGW) standards for heavy bomber requirements, and as such featured three intersecting runways, all 150 feet in width. The main runway (03/21) was 6,000 feet and aligned to the prevailing wind direction; the other two were 4,300 (13/32) and 4,200 (08/26) feet long, respectively. The perimeter track/taxi-way that encircled the actual flying field joining the ends of each runway by means of an approach apron was 2.7 miles long and 50 feet wide. Each runway had a shallow gully on either side, and about every thirty feet, drain cover grates were built into the gullies leading to soak-away drains. Branching off from the perimeter track were the fifty "loop" type dispersal points for the aircraft—twenty doubles and ten single loops—and as the name suggests, this was simply a loop of concrete adjoining the taxiway. These loop-type dispersal points that were fifty feet in width and set back 150 feet from the perimeter track were sometimes referred to as "spectacles" due to their appearance, especially when viewed from the air. The loops were found to be

The control tower as it was in 1944-45. Standing on the balcony (L to R) are Col. A.J. Shower, Col. A.F. Herzberg, and unknown.

better for maneuvering the aircraft and each accommodated two B-24 Liberator aircraft. Both the runways and perimeter track had a concrete screed finish.

Two "T2" type hangars measuring 240 feet long, 120 feet wide, and 39 feet high were erected for major aircraft overhauls. These were rectangular, steel-framed buildings clad with corrugated steel sheeting and fitted with heavy steel sheet-clad sliding doors at either end. On completion, the hangars were painted with black bitumen. Each of the hangars accommodated two and a half B-24s—it is assumed that the half would be either the front or rear section of a plane.

The airfield had two aviation gasoline storage installations with a total holding capacity of 162,000 gallons; the larger, with a holding capacity of 90,000 gallons, was on the east side of the field, about 300 feet to the west of the entrance to Salhouse rail station and about 300 feet north of Dakenham Hall Farm. The other storage facility, on the southwest side of the field, had a capacity of 72,000 gallons and was about 200 feet south of hardstand number 44. Additionally, the airfield had two bulk lubrication storage tanks, each with a holding capacity of 3,500 gallons, about midway between the airfield's main entrance and the "T2" hangar. Also, for the motor transport section, a gasoline storage tank of 5,000 gallons was constructed near the vehicle maintenance/ workshop area.

The control tower stood in the center of the airfield and was a building with a flat roof, brick construction,

The control tower in 1944-45.

The Tower in 1996 as a car junkyard.

and cement rendered walls; it was sited to see all extremities of the flying field. The three elongated windows on both the upper and lower floors on the east side of the "Tower" overlooked the main runway, as did the balcony on the second floor. The balcony also extended a few feet onto the north and south walls, the extension on the south wall giving access to the outside metal stairway to the roof and radio building.

Note: In 2007, the control tower was fully restored, both internally and externally. Following this extensive and expensive internal restoration, the Tower is now used as an office block. The coordinates for the Tower, based on map datum WGS 84 (taken on Thursday, December 26, 2002, at 1108 hours UT from the center window, overlooking the main runway) are Lat. N52° 40′ 22.5″ Long. E001° 22′ 36.6″ and 80 feet above sea level.

A number of buildings of varying size and design were erected on the "technical site" that adjoined the flying field. All buildings had a classification, such as permanent brick buildings, temporary brick buildings, Romney buildings, Seco buildings, and Nissen huts. The permanent brick buildings were very few in number, but those under this classification were the Control Tower, the AM Bombing Teaching building, Bomb Sight store, RU Pyro store, Electricity Generating site, Gymnasium, and the Speech Broadcasting building. Numerous brick-constructed blast shelters were interspersed in all areas for protection in the event of a bombing or strafing attack.

A fairly large bomb storage area was built on the extreme northern edge of the airfield, about one mile from the accommodation site and a similar distance north of the technical site. Roads leading off the perimeter track serviced the storage area.

Mark II airfield lighting was installed on the field.

Rackheath Hall was surrounded by park areas, with a vast number of trees providing natural camouflage for the accommodation sites. About 200 Nissen huts and a smaller number of Seco buildings were erected to accommodate 2,894 personnel. In addition to the accommodation and ablution buildings, the base Hospital/Sick Quarters, Chapel, Bulk Food Stores, Operations Block, Gymnasium, Cinema/Theatre, Officers and Enlisted Men's Clubs, and Mess facilities for Officers and Enlisted Men were built on the west side of Green Lane West, quite some distance from the flying field/technical site area.

Rackheath's control tower, winter 2008-09.

Concrete roadways were laid down for access to all of the buildings on both the flying field/technical sites and the accommodation/messing sites. Also, a sewage treatment plant and filter beds were built on the northern side of the main Norwich-Wroxham road and about a quarter mile on the west side of Stone Hill; the sewage plant is still in use.

The airfield was finally completed on 14 February 1944, and taken over by the Air Ministry.

During the seventy-five weeks it took to build the airfield, which occupied in excess of 1,200 acres, 556,000 tons of soil were excavated, 504,000 cubic yards of concrete were laid, and in excess of 4,000,000 building bricks were used. The construction also involved the installation of ten miles of cable conduit, ten miles of drainage pipes, eight miles of soak-a-way drainage, eight miles of piped water mains, five miles of sewer piping, and ten miles of roadways. At the time, the cost of building Rackheath was $250,000. Analyzing the cost, it would appear the flying field cost approximately $125,000 and the buildings and services cost the remaining $125,000.

The airfield was officially placed in the care of the Royal Air Force. The RAF officially handed control of the airfield over to the 467th Bombardment Group at the flag ceremony on 12 April 1944, at which time the RAF Ensign was lowered and the US Stars and Stripes was raised. This timing may appear unusual, as the Group officially took up occupation on 12 March 1944, flew its first operational mission on 10 April, and on the twelfth was flying its third mission. Also, the first, albeit small, contingent of the US 8th Air Force had arrived on the base on 10 September 1943, as part of the 1229th Quartermaster Company Service Group (AVN).

USAAF Field 145 at Rackheath, Norfolk, England, was the closest UK heavy bomber base to Germany.

Details Relating to the Village of Rackheath, Where a WWII Airfield Was Built, and Also Where over 5,000 USAAF Personnel Were Based During 1943-45

Rackheath was a typical English village in 1944-45, and had a population in the region of 400; today, its population is about 1,750. Rackheath is only five miles from Norwich, and from there one can take a train to London.

The village of Rackheath covers about 2,000 acres approximately four and a half miles northeast by north of the city of Norwich, Norfolk, England. It is an agricultural area, as it has been for several centuries, the land being light and sandy, with chalk sub-strata. The main farming crops today are wheat, barley, and a mixture of root crops. However, the village is virtually unrecognizable, compared to how it appeared in September 1943, when members of the 467th Group's first ancillary unit arrived. Apart from one or two road closures, there were no effective or significant changes in the village from 1943 to July 1945, when the American servicemen were based at Rackheath.

Rackheath is steeped in history that can be traced back to just before the first millennium. The name of the place reveals something of its history and character. The name Rackheath is thought to have derived from the words "Ragi" or "Rager"—the name of a person, probably the head of an early settlement—and "Heider" or "Heath," which describes the character of the district. It is a strong possibility the name "Ragi" or "Rager" came about from the Danish word "Ra," or stream. Several centuries back, this may have had some connection with "Dobbs Beck," a small stream flowing in the northern part of the village about a quarter mile to the east of "All Saints" Church. Referring to the characteristics of the "heath land," the southern part of the village for several centuries was nothing more than heath or scrubland interspersed with small wooded areas, and remained as such until 1800.

There is evidence of a settlement in the area before 1000 AD. In the year 1050—some sixteen years prior to the Norman invasion—the emerging Saxon or Danish settlement was known as Ra-Cheisham, Racheia, or Rakeia. Analyzing the word "Ra-Cheisham": first "Ra"—an abbreviation of the name of the settlement leader "Ragi"; then "Cheis," from the word "Heider" (heath); and finally "Ham," being the name for a settlement of the Anglo-Saxon invaders from the European continent.

Rackheath consisted of two separate parishes—Magna (great) and Parva (little)—until conjoined in the year 1422. The village is listed under entry number 191 in the *Domesday Book*: a unique tax record of landholdings taken in 1087 to establish how much arable land, woodlands, number of animals, etc., was owned, and by whom in all areas of England. The population of the village in 1086 was twenty-two people, who resided and farmed in the northern area (Magna).

At that time, the hamlet enjoyed a reasonable level of prosperity, as indicated by the presence of a windmill in Rackheath Magna. Records In 1250, Rohesia de Blakenham leased the mill to Robert de Martham; the lease agreement made provision for Rohesia and her tenants to enjoy priority service at the mill for the grinding of their wheat. It was also during that period the beautiful little church of flint stone construction and dedicated to "All Saints" was built in Magna.

The gentry and lords of the manor were attracted by the hunting prospects that the area afforded, and around 1253, Robert de Bruys was given the right to hunt on the lands in the Rackheath area.

Rackheath's All Saints' Church.

Through the years 1315 to 1590, there were at least nine different Lords of the Manor of Rackheath, which included various members of the Est, Yelverton, Philibert, and Helme families. From 1300 to 1600, it was the usual practice for reasonably wealthy families of good status to obtain church positions for the younger heirs to secure a respected role in the parish or beyond. An example of this is the appointment of Robert Est as Rector of Magna in 1300, presented by his father, Lord of the Manor Simon Est.

Rackheath is recorded in the *Liber Regis* (the "King's Book") under the heading "Rackley"—alias "Rackheath Major"—and dated 1535. This came about when King Henry VIII issued the order that the value of all church livings be obtained and recorded.

In 1591, Thomas Pettus—a former sheriff (1566) and mayor (1590) of Norwich—purchased the Rackheath estate from William Helme. Following the death of Thomas Pettus in 1597, his son John (born in 1550) inherited the estate, and in 1600, was knighted by Queen Elizabeth I. The population of the village in 1600 had increased to about fifty souls. The Rackheath estate remained with the Pettus family until 1780, and it was during the 189 years the estate was under their ownership that the first Rackheath Hall was built. (It is understood there are many families named "Pettus" living in the US today, a considerable number of them residing in the state of Missouri—a number of American Pettus ancestors have visited Rackheath over the past thirty years.) In 1780, the Pettus family sold the Rackheath estate to Sir Edward Stracey (the first Stracey baronet).

The "Green Man" Inn was built sometime during the first half of the eighteenth century and is shown on Faden's 1797 map of Rackheath.

In 1820, the village population had increased to approximately 250, and in the same year, the "new" Rackheath Hall was built. This hall—a beautiful, large white brick building of Italianate style standing in the center of an attractive and wooded park—was the residence of various Stracey family members for 129 years, and was first occupied by the family of the first baronet Sir Edward to the seventh Sir Edward Paulet (who died in 1949). From the time the hall was built, it had its own piped water supply pumped through about one mile of underground cast iron pipes by a "ram" pump at a water spring near where "All Saints" Church stands. Also, it had its own acetylene gas production plant for the 200 gas lamps installed (changed to electric lighting in 1919). The entrance to the long driveway across the park and leading to the hall was embellished by fine wrought-iron gates, referred to locally as "The Golden Gates." The gates were made by Barnards Iron Works in Norwich and purchased by Sir George Stracey (the third Stracey baronet) at the Great Exhibition in London in 1851.

In 1850, Sir Edward H.J. Stracey arranged for the National Society School with attached Master's house to be built just off the northern side of the main Norwich-Wroxham road, at the top of Stone Hill. The population had increased to 281 in 1854, with fifty-three houses in the village.

Mrs. Harrison—wife of the Rector, Reverend Thomas Harrison (Rector 1864-1899)—paid for a "reading room" to be built in 1881, on land given to her by her Uncle, Sir Henry J. Stracey. The "reading room" served the village as the only meeting room apart from the school from 1881 until 1938.

"The Golden Gates" of Rackheath (c 1885-1890). (Photo courtesy of Norfolk Records Office)

In 1908, the county education authorities built a new school to accommodate ninety children. The school was sited just off the western end of Green Lane West and was in daily use until September 2003, when the new and much larger replacement school that was built on the southeast side of the airfield was opened.

Rackheath's Green Man Inn.

There were military personnel stationed in the village during WWI, as Rackheath Hall was occupied from November 1917 by a number of personnel of the British Army, when the 64th Highland Division operated an Officer's School of Instruction there.

In 1921, the village population was 295, reflecting an increase of fourteen souls over a period of sixty-seven years; but over the next ten years, leading to 1931, the number of inhabitants grew steadily, with a population count of 340. No records are available, but it is a reasonable assumption that, during the years 1939 to 1945, the population was in the region of 320 to 360, excluding those away from home serving in the armed forces.

The village post office was in the right-hand lodge at the Golden Gates, as one entered from the main road. The Postmaster in 1925 was Mr. Herbert William (Bert) Bidwell (the nearest telegraph office in 1925 was at the post office in the adjoining village of Salhouse). The

Rackheath Hall, built in 1820.

village also enjoyed the services of various blacksmiths from at least the 1790s through the late-1930s. From the late-1920s to the beginning of 1943, a village store was operated by Mr. James C. Curtis on Barrack Row, off Green Lane West. There was a small confectionery shop built into the eastern end cottage at the top of Stone Hill in the ownership of Mrs. Edith Crane.

The Sole and Heel Pub, Rackheath, in 2009.

In the mid to late 1930s, the second public house (inn), known as the "Sole and Heel," was built.

During 1938, the first village hall was built (destroyed by fire in November 1973) on a site provided by Sir Edward Paulet Stracey, who also gave a generous donation towards the building costs. This village hall, fitted with gas lamps fueled by a small, external, acetylene gas-generating plant, replaced the redundant "reading room" as a meeting place. It also served a very special and important purpose during the years 1940 to 1941, as young children were evacuated to rural areas from the major cities in the southern part of England, such as London and other possible targets for enemy bombing raids, and a number of these "evacuees" were sent to Rackheath. Consequently, as the school was unable to accommodate this extra influx of children, the village hall served as a temporary classroom.

Nissen Huts at Site #8, 790th Squadron personnel accommodations.

Without any doubt, both village and inhabitants benefited greatly from the kindness and generosity received during the years 1591 to 1949, when the Pettus and Stracey families resided in Rackheath. This was expressed in forthright fashion in their assumption of the costs of repairs and improvements to All Saints' Church. Maintaining this tradition of civic benefaction in 1943, the Stracey family transferred the site for the new "Holy Trinity" Church (built in 1959) to the Norwich Diocesan Board.

Sir Edward Paulet Stracey and his family resided in the hall throughout WWII. This included the years when the airfield was being built, and a vast number of corrugated iron-sheeted Nissen huts and Seco buildings were erected as living accommodations over a considerable area of the park, to be followed in September 1943 with the arrival of the first elements of the 467th Bombardment Group.

German aircraft dropped bombs on Rackheath during 1940-1943, but fortunately, no one sustained any injury. This undoubtedly came about through a decoy airfield built in the fields north of the main Norwich-Wroxham road. Most of the dummy airfield was in the adjoining parish of Crostwick, behind and to the north of All Saints' Church and to the west of Dobbs Lane. It was originally built as a decoy airfield for the RAF station at Horsham St. Faith (Horsham was later to become the 458th Bomb Group's base). This decoy airfield—manned by RAF personnel whose accommodation was a wooden hut in a nearby field—consisted of one "long grass strip" complete with landing lights on either side and at each end. When enemy aircraft were reported approaching the area, the runway lights were switched on; an underground generator supplied the electricity. This decoy airfield was quite effective and was bombed on several occasions; an RAF Wellington bomber attempted to make an emergency landing on this field that resulted in the bomber crashing. Mrs. Betty Willis, who at that time was a teenager living with her parents at the post office in the right hand side lodge at the Golden Gates, recalls bombs falling and exploding in the woods close to Beeston Lane sometime during those years. In fact, it was one of those bombs that brought down the ceiling in the cottage off Beeston Lane where Mr. Frank Sewell resided. (Frank Sewell was one of many employed to fell trees when the site was being cleared for the building of the airfield at Rackheath.)

Records reveal the dates and bombs (number and type) dropped on Rackheath and the adjoining village of Crostwick during bombing raids by the German Luftwaffe in 1940 to 1943. Without doubt, many of the bombing raids during 1940-1941 were due to the decoy airfield in the parishes of Crostwick and Rackheath.

Date	Parish	Type of Bombs	Number Dropped
31 August 1940	Rackheath	High Explosive	8
14 February 1941	Crostwick	Incendiary	20
15 February 1941	Crostwick	Oil (Incendiary)	1
25 February 1941	Crostwick	High Explosive	16
26 February 1941	Rackheath	High Explosive	6
28 February 1941	Crostwick	High Explosive	10
14 March 1941	Rackheath	Incendiary	25
28 March 1943	Rackheath	Incendiary	500
22 April 1944	Rackheath	High Explosive	5(a)
4 October 1944	Crostwick	V2 Long Range Rocket1(b)	

Note: (a) The only casualties recorded and attributed to any of the above mentioned bombing raids relate to two 467th Bombardment Group ground personnel, one of whom was unfortunately killed and the other injured in the raid on 22 April 1944. The seventeen flight crew members KIA on 22 April 1944 when the two B-24s crashed (one at Barsham and the other at Withersdale Street, Mendham—both in the county of Suffolk) are not included, as they were not actually KIA by the bombs dropped by German aircraft. However, it is acknowledged that the loss of those seventeen crew members was directly caused by some of the Luftwaffe aircraft participating in the attack that evening.

(b)The V-2 long-range rocket that fell at Mud Lane, Crostwick, on 4 October 1944, at 5:40 p.m. The crater made by the rocket was only a few feet from the boundaries where all three parishes (Crostwick, Spixworth, and Rackheath) link. Further reference to this incident is made in the sub-chapter covering October 1944.

The temporary WWII airfield in the parish was to become the "home" for each of the 5,000 veterans of the Group from September 1943 to July 1945. That period of just twenty months was an important stage in the lifetime of each and every one of those veterans. It is appreciated that all of those veterans—irrespective of rank or category—had an important job to do while based at Rackheath, and had neither time nor opportunity to even think about, let alone research, any part of the history of the village in which their airfield was sited. Probably not one individual thought about it at the time, but all those 5,000 veterans were making some contribution to the history of Rackheath. Many details were recorded in some form or other—such as in this book—and are read and discussed many years after their departure from the United Kingdom following the end of hostilities in Europe.

There were no significant changes to the village during the years the American Army Air Force personnel were based at the airfield. Many of the local inhabitants resided in the northern area of the village, although several bungalows and a few houses had been built in the southern part of the village (sometimes referred to as "New Rackheath") in 1938 and 1939. Some of those residences

The crater made by the German V-2 rocket at Mud Lane, Rackheath.

were on either side of the main Norwich to Salhouse road; a few were on the easterly side of Green Lane East. There were also a few bungalows on a small housing estate on the southern side of the main Norwich-Salhouse road, but the development of that site, which commenced in 1939, virtually came to a standstill during the wartime years. Amenities in the southern area were more updated and the properties were connected to both piped water and an electricity supply, whereas in the northern area, neither was available. In those years, the only reasonably modern amenity available to householders in the northern area of the village was a gas supply piped from Norwich used for lighting and cooking. Most dwellings obtained their water from a well in their garden—in some cases a single well was shared between two, three, or four dwellings. The two lodges built at the Golden Gates had to rely on an eighty-two foot deep well in the garden of the left hand side lodge (as one looks towards the park entrance from the main Norwich-Wroxham road) for a domestic water supply, despite the fact a piped water supply was connected to Rackheath Hall at the time it was built. There was no sewage disposal connection to the residences in either the northern or southern areas of the village. The outside lavatories in the northern area were dealt with on a weekly collection basis by a horse-drawn collection tank colloquially referred to as the "honey cart." In the southern part, the reasonably newly built properties were connected to a septic tank and soak-a-way in the garden.

The village general store in one of the dwellings at Barrack Row operated by Mr. James C. Curtis was lost when the cottages were demolished during the construction of the airfield in early-1943. Mr. Curtis opened a smaller shop in part of the pre-fabricated bungalow in which he was re-housed following the erection of two pre-fabricated accommodations on the east side of Green Lane West and nearly opposite the entrance to the base headquarters.

When the American service personnel arrived at Rackheath, social amenities in the village were few, with the majority in the northern area. The "All Saints" Church,

Rackheath Home Guard Platoon, 1940/45.

"Green Man" public house, school, post office, Edith Crane's Sweet Shop, and the village hall—where dances and whist drives were held from time to time—were all in the northern area. The "Sole and Heel" public house was the only social amenity in the southern part; the one remaining amenity—James Curtis's village shop—was approximately at mid-point along Green Lane West, and about equal distances from the northern and southern parts of the village.

The rail track passed through the eastern side of Rackheath, but the village does not have a railway station or stop; the nearest rail station is in the adjoining village Salhouse. The station was easily accessible, but it could be either a reasonable or considerable walking distance, depending where in the village one lived.

During WWII, Rackheath, similar to most villages throughout the UK, had its own Home Guard unit. Capt. Harvey, a local resident, was the commanding officer of the platoon, whose headquarters was at Beech House (near the "Green Man"). Home Guard units were formed all around the British Isles in 1940, to counter invasion by enemy forces.

6

Listing of Combat Missions Flown by B-24H-15 FO 42-52534 *Witchcraft*

Witchcraft Mission #	Group Mission #	Date	Pilot	Crew #	Target	Type	F-T	Fuel Gals
1	1	10 Apr.44	G.W. Reed	62	Bourges, Fr	A/F	6-53	1,840
2	2	11 Apr.44	J.P. Gavin	57	Oschersleben, Ger	A/I	6-53	2,000
3 R/c	3	12 Apr.44	G.W. Reed	62	Schweinfurt, Ger	A/I	3-21	930
4	4	13 Apr.44	G.W. Reed	62	Lechfeld, Ger	A/F	8-06	2,300est
5	5	17 Apr.44	J.R. Bridenbaugh	64	Wizernes, Fr	V/S	3-45	1,235
6	6	18 Apr.44	G.W. Reed	62	Brandenburg, Ger	A/I	7-11av	1.903av
7	7	19 Apr.44	J.A. Roden (see notes)	9	Paderborn, Ger	A/F	5-34	1,300
8 R/nc	9	21 Apr.44	G.W. Reed	62	Zwickau, Ger	A/I	4-00	1,100est
9	10	22 Apr.44	G.W. Reed	62	Hamm, Ger	M/Y	6-18	1,825
10	11	24 Apr.44	E.M. Helton (see notes)	55	Leipheim, Ger	A/F	8-32	2,285
11	12	25 Apr.44	C.H. Brandon	70	Mannheim, Ger	M/Y	8-06	2,245
12	13	26 Apr.44	G.W. Reed	62	Paderborn, Ger	A/F	4-53	1,380
13	15	27 Apr.44	G.W. Reed	62	Blainville, Fr	M/Y	6-40	1,925
14 R/nc	17	1 May 44	G.W. Reed	62	Ruisseauville, Fr	V/S	5-43	1,730
15 R/nc	19	4 May 44	J.K. Newhouse	57	Brunswick, Ger	A/F	4-35	1,630
16	20	5 May 44	G.W. Reed	62	Sottevast. Fr	V/S	4-35	1,380
17	21	7 May 44	G.W. Reed	62	Osnabruk, Ger	M/Y	5-32	1,610
18	22	8 May 44	G.W. Reed	62	Brunswick, Ger	A/I	6-20	1,760
19	23	9 May 44	E. Bryson	56	Florennes, Bel	A/F	5-02	1,460
20 R/nc	24	10 May 44	G.W. Reed	62	Diepholz, Ger	A/F	3-48	1,000
21	25	11 May 44	E. Bryson	56	Epinal, Fr	R/W	8-38	2,515
22	26	12 May 44	G.W. Reed	62	Bohlen, Ger	O/I	8-11	1,820
23	27	13 May 44	G.W. Reed	62	Tutow, Ger	A/F	7-46	2,000
24	28	19 May 44	E.W. Beaney	70	Brunswick, Ger	A/F	6-33	1,680
25	31	23 May 44	G.W. Reed	62	Bourges, Fr	A/F	7-01	1,800
26	33	25 May 44	E. Bryson	56	Mulhouse, Fr	M/Y	7-27	2,100

27	34	27 May 44	G.W. Reed	62	Neunkirchen, Ger	R/W	7-28	1,650
28	35	28 May 44	G.W. Reed	62	Zeitz, Ger	O/I	7-30	2,270av
29	39	2 June 44	G.W. Reed	62	Stella-Plage, Fr	C/D	5-11	1,350
30	40	3 June 44	G.W. Reed	62	Berck Sur Mer, Fr	C/D	3-50	1,135
31	42	6 June 44	G.W. Reed	62	Colleville, Fr	C/D	5-58	1,325
32	44	6 June 44	G.W. Reed	62	Pontaubault, Fr	R/B	7-30	1,900est
33	46	8 June 44	G.W. Reed	62	Pontaubault, Fr	R/B	7-10	1,900
34	47	10 June 44	G.W. Reed	62	Chateaudun, Fr	A/F	6-00	1,690av
35	51	14 June 44	G.W. Reed	62	Beavoir, Fr	M/I	3-47	1,000
36	52	15 June 44	G.W. Reed	62	Evreux, Fr	R/B	5-37	1,800
37	53	17 June 44	S.D. Martin	65	Guyancourt, Fr	A/F	7-02	2,350
38	55	18 June 44	G.W. Reed	62	Wesemunde, Ger	S/Y	7-18	2,000
39	58	20 June 44	G.W. Reed	62	Ostermoor, Ger	O/I	6-11	1,750
40	60	21 June 44	G.W. Reed	62	Berlin, Ger	I/T	8-31	2,500
41	61	23 June 44	G.W. Reed	62	Belloy-sur-Somme, Fr	V/S	4-53	1,200
42 Na/c	63	24 June 44	L.P. Vogt	63	Belle Croix, Fr	V/S	4-58av	1,540av
43 R/nc	68	1 July 44	T.S. Whitsel	73	Beaumetz-les-Aires, Fr	V/S	3-36	1,240
44	69	2 July 44	E.W. Beaney	70	Blanc Pignon Ferme, Fr	V/S	4-49	1,500
45	71	6 July 44	R.E. Evans	58	Kiel, Ger	S/Y	6-14	1,900
46	72	7 July 44	R.E. Evans	58	Lutzkendorf, Ger	O/I	6-48	2,030
47 R/c	73	8 July 44	L.P. Vogt	63	Fisme, Fr	R/B	3-38	1,225
48	75	12 July 44	L.P. Vogt	63	Munich, Ger	M/Y	8-35	2,400
49	76	13 July 44	J.E. Thompson	68	Saarbrucken, Ger	M/Y	6-50	1,875
50	77	16 July 44	L.P. Vogt	63	Saarbrucken, Ger	M/Y	6-34	2,100
51	78	17 July 44	L.P. Vogt	63	Bois de Queue Contessa, Fr	VS	3-49	1,200
52	79	18 July 44	L.P. Vogt	63	Troarn, Fr	T/T	4-45	1,230
53	80	19 July 44	L.P. Vogt	63	Kempten, Ger	A/I	7-51	2,250
54	81	20 July 44	J.H. Zbikowski	54	Eisenach, Ger	A/I	6-47	2,150
55 R/c	83	24 July 44	L.P. Vogt	63	Montreuil, Fr	T/T	5-32	1,550
56	84	25 July 44	L.P. Vogt	63	Montreuil, Fr	T/T	5-22	1,450
57	85	29 July 44	J.E. Thompson	68	Bremen, Ger	O/I	6-07av	1,730av
58	88	2 Aug.44	L.P. Vogt	63	Haut Maisnil, Fr	V/S	5-15	1,700
59	89	3 Aug.44	L.P. Vogt	63	Lille, Fr	O/I	4-17	1,325
60	90	4 Aug.44	H.W. Johnson	69	Rostock, Ger	A/I	7-02	2,475
61	91	5 Aug.44	L.P. Vogt	63	Brunswick, Ger	A/I	7-01av	2,110av
62	93	7 Aug.44	L.P. Vogt	63	Ghent, Bel	O/I	4-22	1,500
63	94	8 Aug.44	R.L. McKenzie	58	Clastres, Fr	A/F	4-22	1,195
64	95	9 Aug.44	L.P. Vogt	63	Saarbrucken, Ger	C/C	5-29	1,800
65	96	11 Aug.44	L.P. Vogt	63	Strasbourg, Ger	M/Y	6-21	1,950
66	97	12 Aug.44	J.K. Newhouse	57	Mourmelon-le-Grande, Fr	A/F	6-59	2,035
67	98	13 Aug.44	C.E. Epting	67	Seine River area, Fr	H/B	4-30	1,525
68	99	14 Aug.44	L.P. Vogt	63	Dole-Tavaux, Fr	A/F	7-20	2,350
69	100	15 Aug.44	L.P. Vogt	63	Vechta, Ger	A/F	5-27	1,550
70	101	16 Aug.44	L.P. Vogt	63	Magdeburg, Ger	A/I	6-02	2,100

71	102	18 Aug.44	J.W. Cravens	62	Woippy, Fr	A/I	8-14	1,980
72	103	24 Aug.44	L.P. Vogt	63	Misburg, Ger	O/I	6-41	1,900
73	104	25 Aug.44	L.P. Vogt	63	Lubeck, Ger	A/I	7-36	2,000
74	105	26 Aug.44	L.P. Vogt	63	Dulmen, Ger	F/D	4-50	1,475
75 R/c	106	27 Aug.44	L.P. Vogt	63	Finow/Oranienberg, Ger	A/I	5-46	1,700
76	109	8 Sept.44	S.T. Gray	64	Karlsruhe, Ger	M/Y	8-33	2,250
77	110	9 Sept.44	S.T. Gray	64	Mainz /Wurmz, Ger	MY	6-33	1,900
78	111	10 Sept.44	E.B. Lackens	71	Ulm, Ger	M/Y	7-25	1,900
79	113	3 Oct.44	S.T. Gray	64	Gaggenau, Ger	I/T	7-29	1,800
80	114	5 Oct.44	S.T. Gray	64	Paderborn, Ger	A/F	5-22	1,800
81	115	6 Oct.44	S.T. Gray	64	Wenzendorf-Stade, Ger	A/I	6-17	1,825
82	116	7 Oct.44	M.M. Ungerer (see notes)	63	Magdeburg, Ger	M/I	6-28	1,925
83	117	9 Oct.44	C.E. Epting	67	Coblenz, Ger	M/Y	5-41	1,700
84	119	14 Oct.44	C.E. Epting	67	Cologne, Ger	M/Y	6-16av	1,740av
85	123	22 Oct.44	S.T. Gray	64	Hamm, Ger	M/Y	5-08	1,450
86	124	25 Oct.44	A.E. Rothchild	68	Neumunster, Ger	A/F	5-48	1,600
87	127	2 Nov.44	N.G. Patton	71	Bielefeld, Ger	M/Y	5-30est	1,500est
88	128	4 Nov.44	S.T. Gray	64	Misburg, Ger	O/I	6-01av	1,775av
89	131	9 Nov.44	S.T. Gray	64	Metz, Fr	T/T	5-54	1,650
90	132	10 Nov.44	S.T. Gray	64	Hanau, Ger	M/Y	7-24	2,000
91	133	11 Nov.44	S.T. Gray	64	Bottrop, Ger	O/I	5-08	1,550
92	134	16 Nov.44	L.O. Graham	66	Eschweiler, Ger	M/I	5-30est	1,600est
93	135	21 Nov.44	S.T. Gray	64	Harburg, Ger	O/I	6-52	1,930
94	136	25 Nov.44	C.E. Epting	67	Bingen, Ger	M/Y	6-14av	1,745av
95	140	4 Dec.44	S.T. Gray	64	Bebra, Ger	M/Y	7-17	2,000
96	141	6 Dec.44	S.T. Gray	64	Bielefeld, Ger	M/Y	6-25	1,600
97	142	10 Dec.44	S.T. Gray	64	Bingen, Ger	M/Y	5-49	1,675
98	143	11 Dec.44	J. Severance	71	Hanau, Ger	M/Y	6-50	2,065
99 R/nc	145	18 Dec.44	G.E. Loveless	61	Coblenz, Ger	M/Y	4-26	1,625
100	146	24 Dec.44	R.A. Meyers	62	Gerolstein-Daun-Ober, Ger	R/R	6-07	2,400
101	147	25Dec.44	J.W. Rice	52	Gerolstein-Mechernich, Ger	C/C	5-11	1,850
102	149	27 Dec.44	J.K. Ross	65	Neunkirchen, Ger	M/Y	6-20	1,700
103	150	28 Dec.44	L.W. Barry	55	Neunkirchen, Ger	M/Y	8-30est	2,500est
104	158	7 Jan.45	G.G. Laszlo	60	Rastatt, Ger	M/Y	7-04	2,150
105	159	10 Jan.45	J.W. Rice	52	Schonberg, Ger	H/B	5-45	2,100
106	161	14 Jan.45	G.G. Laszlo	60	Hallendorf, Ger	I/T	6-35	1,600
107	162	16 Jan.45	G.G. Laszlo	60	Dresden, Ger	M/Y	8-30est	2,500est
108	164	29 Jan.45	J.W. McFarland	73	Munster, Ger	M/Y	5-34	1,500
109	166	3 Feb.45	N.G. Patton	70	Magdeburg, Ger	M/Y	6-55	1,825
110	167	6 Feb.45	J.W. Rice	52	Magdeburg, Ger	M/Y	7-12	1,830
111	171	14 Feb.45	C.D. Barker	69	Magdeburg, Ger	M/Y	6-55	1,875
112	172	15 Feb.45	J.W. Rice	52	Magdeburg, Ger	O/I	6-25	2,190
113	173	16 Feb.45	J.W. Rice	52	Osnabruck, Ger	M/Y	6-00est	2,100est
114 R/nc	X	17 Feb.45	J.W. Rice	52	Aschaffenburg, Ger	A/I	3-15est	900est

115	174	19 Feb.45	J.W. Rice	52	Meschede, Ger	A/I	6-24	1,975
116	175	21 Feb.45	C.D. Barker	69	Nurnberg, Ger	M/Y	8-18av	2,125av
117	176	22 Feb.45	C.D. Barker	69	Hildesheim, Ger	M/Y	7-07	2,030
118	177	23 Feb.45	J.W. Rice	52	Gera, Ger	M/Y	8-03	2,300
119	178	24 Feb.45	J.W. Rice	52	Bielefeld, Ger	M/Y	6-08	2,050
120	179	25 Feb.45	J.W. Rice	52	Schwabisch-Halle, Ger	A/F	8-00	2,100
121	183	1 Mar.45	J.W. Rice	52	Ingolstadt, Ger	M/Y	9-04	2,175
122	184	2 Mar.45	J.G. Phillips	63	Magdeburg, Ger	T/F	7-04	2,200
123	185	3 Mar.45	J.W. Rice	52	Nienburg-Bielefeld , Ger	W/B	7-16	2,050
124	186	4 Mar.45	J.W. McFarland	73	Stuttgart, Ger	M/Y	8-09	2,075
125	191	11 Mar.45	D.M. Rosenthal	54	Kiel, Ger	S/Y	5-53	1,650
126	192	12 Mar.45	J.G. Phillips	63	Swinemunde, Ger	M/Y	7-30	2,035
127	193	14 Mar.45	R.H. Willis	64	Giessen, Ger	M/Y	6-52	1,950
128	194	15 Mar.45	J.C. Wilson	60	Zossen, Ger	A/H	6-52	2,170
129	203	24 Mar.45	M.R. Davis	57	Kirtorf, Ger	A/F	5-56	1,750
130	205	30 Mar.45	R.H. Willis	64	Wilhelmshaven, Ger	S/Y	5-45	1,600
131	206	31 Mar.45	F.J. Jansen	61	Brunswick, Ger	M/Y	6-02	1,950
132	207	4 Apr.45	D.M. Rosenthal	54	Perleberg, Ger	A/F	7-29	1,875
133	210	7 Apr.45	R.H. Willis	64	Krummel, Ger	O/D	6-32	1,785
134	211	8 Apr.45	J.W. McFarland	73	Unterschlauersbach, Ger.	A/F	7-02	2,125
135	216	15 Apr.45	J.W. McFarland	73	Royan, Fr	C/D	8-11	2,150
136	218	17 Apr.45	F.J. Jansen	61	Carlsbad, Czechslovakia	C/C	7-21	2,050
137 R/c	220	21 Apr.45	J.W. McFarland	73	Salzburg, Austria	R/R	7-54	2,000

Note: R/c against mission number = mission recalled/aborted but credited
R/nc against mission number = mission recalled/aborted but *not* credited.
Na/c against mission number = no attack on target but credited.
(a) Against mission 7 = for that mission *Witchcraft* was loaned to 788 Squadron.

Key to abbreviations for Types of Targets:

Abbreviation	Target	Abbreviation	Target
A/F	Airfield	A/H	Army Headquarters
A/I	Aviation Industry	C/C	Communications Center
C/D	Coastal Defenses-Gun Emplacements	F/D	Fuel Depot
H/B	Highway/Road Bridges	I/T	Industrial Targets
M/I	Military Installations	M/Y	Railway Marshalling Yards
O/I	Oil Industrial Sites	R/B	Railway Bridges
R/F	River Ferry	R/J	Road/Highway Junctions
R/R	Railroad Junctions	R/W	Railway Repair Works
S/Y	Shipyards and Docks	T/F	Army Tank Production Plant
T/T	Tactical Targets	V/S	V–Weapon Sites
W/B	River Bridges/Viaducts		

The small letters “av” or “est” in either or both columns headed F-T (Flight Time) or Fuel Gals (gallons of fuel used to top the fuel tanks on return from mission) reflect that there are no actual figures available for *Witchcraft* due to the plane not being refueled. Consequently, the average Flight Time and/or Fuel Gals figure for all of the Group B-24s participating in that mission as shown in Group records is used as a fair indication.

The list of combat missions flown by *Witchcraft* indicates that it flew 137 missions; included in that number are the thirteen missions that were either aborted, recalled, or the target was not attacked. No credit was given for seven of the recalled/aborted missions, but the remaining six were credited. The figures illustrate that *Witchcraft* was credited with 130 combat missions without ever aborting on any combat mission or failing to attack any target, other than under instructions given by the Second Air Force Division HQ Command via the 467th Group HQ. There were no mechanical or crew problem aborts on any of the 137 combat missions that *Witchcraft* flew.

The 130 credited combat missions flown by *Witchcraft* were to five different European countries: Austria, 1; Belgium, 2; Czechoslovakia, 1; France, 33; and Germany, 93.

Note: Sadly, all crew members of three crews that flew combat missions in *Witchcraft* did not survive the European conflict:

1 - Lt. James A. Roden and Crew #9 on 22 April 1944 - flying B-24H-42-52536 – Crashed at Mendham, Suffolk, UK, with all ten crew members KIA following damage from enemy aircraft - Group Mission #10 - Target Hamm, Germany - ("Night Of The Intruders").

2 - Lt. Edwin M. Helton and Crew #55 on 21 June 1944 - B-24H-42-52497 *Osage Express* – following damage by enemy action and crash-landed on the west bank of the Muritz See, near Klink, Germany. All nine crew members were killed by the German SS. Group Mission #60 –Target: Berlin, Germany.

3 - Lt. Maynard M. Ungerer and Crew #63 on 10 November 1944 - B-24H-42-52571 *Snooper*. Soon after leaving the target area (Hanau), "571" was seen with the propeller feathered on #2 engine and losing altitude; it was last seen by crews of the 93rd Bombardment Group about thirty-five miles southwest of Brussels. It was presumed the nine crew members went down with their B-24 while flying over the North Sea. Group. – Group Mission #132- Target Hanau, Germany.

Additionally, four members of Lt. John P. Gavin's Crew #57 were KIA, but Lt. Gavin and five of his fellow crew members survived and became POWs - B-24H-41-28730 *Blonde Bomber* - 29 April 1944 - Group Mission #16. The B-24 was severely damaged during enemy action over the target (Berlin), but stayed airborne for a considerable time, until it crashed a few miles north of Hanover, Germany.

7

Pilots and Crews That Flew Combat Missions in *Witchcraft*

1	**BARKER** – Lt. Cleason D.	Crew #69	3 Missions Credited	*Witchcraft* Mission Numbers **111** (171), **116** (175); **117** (176)
2	**BARRY** – Lt. Learned W.	Crew #55	1 Mission Credited	*Witchcraft* Mission Number **103** (150)
3	**BEANEY** – Lt. Elroy W.	Crew #70	2 Missions Credited	*Witchcraft* Mission Numbers **24** (28); **44** (69)
4	**BRANDON** – Lt. Charles H.	Crew #70	1 Mission Credited	*Witchcraft* Mission Number **11** (12)
5	**BRIDENBAUGH** – Lt. Philip H.	Crew #64	1 Mission Credited	*Witchcraft* Mission Number **5** (5)
6	**BRYSON** – Lt. Eddie	Crew #56	3 Missions Credited	*Witchcraft* Mission Numbers **19** (23); **21** (25), **26** (33)
7	**CRAVENS** – Lt. Joseph W.	Crew #62	1Mission Credited	*Witchcraft* Mission Number **71** (102)
8	**DAVIS** – Lt. Marvin R.	Crew #57	1 Mission Credited	*Witchcraft* Mission Number **129** (203)
9	**EVANS** – Lt. Richard E.	Crew #58	2 Missions Credited	*Witchcraft* Mission Numbers **45** (71); **46** (72)
10	**EPTING** – Lt. Carl E.	Crew #67	4 Missions Credited	*Witchcraft* Mission Numbers **67** (98); **83** (117); **84** (119), **94** (136)
11	**GAVIN** – Lt. John P.	Crew #57	1 Mission Credited	*Witchcraft* Mission Number **2** (2)
12	**GRAHAM** – Lt. Lester O.	Crew #66	1 Mission Credited	*Witchcraft* Mission Number **92** (134)
13	**GRAY** – Lt. S.T. (Jr)	Crew #64	14 Missions Credited	*Witchcraft* Mission Numbers **76** (109); **77** (110); **79** (113); **80** (114); **81** (115); **85** (123); **88** (128); **89** (131); **90** (132); **91** (133); **93** (135); **95,** (140); **96** (141); **97** (142)
14	**HELTON** – Lt. Edwin M.	Crew #55	1 Mission Credited	*Witchcraft* Mission Number **10** (11)
15	**JANSEN –** Lt. Frederick J.	Crew #61	2 Missions Credited	*Witchcraft* Mission Numbers **131** (206); **136** (218)
16	**JOHNSON** – Lt. Howard W.	Crew #69	1 Mission Credited	*Witchcraft* Mission Number **60** (90)
17	**LACKENS** – Lt. Edwin B.	Crew #71	1 Mission Credited	*Witchcraft* Mission Number **78** (111)
18	**LASZLO** – Lt. Geza G.	Crew #60	3 Missions Credited	*Witchcraft* Mission Numbers **104** (158); **106** (161); **107** (162)
19	**LOVELESS** – Lt. George E.	Crew #61	1 Mission Not Credited	*Witchcraft* Mission Number **99** N/C (145 N/C)
20	**MARTIN** – Lt. Sherman D.	Crew #65	1 Mission Credited	*Witchcraft* Mission Number **37** (53)
21	**McFARLAND** – Lt. James W.	Crew #73	5 Missions Credited	*Witchcraft* Mission Numbers **108** (164); **124** (186); **134** (211); **135** (216); **137** (220)

22	**McKENZIE** – Lt. Robert L.	Crew #58	1 Mission Credited	*Witchcraft* Mission Number **63** (94)
23	**MEYERS** – Lt. Robert A.	Crew #62	1 Mission Credited	*Witchcraft* Mission Number **100** (146)
24	**NEWHOUSE** – Lt. James K.	Crew #57	2 Missions 1 Credited & 1 Not Credited	*Witchcraft* Mission Numbers 15 **N/C** (19 N/C); **66** (97)
25	**PATTON** – Lt. Nolan G.	Crew #70	2 Missions Credited	*Witchcraft* Mission Numbers **87** (127); **109** (166).
26	**PHILLIPS** – Lt. John G.	Crew #63	2 Missions Credited	*Witchcraft* Mission Numbers **122** (184); **126** (192)
27	**REED** – Lt. George. W.	Crew #62	30 Missions 27 Credited & 3 Not Credited	*Witchcraft* Mission Numbers **1** (1); **3** (3); **4** (4); **6** (6); **8 N/C** (9 N/C); **9**(10); **12** (13); **13** (15); **14 N/C** (17 N/C); **16** (20); **17** ;(21); **18** (22); **20 N/C**(24 N/C); **22** (26); **23**(27);**25**(31);**27**(34);**28**(35);**29**(39);**30**(40);**31**(42);**32**(44); **33** (46); **34** (47); **35** (51); **36** (52); **38** (55); **39** (58); **40** (60); **41** (61)
28	**RICE** – Lt. John W.	Crew #52	12 Missions 11 Credited & 1 Not Credited	*Witchcraft* Mission Numbers **101** (147); **105** (159); **110** (167); **112** (172); **113** (173); **114 N/C** ("X" N/C); **115** (174); **118** (177); **119** (178); **120** (179); **121** (183); **123** (185)
29	**RODEN** – Lt. James A.	Crew #9 (788th Sqdn)	1Mission Credited	*Witchcraft* Mission Number **7** (7)
30	**ROSENTHAL** – Lt. Donald M.	Crew #54	2 Missions Credited	*Witchcraft* Mission Numbers **125** (191); **132** (207)
31	**ROSS** – Lt. John K.	Crew #65	1 Mission Credited	*Witchcraft* Mission Number **102** (149)
32	**ROTHCHILD** – Lt. Aubrey E.	Crew #68	1 Mission Credited	*Witchcraft* Mission Number **86** (124)
33	**SEVERANCE** – Capt. Joseph	Crew #71	1 Mission Credited	*Witchcraft* Mission Number **98** (143)
34	**THOMPSON** – Lt. John E.	Crew #68	2 Missions Credited	*Witchcraft* Mission Numbers **49** (76); **57** (85).
35	**UNGERER** – Lt. Maynard M.	Crew #63	1 Mission Credited	*Witchcraft* Mission Number **82** (116)
36	**VOGT** – Lt. Leonard P.	Crew #63	22 Missions Credited	*Witchcraft* Mission Numbers **42** (63); **47** (73); **48** (75); **50** (77); **51** (78); **52** (79); **53** (80); **55** (83); **56** (84); **58** (88); **59** (89); **61** (91); **62** (93); **64** (95); **65** (96); **68** (99); **69** (100); **70** (101); **72** (103); **73** (104); **74** (105); **75** (106)
37	**WHITSEL** – Lt. Travis S.	Crew #73	1 Mission Not Credited	*Witchcraft* Mission Number – **43 N/C** (68 N/C)
38	**WILLIS** – Lt. Robert H.	Crew #64	3 Missions Credited	*Witchcraft* Mission Numbers **127** (193); **130** (205); **133** (210)
39	**WILSON** – Lt. Joseph C.	Crew #60	1 Mission Credited	*Witchcraft* Mission Number **128** (194)
40	**ZBIKOWSKI** – Lt. Joseph H.	Crew #54	1 Mission Credited	*Witchcraft* Mission Number **54** (81)

Note: Names of pilots are shown alphabetically.

(a) The *Witchcraft* Mission Number shown as X **N/C** **(**X N/C) indicates the mission was not given a credit rating.

(b) The number in **bold print** relates to the actual *Witchcraft* mission number and the bracketed figure is the 467th Group Mission Number.

(c) A total of forty pilots and crews flew *Witchcraft* on combat missions.

(d) As the list indicates, *Witchcraft* was flown on a total of 137 combat missions, of which 130 were given a credit rating. The seven missions not given a credit rating were due to the crews being recalled due to inclement weather conditions over Europe. Details relating to combat missions having to be aborted are stated in the appropriate mission details as shown in Chapter Eight.

(e) Group records reveal that *Witchcraft* was loaned to the 788th Squadron for the combat mission to Paderborn, Germany, on April 19, 1944. That was the seventh combat mission flown by both the 467th Group, as well as the seventh for *Witchcraft*. Other than that one occasion, *Witchcraft* was never loaned to another squadron while serving with the 467th Bombardment Group at Rackheath.

8

Details of Combat Missions That *Witchcraft* was Assigned to Fly

Witchcraft prior to flying its first combat mission.

Mission 1 – 10 April 1944 to Bourges, France
Group Mission #1 – Target – Luftwaffe Airfield
On the morning of 10 April 1944, thirty B-24s—including *Witchcraft* flown by Lt. George W. Reed and his Crew #62—were assigned the mission to Bourges. The planes, each loaded with 6 x 1,000-lb. GP (general purpose) bombs, commenced take-off from Rackheath at 0600 to attack the Luftwaffe airfield at Bourges, in German-occupied France.

Col. Shower flew as Group Command Pilot, with Lt. Kenneth Driscoll and Crew #7 from the 788th Squadron in B-24H 42-52623 *Wabbit*; Maj. Salzarulo flew as Deputy Group Lead with Lt. George Tormoen and Crew #15 on B-24H 42-52548 *Jaw-Ja-Boy*, also from the 788th Squadron. Maj. Walter Smith flew as the second Squadron Lead with Lt. Richard Campbell and Crew #53 on B-24H 42-52571 *Snooper* from the 790th Squadron, and Capt. Stanley Neitzel flew Deputy Squadron Lead with Crew #70 on B-24H 41-29270 *My Wild Irish Rose*, also from the 790th Squadron.

The estimated time of return was made known to the personnel on the ground in time for them all to gather 'round the perimeter strip to welcome the crews on their return. It was an

The airfield at Bourges, France, on 10 April 1944.

unusually beautiful day in England, and the clear blue skies permitted the sun to shine its warm rays on the crowd waiting to greet the returning aircraft. The Group B-24s flew over the base in perfect formation. A quick count revealed all aircraft had made it back to base, and every man on the field was thrilled to see their friends return safely. Following the debriefing, the interrogation reports indicated that neither flak nor enemy aircraft were encountered, and the crews on that first mission referred to it as a "milk run." Two of the aircraft had failed to attack due to mechanical problems, and two failed for other reasons. The remaining twenty-six aircraft dropped 149 x 1,000lb GP bombs. Aerial photographs showed good results were achieved, although one of the squadrons was slightly west of MPI (Mean Point of Impact).

Lt. John P. Gavin and Crew #57.

The B-24s had good fighter cover by P-47s and P-51s.

Group records indicate that *Witchcraft* was airborne for 6 hours 53 minutes and following return to base, it took 1,840 gallons to top off its fuel tanks.

Mission 2 – 11 April 1944 to Oschersleben, Germany
Group Mission#2 – Target – Focke-Wulf aircraft plant
Twenty-seven B-24s, including *Witchcraft* flown by Lt. John P. Gavin and Crew #57, were assigned to attack the Focke-Wulf aircraft plant; each plane was loaded with 52 x 100-lb. type 1B incendiary bombs. The Group B-24s, led by Lt. Col. Allen F. Herzberg flying in Lt. Lominack's B-24 "52350" with Crew #28, commenced take-off from Rackheath at 0715.

A total of 1,361 bombs were dropped on the primary target and thirty-two were dropped on a target of opportunity. Good fighter protection was provided by P-38s and P-47s. Moderate flak and fighter opposition was encountered, and the results of the mission were claimed as good, although bombs fell on the airfield and the factory was not destroyed.

Group records reveal that the flight time for Lt. Gavin's crew was six hours fifty-three minutes, and 2,000 gallons were used to top off the fuel tanks in *Witchcraft*.

Left to right are Master Sgt. Joe Ramirez, Cpl. Joe Vetter, Sgt. Ray Betcher, and Staff Sgt. George Dong with *Witchcraft* on completion of her second combat mission.

Mission 3 – 12 April 1944 to Schweinfurt, Germany
Group Mission#3 – Target – Primary – Schweinfurt, Germany
Secondary – Focke-Wulf aircraft plant at Oschersleben, Germany
Twenty-seven aircraft, including *Witchcraft* and its original Crew #62 (Lt. George W. Reed's crew), were assigned the mission. Each plane was loaded with 52 x 100-lb. incendiary bombs and scheduled take-off time was 1012.

After assembly, and having reached the French coastline, the mission was recalled by the Second Bombardment Division due to unexpected bad weather over the target.

Having reached enemy occupied territory, this mission was given a credit rating.

The flight time recorded for 42-52534 on this aborted mission was three hours twenty-one minutes and 930 gallons were used to top off the fuel tanks in *Witchcraft*.

Mission 4 – 13 April 1944 to Lechfeld, Germany
Group Mission #4 – Target – Airfield Installations
For the mission to Lechfeld, the 467th Group put up twenty-eight planes, including *Witchcraft* flown by Lt. George W. Reed and Crew #62. The B-24s, each carrying 50 x 100-lb. incendiary bombs, commenced lift-off from Rackheath at 1015 for the estimated 8½-hour mission—the longest yet flown by the Group. One plane aborted during assembly due to mechanical problems and another dropped out of formation due to an engine problem that developed over Germany, but dropped its bomb load.

Only twenty-three of the remaining twenty-six Group ships dropped their bombs on the target. One of the three that failed to bomb the target was due to a bomb rack mechanical failure; another dropped some of its bomb load on a village in Germany and some in the Channel; and the third ship—42-52535 *Katy* from the 789th Squadron (flown by Lt. Ernest Caluori and Crew #31)—was severely damaged. It was last seen going down with a fire in the left wing, and resulted in four crew members KIA and six taken POW. The bombing results rated as not good, since one flight dropped its bombs 3,000 feet southeast of the MPI and the other flight released their bombs 2,000 feet east of the MPI. The crews encountered moderate flak and fighter opposition, and the Group B-24s sustained considerable battle damage.

Group records show that *Witchcraft* had a recorded flight time of eight hours six minutes, but the quantity of fuel used is unknown.

Mission 5 – 17 April 1944 to Wizernes, France
Group Mission #5 – Target – V-1 Flying Bomb Sites
Only ten B-24s—including *Witchcraft* flown by Lt. Joseph R. Bridenbaugh and Crew #64—were assigned to hit the *No Ball* sites at Wizernes.

The planes, each loaded with 8 x 1,000-lb. GP bombs, commenced their take-off at 1350.

One B-24 failed to attack due to bomb rack malfunction. The formation was guided by PPF (Pathfinder Flares), and 72 x 1,000-lb. GP bombs were released over the target at an altitude of 22,500 feet. Flying in each of the five PPF ships was a 467th Group member: Maj. Albert L. Wallace (791st), Maj. Robert L. Salzarulo (788th), Maj. Garnet B. Palmer (789th), Capt. Robert W. Doenges (789th), and Capt. Fred E. Holdrege (790th). Each PPF ship led two of the 467th Group B-24s. Unfortunately, the results were unknown due to the target being completely covered by overcast. Light and inaccurate flak was encountered and no enemy aircraft were seen. Fighter escort for the B-24s was provided by P-47s.

Group records reveal that the flight time for *Witchcraft* was three hours forty-five minutes and 1,235 gallons of fuel were used to top off her fuel tanks.

Mission 6 – 18 April 1944 to Brandenburg, Germany
Group Mission #6 – Target – Arado aircraft plant
Twenty-seven B-24s commenced take-off from Rackheath at 1040, including *Witchcraft* flown by Lt. George W. Reed and Crew #62. Each plane was loaded with 50 x 100-lb. incendiary bombs.

Twenty-four aircraft bombed the target; one plane had engine problems and turned back at the IP (Initial Point), and two aircraft returned to base early due to engine failures, but released their bombs over Germany.

Col. Albert J. Shower led the Group B-24s, with Lt. Charles Grace and Crew #77, from the 791st Squadron, flying 41-29375 *Lil' Peach*.

Anti-aircraft flak was moderate and no enemy fighter aircraft were encountered. The target was heavily clouded over, but reconnaissance reports revealed the bombing results were fair.

Fighter escort was provided by P-38s, P-47s, and P-51s. A good day for the Group, as no aircraft loss or crew casualties were incurred.

Lt. Reed recorded a flight time of seven hours forty-five minutes in his flight log. The number of gallons used to top-up the fuel tanks in *Witchcraft* after this mission is unknown, but average gallons used that day for each B-24 is shown in Group records as 1,903 gallons.

Lt. J.A. Roden's Crew # 9. Rear (L to R): James A. Roden (P), Wellington E. Landis (N), James R. Howe (G), and Charles D. McGonigle (BTG). Front (L to R): Louis J. Violette (E), George E. Carter (RO), and Richard F. Horak (TG). Note: J.H. Maxey (CP), Riley E. Orr (G), and Robert E. Wilson (B) are not in the photo.

Mission 7 – 19 April 1944 to Paderborn, Germany
Group Mission #7 – Target – Luftwaffe Airfield
Twenty-seven of the Group's B-24s, including *Witchcraft* flown by Lt. James A. Roden and Crew #9 (*from 788th Squadron), commenced take-off at 0730. The ships each carried a mixture of 100-lb. GP and 160-lb. IB.

Maj. Walter R. Smith led the first squadron with Lt. Bill. F. Moore and Crew #11, and Lt. James A. Secaffico flew as deputy first squadron lead with Lt. Romeyne W. Werdung and Crew #3. Capt. Fred Holdrege led the second squadron with Lt. Carl. V. Schott and Crew #51, and Capt. Stanley J. Neitzel flew as deputy second squadron lead with Lt. Richard Campbell and Crew #53.

All aircraft bombed the target. A few of the bombs dropped within 1,000 feet of the MPI, with the concentration between 1,000 and 2,500 feet short of the MPI; consequently, the results were classified as fair. Flak was meager and no enemy fighter opposition was encountered. Good fighter escort was provided by P-47s and P-51s.

Another good day for the 467th, as no aircraft were lost nor casualties incurred.

Group records indicate that *Witchcraft* was loaned on that one and only occasion to another squadron. The records reveal the flight time for Lt. Roden and his crew was five hours thirty-four minutes, and 1,300 gallons were used to top-up the fuel tanks in *Witchcraft* following the mission.

Mission 8 – 21 April 1944 to Zwickau, Germany.
Group Mission #9 – Target – aircraft plant
Thirty-two aircraft, including *Witchcraft* flown by Lt. G. W. Reed and Crew #62, commenced take-off at 0600 hours. Each B-24 was loaded with a mixture of 500-lb. GP and 100-lb. IB.

As most of the B-24s failed to assemble due to bad weather and severe icing, the mission was aborted and the aircraft were recalled. No credit was given for the mission.

Lt. Reed's flight records indicate take-off time to landing *Witchcraft* was four hours. The quantity used to top-up the fuel tanks is unknown.

Mission 9 – 22 April 1944 to Hamm, Germany
Group Mission #10 – Target – Railroad Marshalling Yards
This mission was a planned and premeditated, late take-off "surprise" attack, with the intention of arriving over the target during early evening, at an hour when the enemy would least anticipate an attack. The time of the strike would be well beyond the hours when the usual daytime American bomber raids were made, and a few hours too early for the usual time of the RAF night attacks. The purpose was to "catch out" and destroy the railroad repair

equipment that the German work force brought out very late afternoon/early evening—during the lull between the daytime and nighttime bomber raids—to repair bomb-damaged railroad tracks.

The 467th Group assigned twenty-eight B-24s, including *Witchcraft* flown by Crew #62 (Lt. George W. Reed's crew). The twenty-eight planes were loaded with an overall total of 730 x 500-lb. GPs and 142 x 100-lb. IBs.

Take-off commenced at 1630, with Col. Shower leading the Group with Lt. R. Campbell and Crew #53, and Lt. C.H. Brandon flying as deputy lead with Lt. R.D. Sheehan and Crew #61—both from the 790th Squadron.

All aircraft reached the target and twenty-six dropped a total of 132 x 500-lb. GP and 676 x 100-lb. IB bombs in the target area. The results were rated very good, with a very high number of bombs dropped in the MPI area. One plane had a bomb bay rack malfunction, causing 10 x 500-lb. GP bombs to fall on a small village just beyond the IP. Another B-24 had a problem opening the bomb bay doors and released its 54 x 100-lb. IB bombs over another small village. Heavy and intense flak was encountered on the route to and over the target area.

P-47s and P-51s provided escort protection for the B-24s during part of the flight. No enemy aircraft were seen or encountered until the Group airplanes commenced preparations to land at Rackheath, having just about completed the six-hour mission.

The flight time on this mission for *Witchcraft* and Crew #62 is shown as six hours eighteen minutes in the flight logs of both Lt. Reed and Lt. John Oder. Group records reveal that 1,825 gallons were used to top up the fuel tanks in *Witchcraft* after landing.

Some comments relating to this mission:

In the darkness, as Second Bombardment Division B-24s were flying over the North Sea on their homeward flight back to their various bases, they were followed by undetected enemy aircraft. The 467th aircraft were preparing to land when the intruding enemy aircraft attacked, and two B-24s crashed after being severely damaged. One was 788th Squadron B-24 42-52536, flown by Lt. James A. Roden and Crew #9, that crashed at Withersdale Street, Mendham, Suffolk, with the loss of all ten crew members. The other B-24 lost that evening was 42-52445 from the 791st Squadron, flown by Lt. Stalie C. Reid and Crew #88. Three of the crew members parachuted out of the burning B-24 before it crashed in a field opposite the village school at Barsham, Suffolk; Lt. Reid and six of his crew members lost their lives.

Besides attacking the 467th Group's B-24s as they were entering their respective landing patterns, the intruding Messerschmitt 410A/1 fighter-bomber aircraft also strafed and dropped five 50-kg high explosive bombs on the airfield at Rackheath, causing some damage to the aircraft. One member of the ground personnel—Pfc. Daniel E. Miney from the 1229th Quartermaster Service Company—was killed in the bombing attack, and Pat Mahoney, from the same company, was injured. Pfc. Miney was the only member from the 467th Group ground echelon killed in action during the time the Group was at Rackheath.

The Group suffered its heaviest combat loss up to that mission, with the loss of two aircraft and seventeen flight crew members killed and four wounded.

Comments by the Author relating to Group Mission #10

It has been erroneously mentioned in various books and articles that the reason for the late take-off time for this mission was due to bad weather conditions over the target, and that the take-off time was delayed several times throughout the day, until late afternoon clearance was given. The fact is, the unusually late take-off time (1630 hours) for a daytime combat mission over enemy territory was pre-planned. Documents amongst Group records, plus extracts from letters written by Richard Campbell, Kenneth Driscoll, Louis Schiavo, John (Jack) Stevens, and extracts from Anthony (Tony) Bell's diary as printed hereunder, completely establish this fact. They also dispel the myth of "bad weather reports over target area" as being the reason for the late take-off time for the mission to Hamm on 22 April 1944, that has appeared in various publications.

Lt.Col. John E. (Jack) Stevens (USAF Retired)—a 2/Lt. and crew leader of Crew #89, 791st Squadron, during this mission, wrote the following:

> Here is an account of the scariest mission that my crew and I were on.
>
> We didn't go on a mission on the morning of April 22, 1944, but soon after noon, the twenty-eight crews who were alerted to fly that day were

called to a mission briefing. There, we learned take-off was 4:30 PM; our target was the railroad marshalling yard at Hamm, Germany. Bomb loads were either 500-lb. general purpose or 100-lb. incendiaries; bombing altitude was 27,000 feet; and weather was forecast to be clear for the whole mission.

We made a routine take-off and assembly, joined the bomber stream as scheduled, and proceeded on course. We encountered flak along the route and in the target area, but I don't recall any fighter attacks. After we turned onto the bomb run, I could see the marshalling yard up ahead very clearly (one of the few times). Smoke was rising from bomb hits by earlier groups.

We bombed at approximately 7:30 PM, rallied off the target, and headed home. As we came across Holland, it started to get dark at our altitude, and I saw running lights of several of our planes go on. I thought that would help enemy anti-aircraft gunners track us and commented about it to my crew, but because of the radio silence rule, didn't bring it to our leader's attention.

We let down as we came across the English Channel and, of course, the lower we went, the darker it got. After we sighted England, I turned on my running lights and it seemed that all we had to do was go through our normal formation approach and landing procedures, and we'd have another mission behind us. By the time (about 10:00 PM) we neared traffic altitude, it was real dark. I couldn't see any ground lights, but figured that was because of England's strict blackout. All I could see of the plane I was flying on was its red wing tip light, the vertical line of blue formation lights on the rear edge of each rudder, and the horizontal line of blue formation lights on top of the fuselage. I found it difficult to hold formation because the lines of lights on the rudders seemed to switch places with each other.

Our formation went into a left turn and I thought, "Oh, good, we're going into our landing procedure." I recalled instructions the 8th Air Force indoctrination team gave us about a "funnel of lights" we'd be able to see as we approached an airfield at night; the funnel would lead into the active runway. I had the crew looking for that "funnel of lights," but no one could see any ground lights. Our formation circled around several times, and I was getting bleary-eyed trying to concentrate on those lines of blue lights on the plane I was flying on.

We had heard no radio transmissions, and with more than a hundred 2nd Air Division planes flying around East Anglia in darkness, I got to thinking about the likelihood of mid-air collisions. I told the crew I was going to leave the formation and asked Will Rapp, our navigator, to tune up the radio beacon for an Automatic Radio Direction Finding (ADF) approach to our field. The beacon was working and we homed in on it, then took up the 35 degree heading to our field; but again, none of us could see any lights, much less a "funnel of lights." We checked the beacon frequency and tried a second approach, but still couldn't see any lights of any kind.

I assumed there was some problem affecting the lights at our field, but with all the airfields in the East Anglia area, some others would be working. So, I told the crew I'd start a wide turn and for them to look for any lights, and that we'd land at the first field we saw. After a short while, we saw a fire and determined it was on an airfield. Because we couldn't see any electric lights there either, I assumed there was an area electrical outage. I remarked to my crew that the people at that base were trying to be helpful by lighting a fire for their returning planes, and I went into a normal landing pattern. As we came down the final approach our copilot, Ray Smith, grabbed my arm and said, "Jack, that's a B-24 burning" [it was Capt. Alvin D. Skaggs's ship *Vadie Raye - P.W.*]. I looked up and, sure enough, it was a B-24 completely engulfed in flames. We landed, turned off at the end of the runway, and cut the engines, but left the "putt putt" and running lights on so no one would run into our plane.

An operations jeep came out and the driver asked us to turn off our lights. I said we didn't want anyone running into our plane, and he assured us that base personnel would take care of the plane. We piled into his jeep and headed towards Operations. The driver didn't have any lights on and I saw soldiers walking alongside us on the taxi strip we were on; I told the driver to turn on his lights or he'd hit one of the men. He responded, "Don't you know this field is under attack by German planes?" Oops! Maybe that's why the complete blackout—including the absence of any "funnel of lights."

We had landed at Seething (USAAF Airfield No. 146, home of the 448BG), and I reported to the Group Commander, who was outside the Operations Building, firing a carbine at German planes as they flew past. He asked about casualties and plane damage. I said we had no casualties and started to tell him the location and size of flak damage we'd received. He stopped me to ask if the plane was flyable and, when I assured him it was, he had our base notified and had someone take us to the Mess Hall and arrange for quarters for us—there were quite a few empty bunks that night. The German planes left soon after we landed (I guess they learned we were there) and things started to calm down.

After breakfast next morning, we flew back to Rackheath and learned that one man [PFC Daniel Miney, 1229th Quartermaster Service Company – *P. W.*] was killed and some property damaged by bombs. Then, we learned that Stalie Reid and his crew [including other former 7th Anti-Submarine Group members Bombardier Lt. Louis A. Alier and Radio Operator T/Sgt. Walter W. Kovalenko – *P. W.*] had been shot down. Three of the crew managed to bail out, but the rest were killed.

When we got back to our Nissen hut, our uniforms were gone. However, after a short dialogue with our hut mates, they flashed big grins and brought our uniforms out from their lockers. They knew we were at Seething and would be back, but wanted us to think we'd been declared missing and that our effects had already been picked up; a somewhat morbid way to say "welcome back."

Because Stalie Reid and his two crew members were 7th Anti-Sub members, Col. Shower had me represent the 467th Bomb Group at their burial at Cambridge a few days later.

Retired Col. Richard J. Campbell was a pilot with the 790th Squadron (his rank at the time of the mission was 1/Lt). Col. Campbell's following letter was published in the 467th Group Association Journal *Poop from Group*, Vol 12 – No.1, dated March 1, 1993:

> There were two missions to Hamm, Germany: the first on 22 April '44 and the second on 22 October '44. I flew as Lead Aircraft Commander, with Col. Albert Shower as Group Lead Command Pilot, on the first (April) mission.
>
> I do remember the intelligence briefing for the mission. We were told the reason for a late take-off. The Germans had developed high-skilled and well-trained railroad repair crews. They had the ability to get two lines operating in a bombed marshalling yard in a very short period of time. They were using special equipment mounted on railroad cars. Our mission was to catch one of these units while it was operating.
>
> Heavy flak was encountered along the route and in the target area. Enemy aircraft were not encountered until the aircraft were nearly back to their bases. Several German aircraft followed the formation back to the coast. The weather was clear and it was just turning dark. A small number of German twin- and single-engine fighters came into the traffic of the base and attacked planes as they landed.

Anthony (Tony) Bell—former S/Sgt Radio Operator on Lt. James A. Mikkelsen's Crew #84 of the 791st Squadron— wrote the following diary entry concerning this mission (note the briefing time):

> April 22, 1944 – We were briefed at 1300. Our take-off time was 1638. We climbed and assembled OK, except Wescott's crew [Lt. W.L.Wescott's Crew #87, flying 41-29369 *Tender Comrade* – *P. W.*] was supposed to be on our left

> wing, but we never saw their ship during the whole trip.
>
> Our target was the marshalling yards at Hamm, and the 1st, 2nd, and 3rd Divisions are scheduled to hit it all in one day! We're last to go in on the target.
>
> We were hit bad by flak, and our nose gunner Lyvers [Staff Sgt. Joseph P. Lyvers – *PW*] was hit in the back of the neck, but he was OK. A large piece hit the windshield and busted it, and another piece just missed my shoulder by a fraction of an inch—as a matter of fact, I thought I was hit, but I wasn't. We lost an engine, and also the formation again! We got flak all the way back and lost two airplanes. Boy, it was accurate today! Our ship had 37 holes in it. Our take off time was pretty late. This made us return at night and we are just Day Bombers, and don't know anything about flying formation at night.
>
> Anyway, here we are again over enemy territory by ourselves, without the formation and no fighter escort. Perkins, our Tail Gunner [Sgt. Fay E. Perkins – *P.W.*], called in, reporting about 30 or 40 airplanes way behind us, but he couldn't identify them. We were supposed to be "last out of Europe," so who the hell were these guys? We considered slowing down for the benefit of their protection, but didn't. At the French coast, the Germans shot everything they could at us! We were low enough to receive anything, even 37-mm fire, but fireworks! I'll swear they fired fireworks into the sky, but they were well below us!
>
> When we got to the English coast, the damn English fired on us! I couldn't authenticate, because my authentication tables ran out an hour earlier! So much for late take-offs!
>
> We finally got to our field and the mini pinpoint runway lights were turned on for us. Then, just as we were committed to land, they went out! Mikk [Lt. J. Mikkelsen, Pilot – *P.W.*] turned on our landing lights and set down, taxiing to the end of the runway. Wow! Could you believe it? We're home!
>
> Just about then we were informed by a stuttering, stammering ground officer to shut our lights, as the field was under attack by German bombers and fighters. Damm! Now, it was clear who that was flying behind us! They stood back until it got dark enough to pass us, left us alone so we wouldn't radio their presence, sneaked in with an American formation, and preceded to have a turkey shoot when our ships started to land. We lost two bombers and two crews, one ground man, and one ground man injured. But our crew lucked out again! Damm – what a day!

Finally, a letter written by retired USAF Maj. Kenneth Driscoll, who also flew on that particular mission as a 1/ Lt. pilot in the 788th Squadron. His letter was published in *Poop from Group* Vol. 11, No. 1, dated 1 March 1992. Maj. Driscoll wrote:

> During 1944, I had flown five daylight B-24 bombing missions with the 467th Bomb Group and thirty secret night missions with the $801^{st}/492^{nd}$ Bomb Group, dropping spies and supplies to support the French underground forces. But one mission in particular stands out above the other thirty-four, and that is the 467th Bomb Group mission to Hamm, Germany, on 22 April 1944. That was the third combat mission for my crew.
>
> HQ 8th Air Force decided to pull a "surprise" attack on Germany. Our target was the railroad marshalling yards at Hamm, Germany.
>
> The "surprise" was that the 8th Air Force was to hit the target about an hour before dark and catch the Germans unprepared to retaliate with anti-aircraft guns (flak) and fighters.
>
> After bombing the target, we were to fly in formation back to the coastline. Upon reaching the North Sea coastline, darkness would be setting in.
>
> At our afternoon briefing, our instructions were that when it got dark, we were to break formation, turn on our running lights, and each crew was on its own to return to base.
>
> The Group aircraft took off as scheduled late in the afternoon/early evening. My Squadron, the 788th, was not leading the Group. My crew was flying number 2 position (deputy lead) in the

squadron formation. I do not recall who our squadron lead pilot was.

The Group got into formation at about 24,000 feet at the assigned radio beacon north of our base, Rackheath. At the designated time, the Group turned east and joined other Groups flying in formation at the Division assembly line. When we crossed the North Sea, our altitude was approximately 27,000 feet.

After dropping bombs, the flights turned to the right of the target and reformed [sic] into the normal Group formation configuration for the return flight.

The flight to the coast was routine, with the exception of having to keep extra power on the three good engines to enable us to keep in formation. [About ten minutes before reaching the IP, Lt. Driscoll's plane got hit by flak that put number 2 engine out of use – *P.W.*]

Just prior to reaching the coast in semi-darkness, enemy anti-aircraft guns shot some tracer shells at us. They resembled the bright white Roman candles used at 4th of July celebrations. There were 10 or 15 of them. I saw them passing nearby to the right of us. They were going straight up. Because my field of vision was cut off at the top of the copilot's window, I could not follow them up. I had never seen anything like that before.

Shortly thereafter, we crossed the coastline and headed back across the North Sea. When we were out over the water about 15 miles, darkness was becoming a reality.

Shortly after dropping back out of formation, we turned on our running lights and started a very slow descent. This allowed me to reduce the power and take the strain off the three good engines.

When full darkness came, I started to fly by instruments, which was normal procedure on night flights over water. The navigator, Lt. Harold Pantis, kept getting electronic fixes. He kept us all informed over the intercom as to when we would make landfall near Great Yarmouth, and the estimated time of arrival (ETA) over our base at Rackheath. We did not see the lights of other aircraft. The formation had pulled ahead, as they were flying faster than we were.

When the ETA at the base was up, the navigator called over the intercom and said the base was directly below us. I banked the aircraft to the left and looked down. I could see absolutely no base lights or runway lights; everything was blacked out.

I made about six passes across the blacked-out base. The entire countryside was very dark, with no lights or landmarks visible. . . After circling about three more times, the runway lights were turned on. I immediately entered a normal traffic pattern. As usual, landing lights were turned on during the final approach. The tower still maintained radio silence. We landed and rolled to near the end of the runway, turned right onto a taxiway, turned off our landing lights, and started to taxi back to our parking area. Periodically, the landing lights were turned on for a very short time to assist me in taxiing the aircraft in.

When we got about halfway down to our parking area, military personnel in a jeep flagged us down and I stopped the aircraft. We were then informed that German fighters and fighter-bombers were in the area and had hit the base. The German planes had intermingled in the darkness with the 8th Air Force planes coming back across the North Sea and were not detected when crossing the English coast.

I never received an explanation why the tower did not break radio silence and instruct us to turn off our lights, scatter in a northerly direction, and return in a half hour or so. It is possible that the first few returning aircraft were advised of the situation. At that time, I estimated we were about 8-10 minutes away and 20-25 miles out from the base. With VHF radios, we should have been able to pick up tower transmissions at that distance.

The German fighters probably did not try to shoot down any of our aircraft while intermingled with us coming in over the North Sea. That action would have been detected and their surprise attack ruined. Our incoming aircraft would have been alerted and appropriate disbursal information

> given to us. The ground bases and anti-aircraft gun sites would also have been alerted earlier.
>
> This was a fighter pilot's dream: to be undetected among hundreds of enemy bombers flying at night with their running lights on and their guns secured (unmanned for landing).

Irrelevant to the reason for the late take-off, it is worthwhile referring to the entry made by Staff Sgt. Radio Operator Tony Bell (Crew #84, 791st Squadron) in his diary on the mission. Tony wrote:

> Our landfall on the English coast was not only after darkness fell, it was also one full hour after our verey pistol color code authentication tables ran out!

Responding to Maj. Driscoll's letter, Tony wrote:

> I wonder if Kenneth Driscoll remembers the heavy flak the British sent us as we flew around with our navigation lights on, firing one-hour-old authentication flares! I'll never forget the colors: Yellow/Yellow/Red! The more we fired, the more the Brits would respond!

Lt. Louis Schiavo, who served with the 790th Squadron as a pilotage/navigator, wrote a letter to the author regarding the Hamm mission, in which he mentioned in detail about an interesting incident:

> I flew as Pilotage Navigator in the nose turret on that mission. Up to this time, bombardiers had a trying time locating their targets or aiming points on approaching a target due to the poor position of the bombsight viewing window. It was decided to have a navigator in the nose turret, where forward visibility was good, to assist the bombardier in locating and identifying the target. With this arrangement, during the attack on Hamm, we were able to attack the target with considerable success and then turn towards the Dutch coast for return to base. The thing that impressed me most as we headed back to Rackheath was the bursting Flak shells in the dark. Seen in daylight, the Flak bursts appeared as harmless, black puffs of smoke, but seen up close and personal in the dark of evening, they appeared as blood-red bursts of fire and smoke. We were relieved to depart the Dutch coast and head for Rackheath. By the time we reached our base, it was quite dark.
>
> Since we flew as Lead Aircraft [flying with Lt. Richard Campbell and Crew #53 on '571 *Snooper - P.W.*] with Col. Shower as Command Pilot on our plane, we were scheduled to land first. The flight from the Dutch coast was uneventful, and we were letting down to the runway for a landing. As usual, I left the nose turret and took a position on the flight deck between Col. Shower (flying in the right hand seat) and the pilot in the left seat. Just before we were about to touch down on the runway, a dark form passed us on the right side, then swooped down directly in front of us, as if to land on our runway. Col. Shower called, "Did you see that? He cut us out as we were about to land. Did anyone get that SOB's aircraft number?" As we pulled up to make another run at landing, an explosion took place just ahead of us on the ground, on or near the runway. We quickly circled and landed just as all the landing lights were being extinguished. We taxied to a hardstand and exited the plane, unsure of what was going on around us.
>
> During my tour of duty in the ETO, we never took off late on a mission again.

The following is a brief comment made by Lt. John G. Oder (790th Squadron and original crew copilot of *Witchcraft*) that he entered in his flight record for 22 April 1944 after flying the Hamm mission:

> 4-2-44 mission #4 [John's actual mission number - *P.W.*] – R.R. Yards Hamm – Results Good – Heavy Flak – Ten holes in ship – Jerry followed us home – Hectic night landing.

Mrs. Phyllis A.G. Smales well remembers the German aircraft flying over Rackheath late that evening of 22 April 1944. In her letter, Mrs. Smales wrote:

During the WWII years until October 1944, I lived with my parents in a farmhouse—Mousehold Farm, Rackheath, close by the Norwich-Cromer railroad track and about 100 yards from the southeast edge of the airfield. Also, I worked for the American Red Cross on the base at Rackheath; I commenced working there about mid-January 1944.

It was our usual habit to watch the crews coming back with their planes. However, I remember very well that night of April 22, 1944, when the German planes followed the Group *Liberators* back to the airfield; in fact, both my mother and I watched what was happening from my bedroom window. That night, the *Liberators* kept flying around and we wondered why; we managed to pick up "pieces of conversations" on the short wave radio that we had. It then became obvious as to what was happening, and that there were German aircraft in the area over or near to the airfield. I still remember those loud, thud-like bangs and the flashes caused by the exploding bombs being dropped on the nearby airfield and our house shaking with each explosion.

Denis Sporle, a resident of Barsham, Suffolk, remembered the crash of B-24H-15 FO 42-52445 from the 791st Squadron the night of 22 April 1944. The following is an extract from notes taken during a conversation and interview with Denis in August 2000:

Denis vividly recalls that Saturday evening, April 22, 1944. His father, Special Police Constable George Sporle, was on duty at Ink Factory Hill, about a mile to the east of Barsham school, on the Beccles – Bungay road. Denis—although only eleven years of age at the time—recalls that his mother awakened him and his two sisters, and told them to get downstairs immediately. Within seconds, they were down the stairs, and his mother then pushed he and his sisters under the table in the living room for safety; they could hear anti-aircraft guns firing, to all appearances indicating an air raid. The time was about 10:15 PM, and about then, Denis remembers hearing a very loud bang and rumbling noises from close by; within a few minutes, his father arrived home and mentioned that an airplane had crashed nearby, in the field across the road opposite the village school. Denis recalls his father mentioning that he was on duty at Ink Factory Hill, about one mile to the east of Barsham school, on the Beccles-Bungay road, when he saw a plane on fire flying low over the Waveney Valley, approaching from the southeast and gradually losing height. His father thought it was going to crash on or very close to the area where we lived. Next morning, they walked up the lane next to their house to the adjoining road on their way to attend services at the village church. It was then he [Denis] saw the wreckage of the aircraft in the corner of a field very close to the road; the tail section, complete with stabilizers, was in a field on the other side of the road.

The Luftwaffe Aircraft Involved in this "Intruder Attack"

Kampfgeschwader 51 "Edelweiss" was one of the Luftwaffe's most distinguished bomber units, having been in the Battle of Britain in 1940, and later in the air offensive against Russia, as well as in other offensives. In early April, KG51 was based at Gilze-Rijen, Holland, in early 1944, and it was soon after arrival there that part of KG51 converted from its former bomber status and became a fighter force equipped with Me-410 fighter aircraft.

Maj. Dietrich Puttfarken, a squadron commander, formed and commanded a special long-range night fighter *Staffel* of KG51. The unit had only acquired operational status just prior to 22 April due to the small number of aircraft and crews available. But this small unit planned to take advantage of the opportunity offered by following the 8th Air Force bombers as they crossed the coastline on their homeward flight across the North Sea. The Luftwaffe fighter-bombers "tailed" the unaware crews in their B-17s and B-24s as they crossed the English coastline and approached their respective bases, and it was soon after that KG51 aircraft commenced their attack on the 8th Air Force planes. That small force of Luftwaffe fighter-bombers wreaked havoc on the returning Fortress and Liberator bombers by their surprise attack. They not only shot down several of the American bombers from various Groups, but also dropped small, high-explosive bombs on airfields and strafed a number as well. At Rackheath, Private Daniel E. Miney from the 1229th Quartermaster Company Service Group was killed, and another member—Pvt. Michael P. Mahoney—was injured.

A bungalow on Green Lane East, Rackheath (about 100 yards on the east side of the "Sole and Heel" public house) was badly damaged by one of the bombs that night.

However, on this particular "intruder mission," KG51 lost two Me-410s: OK+HP (serial number 420450) and 9K+MN (serial number 420314). OK+HP, flown by *Oberleutnant* Klaus Kruger and his radio operator, *Feldwebel* Michael Reichardt, were both killed when their aircraft crashed at Ashby St. Mary, about six miles southeast of Norwich, after sustaining severe damage from gunfire. The other KG51 plane (9K+MN) was ironically piloted by the Squadron Commander, Maj. Dietrich Puttfarken, and both he and his radio operator, *Oberleutnant* Willi Lux, along with their Me-410, were lost without any trace. It can only be assumed that Maj. Puttfarken's airplane either received some severe damage from gunfire or developed a major mechanical problem while flying back to KG51's base at Gilze-Rijen, Holland, and crashed into the North Sea.

Mission 10 – 24 April 1944 to Leipheim, Germany
Group Mission #11 – Target – Airfield and aircraft plant
For the mission to Leipheim, the Group put up twenty-eight B-24s. *Witchcraft* was flown by Lt. Edwin M. Helton and Crew #55. The planes, each loaded with 10 x 500-lb. GPs, commenced take-off from Rackheath at 0750. Two of the B-24s aborted and returned to base due to mechanical problems.

Col. Albert J. Shower flew with Lt. James D. Swearingen and Crew #78 of the 791st Squadron in B-24 41-29375 *Lil' Peach*, leading the Group and 96th Combat Wing formations.

The 467th's planes dropped a total of 260 bombs on the target from 18,000 feet, and the results were rated excellent, with the bombs concentrated on the MPI. Everything went well for the Group: clear weather, flak was mild, and no enemy fighters seen. The B-24s had good fighter cover support provided by P-38s, P-47s, and P-51s.

Group records reveal the flight time for *Witchcraft* was eight hours thirty-two minutes and the fuel tanks were topped up with 2,285 gallons after the mission. Note: For his outstanding leadership on this mission, Col. Shower was awarded the Distinguished Flying Cross.

Mission 11 – 25 April 1944 to Mannheim, Germany
Group Mission #12 – Target – Railroad Marshalling Yards
Twenty-two aircraft, including *Witchcraft*, flown by Lt. Charles H. Brandon and Crew #70, and carrying a total load of 878 x 100-lb. GPs and 163 x 100-lb. IBs, commenced take-off at 0655. Many of the aircraft were late taking off due to the bomb load instructions arriving late at Rackheath from headquarters. Due to the delay, the Group aircraft were unable to reach their designated flight position in the formation.

Lt. Col. Herzberg led the Group, flying with Lt. R.M. Werdung and Crew #3 in 41-29373 *Flak Magnet* from the 788th. Lt. W.F. Moore and Crew #11 on 41-29408 *Valiant Lady*, from the 788th Squadron, flew deputy lead. Lt. Moore's ship developed engine problems over the Paris area and had to abort and return to base, and Lt. Baxter Hensley and Crew #90 in 42-52530 *Bugs Bunny* (791st Squadron) filled the gap in the formation. Maj. Leonard M. McManus led the second squadron and flew with Lt. C.V. Schott and Crew #51 in 42-52512 *Baff'ling Bratt* from the 790th Squadron.

Lockheed P-38s, Republic P-47s, and North American P-51s provided excellent escort. Anti-aircraft fire was reasonably accurate, and although enemy fighter aircraft were seen attacking other formations, they did not approach the 467th. Five aircraft dropped 200 x 100-lb. GP and 60 x 100-lb. IB bombs on various targets of opportunity after becoming separated from the formation. 278 x 100-lb. GPs and 83 x 100-lb. IBs were jettisoned over the English Channel to decrease fuel consumption. The remaining 400 x 100-lb. GPs and 20 x 100-lb. IBs were brought back to base. The mission rating is unknown, but in view of the small tonnage of bombs dropped on various targets, it probably would not have achieved a high rating.

It is reasonable to state that the delay in arrival of the bomb load instructions was not at all helpful for this mission. Good fortune was holding with the Group and it did not suffer any loss of aircraft or incur any crew casualties.

Group records indicate the flight time for Lt. Brandon and Crew #70 was eight hours six minutes, and 2,245 gallons filled up the fuel tanks of *Witchcraft*.

Master Sgt. Joe Ramirez and his team at hardstand #32, awaiting return of *Witchcraft*.

Mission 12 – 26 April 1944 to Paderborn, Germany
Group Mission #13 – Target – Primary – Airfield
Secondary – Targets of opportunity at Osnabruck

Witchcraft and Lt. G.W. Reed and Crew #62 were assigned along with twenty-seven other 467th Group B-24s and crews the mission to Paderborn. The planes—each loaded with 10 x 500-lb. GP bombs—commenced take-off from Rackheath at 0630. Lt. H. Monefeldt and Crew #32 flew 42-52525 *Six Bits* and led the Group; Lt. Edward K. and Maj. Walter Smith flew with Lt. Leonard Lominack and Crew #28 on 41-29363 as Deputy Group lead—both aircraft and crews were from the 789th Squadron.

Paderborn was not bombed due to heavy undercast covering the area. Twenty-four aircraft dropped their bombs in the Minden/Osnabruk area. One B-24 jettisoned its bombs in the English Channel due to mechanical problems, and three aircraft brought their bombs back to base. Due to the heavy overcast, it was impossible to assess the damage.

Master Sgt. Joe Ramirez carrying out an oil change on *Witchcraft*.

No enemy fighter aircraft were sighted, but the crews encountered very intense and heavy flak that caused varying degrees of damage to fifteen of the Group B-24s and injuries to three crew members; however, no aircraft were lost. P-38s, P-47s, and P-51s provided good escort cover.

The flight records of both Lt. Reed and his copilot, Lt. Oder, show the flight time for *Witchcraft* and Crew #62 was five hours fifteen minutes, as well as the comment "Two holes in ship." Group records show flight time for *Witchcraft* as four hours fifty-three minutes and 1,380 gallons was used to top up her fuel tanks.

Mission 13 – 27 April 1944 to Blainville, France
Group Mission #15 – Target – Railroad Marshalling Yards

Witchcraft, flown by Lt. George Reed and Crew #62, joined twenty-three other Group bombers attacking the railroad yards at Blainville, France. Twenty-three of the ships were each loaded with 12 x 500-lb. GP bombs and one was loaded with 10 x 500-lb. GPs and 2x100-lb. IBs.

As it was a late take-off, Staff Sgt. Bob McEwen decided he had time to do some laundry.

Col. A.J. Shower flew with Lt. J.J. Swearing and Crew #78 on B-24 41-29375 *Lil' Peach* from the 791st Squadron and led the 467th's planes, which commenced take-off at 1527.

Only twenty of the planes bombed the target due to three planes making an early return to base due to mechanical problems; one ship bombed Verdun with another group. However, the twenty planes that reached the target dropped a total of 238 x 500 lb GPs and 2 x 100bd IBs from 17,500 feet. The results were rated "only fair." The flak was light and no enemy aircraft were seen. The B-24s were given good fighter support cover by P-38s, P-47s, and P-51s.

The flight logs of Lts. Reed and Oder contain an entry of six hours fifteen minutes, whereas Group records show a flight time of six hours forty minutes. Group records also reveal that the fuel tanks of *Witchcraft* were topped up with 1,925 gallons following the mission.

A new unit that had recently arrived from the United States was attached to the 790th Squadron for a few days during the month. This unit, occasionally referred to as the "Buck Rogers outfit," had been trained to use a special type of bombing equipment. Their particular technique was a mystery that remained unsolved at the time of their sudden transfer to the 458th Bombardment Group at Horsham St. Faith. (Later, this equipment was known as "Azon.")

Mission 14 – 1 May 1944 to Ruisseauville, France.
Group Mission #17 – Target – V-Weapon Site (V-1 Flying Bombs)
Twenty-two of the Group's B-24s, including *Witchcraft* flown by Lt. G.W. Reed and his Crew #62, were assigned for the mission to Ruisseauville. The planes, each loaded with 10 x 500-lb. GP bombs, commenced early morning take-off at 0445.

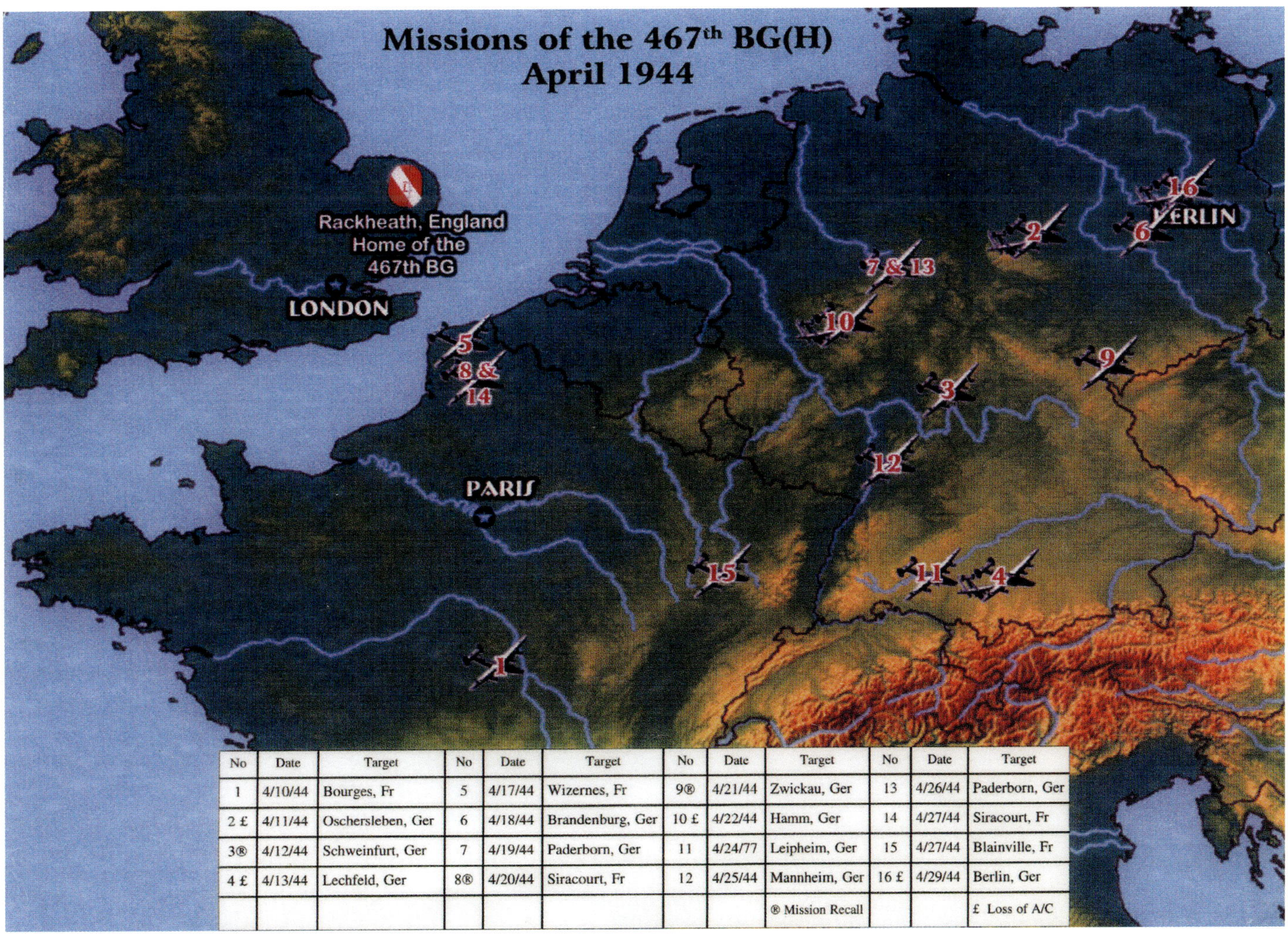

No	Date	Target	No	Date	Target	No	Date	Target	No	Date	Target
1	4/10/44	Bourges, Fr	5	4/17/44	Wizernes, Fr	9®	4/21/44	Zwickau, Ger	13	4/26/44	Paderborn, Ger
2 £	4/11/44	Oschersleben, Ger	6	4/18/44	Brandenburg, Ger	10 £	4/22/44	Hamm, Ger	14	4/27/44	Siracourt, Fr
3®	4/12/44	Schweinfurt, Ger	7	4/19/44	Paderborn, Ger	11	4/24/77	Leipheim, Ger	15	4/27/44	Blainville, Fr
4 £	4/13/44	Lechfeld, Ger	8®	4/20/44	Siracourt, Fr	12	4/25/44	Mannheim, Ger	16 £	4/29/44	Berlin, Ger
								® Mission Recall			£ Loss of A/C

467th Bombardment Group Combat Missions, April 1944.

About halfway across the English Channel, a solid undercast was encountered that extended into France and obliterated the target, so the mission was aborted.

The flight records of both Lts. Reed and Oder reflect a flight time of six hours, whereas Group records show a flight time of five hours forty-three minutes for *Witchcraft*, and that 1,730 gallons were used to top up the fuel tanks in "Witch." The mission was not given a credit rating.

Mission 15 – 4 May 1944 to Brunswick, Germany
Group Mission #19 – Target – Wagram Airfield and Airfield Assembly Plant
Twenty-six 467th planes—including *Witchcraft*, flown by Lt. James K. Newhouse and Crew #57—were assigned the mission to Brunswick, Germany. The B-24s, each carrying 20 x 250-lb. GP bombs, commenced take-off at 0651. Four of the B-24s made an early return to base due to mechanical problems.

The mission was aborted due to bad weather and the remaining twenty-two planes were recalled before reaching enemy territory.

The flight time for *Witchcraft* is shown in Group records as four hours thirty-five minutes; the records also reveal 1,630 gallons were used to top up her tanks.

The mission was not given a credit rating.

Mission 16 – 5 May 1944 to Sottevast, France
Group Mission #20 – Target – V-Weapon Site
To attack the V-Weapon site near Cherbourg, France, the Group put up twenty-four B-24s, including *Witchcraft* flown by Lt. Reed and Crew #62.

Lt. Keith Newhouse and Crew # 57. Rear (L to R): Louis Bober, Truman Simpson, Harold Smith, and Keith Newhouse. Front (L to R): John Hollick, Malcolm Wentz, Joseph Kobel, Edward Twogood, L.E. White, and Bruno Ravetti.

The planes—each loaded with 10 x 500-lb. GPs—commenced lift-off from Rackheath at 0453. Great difficulty was encountered in assembly due to dense contrails, and the failure of the PFF ship to appear on schedule added to the confusion. Two aircraft returned to base due to mechanical problems, and a third returned due to an acutely ill radio operator.

Six of the seven planes that reached the target dropped their bomb loads from 24,000 feet; the seventh left the formation before the second run due to running low on fuel. Twelve of the Group ships joined a formation that had abandoned the mission, and two others did not reach the target due to losing their formation in the clouds. There was no enemy air opposition, although some flak was encountered. The bombing results were indeterminate due to heavy clouds over the target area. P-47s gave good support cover for the B-24s.

Group records indicate the fuel tanks of *Witchcraft* were topped up with 1,380 gallons, and also show a flight time of four hours thirty-five minutes, although Lt. Reed's log shows a flight time of five hours.

Mission 17 – 7 May 1944 to Osnabruk, Germany
Group Mission #21 – Target – Railroad Marshalling Yards
For the mission to Osnabruk, the Group assigned thirty-four aircraft, all loaded with 52 x 100-lb. IBs. The aircraft, including *Witchcraft* flown by Lt. G.W. Reed and Crew #62, commenced take-off at 0600.

Twenty-four of the 467th B-24s flew with the 458th Group and ten with the 44th. Maj. McManus led the formation in Lt. Werdung's ship 42-94881 (Crew #3 from the 788th Squadron) and flew with the 458th Group. Lt. Brandon, with Lt. Harry D. Wills (Crew #2 from the 788th Squadron), led the ten planes that flew with the 44th Group. Three of the ships made an early return to base: one due to personal error and the remaining two due to mechanical malfunctions.

A total of 1,612 bombs were dropped on the target, 104 were jettisoned in the Channel, and fifty-two were brought back to base. A solid undercast prevented the observation of bombing results. Extensive flak was encountered and caused damage to eight of the Group's B-24s, but no enemy fighter aircraft were seen. Fighter escort was provided by P-47s.

A flight time of six hours thirty minutes was recorded in Lt. Reed's flight log for *Witchcraft* and Crew #62.

Group records show the flight time for *Witchcraft* as five hours fifty-two minutes, and 1,610 gallons were used to top up the fuel tanks.

Mission 18 – 8 May 1944 to Brunswick, Germany
Group Mission #22 – Target – Wagram Airfield and aircraft plant near Brunswick
Thirty-three aircraft and crews were assigned to fly the mission, including Lt. G.W. Reed and Crew #62 in *Witchcraft*. The planes, each carrying 52 x 100-lb. IB, commenced take-off at 0610. Three ships returned to base early because of mechanical failure; two of the planes brought their bombs back to base and the third jettisoned its bombs in the Zuider Zee.

The first squadron flew high right on the 466th Bomb Group; the second squadron flew high right on the 458th Group; and the third squadron flew low left on the 392nd Group. Maj. Palmer, in Lt. Monefeldt's plane, led the squadron that flew with the 466th Group; Capt. Beatty, in Lt. Swearingen's B-24, led the squadron that flew with the 458th Group; and Capt. Doenges, in Lt. Charles W. Grace's ship, led the squadron that flew with the 392nd Group.

Flak was generally mild, but enemy aircraft were very active, despite good fighter support by P-38s, P-47s, and P-51s. A large number (45–60) of Me-109s attacked the Group formations. Lt. Charles D. Harrison's plane was attacked by six or seven Me-109 fighters just after leaving the target and was seen to turn on its back and go down, but four members of the crew bailed out and were taken POW by the Germans. Lt. Harrison and five of his crew members (Crew #18 – 788th Squadron) were KIA.

Nine of the 467th Group planes received minor battle damage and two suffered major battle damage. B-24H-42-52542 *Stinger*, piloted by Lt. Thomas H. Murphy, had two engines knocked out, its right wing damaged, its top turret dome knocked off, its radio and electrical connections severed, and its landing gear damaged. Unbelievably, the crew managed to fly it back to Norfolk. Lt. Murphy and his copilot instructed the crew members to bail out and then brought the ship down on one wheel at Watton, Norfolk; the plane was salvaged by 3 SAD on 9 May 1944. Staff Sgt. George Hamilton, flying on Lt. J.D. Swearingen's B-24 as a waist gunner (Crew #78 – 791st Squadron), was badly wounded while flying the mission and died before the ship landed. (Sgt. Hamilton was one of three survivors from Lt. Stalie Reid's Crew #88 who bailed out just before their B-24 42-52445 crashed at Barsham, Suffolk, the night of 22 April 1944, after their ship was attacked by German aircraft.)

Overall losses by the Group were one B-24 lost over the continent to enemy action; one B-24 salvaged due to crash-landing at Watton; and seven crew members KIA, five wounded, and four taken POW. Claims by Group gunners for enemy aircraft were two destroyed, one probably destroyed, and four damaged.

The bomb drop by PFF was from 20,000 feet, but clouds prevented the observation of results.

Lt. John Oder mentioned in his flight log that *Witchcraft* received slight damage: "two holes in the ship." Also recorded in his log is the entry of six hours fifteen minutes as the flight time, whereas Group records show a flight time of six hours twenty minutes, and that 1,700 gallons were used to top up the fuel tanks in *Witchcraft*.

Mission 19 – 9 May 1944 to Florennes, Belgium
Group Mission #23 – Target – Luftwaffe Airfield
The 467th assigned twenty-eight aircraft, including *Witchcraft* flown by Lt. Eddie Bryson and Crew #56, for the mission to attack the airfield at Florennes, Belgium. The B-24s, each carrying 40 x 100-lb. GPs, commenced take-off from Rackheath at 0600.

Col. A.F. Herzberg flew with Lt. Robert Sheehan and Crew #61 in 42-5034 *Messie Bessie* from the 790th Squadron, leading the Group B-24s, and Capt. Arthur R. Garner, who flew with Lt. George E. Tormoen and Crew #15 on B-24 42-94881 from the 788th Squadron, led the second squadron.

One plane returned early on account of flak damage to an engine just before reaching the target. Another aircraft brought its bombs back to base because its bomb bay doors failed to open and the linkage broke, making it impossible to salvo the bombs. The remaining twenty-six B-24s bombed the target and dropped a total of 1,021 bombs, achieving good results, despite the fact that forty-two bombs were brought back to base and fifty-seven were jettisoned, some of them in the English Channel.

No enemy aircraft were encountered, although some were seen in the distance. Flak was moderate but fairly accurate, and five of the Group's B-24s received minor damage. The B-24s had good fighter support cover provided by P-38s and P-47s. A good day for the Group, as no crew casualties were incurred and no aircraft were lost.

Group records indicate the flight time for *Witchcraft* was five hours two minutes, and it took 1,460 gallons to top up her fuel tanks.

Mission 20 – 10 May 1944 to Diepholz, Germany
Group Mission #24 – Target – Luftwaffe Airfield
Twenty-four B-24s and their crewss—including *Witchcraft*, flown by Lt. G.W. Reed and Crew #62—were assigned for the mission to Diepholz.

The planes carried a total load of 570 x 500-lb. GP and 364 x 100-lb. Incendiary bombs and started take-off from Rackheath at 0545.

Brigadier General Walter Peck and Col. Albert J. Shower were the Command Pilots in the lead ship, flown by 1/Lt. Lowell .J. Hanna and Crew #76 in 42-94963, from the 791st Squadron.

Due to the very bad weather conditions encountered, the aircraft were recalled at about 0830. All airplanes brought their bomb loads back to base.

The flight log of Lt. Reed shows the flight time for *Witchcraft* as four hours zero minutes, whereas Group records show three hours forty-eight minutes, and also that it took 1,000 gallons to top up the fuel tanks.

The mission was not given a credit rating.

Mission 21 – 11 May 1944 to Epinal, France
Group Mission #25 – Target – Rail Locomotive Repair Works
For the mission to attack the locomotive repair shed at Epinal, the Group assigned twenty-nine B-24s, including *Witchcraft* flown by Lt. E. Bryson and Crew #56.

The planes, each loaded with 5 x 1,000-lb. GP bombs, commenced take-off from Rackheath at 1010. Col. Shower flew with Lt. R.M. Werdung and Crew #3 in B-24 42-94881 from the 788th Squadron and led the formations.

Seven of the planes made an early return to base: five due to mechanical problems, one due to the pilot being unable to get his plane above 10,000 feet, and one that was damaged by flak near Chartres. One of the B-24s that made an early return dropped the five bombs it was carrying in the Channel, while the other six brought their bombs back to base.

Flak was intense and accurate as the planes approached the target, but really light when they were over it, although it caused minor damage to three of the Group planes. The fact the flak was light and the absence of enemy fighter aircraft influenced the Group in making a second run over the target, as the first run was a failure due to clouds and unexpected winds. The remaining twenty-two B-24s dropped their total of 110 bombs on the target from 18,000 feet. The results were rated only fair. P-38s, P-47s, and P-51s provided good fighter cover.

Lt. William T. Shoup (Crew #54 – 790th Squadron) reported over the VHF that the gasoline supply on his plane was low shortly after passing the Group Rally Point. His plane (42-50354 *Messie Bessie*) was last seen heading towards Switzerland. A report from POW at the 2nd Air Division stated the B-24 made a normal landing in Geneva, Switzerland, and that the ten crew members were interned but unharmed. That was the final combat mission flown by the 788th Squadron (1st establishment).

A flight time of eight hours thirty-eight minutes is shown in Group records, and 2,515 gallons were used to top-up her fuel tanks.

Mission 22 – 12 May 1944 to Bohlen, Germany
Group Mission #26 – Target – Synthetic Oil Plant, Power Plant and Gas Works
Secondary Target – Merseburg, Germany.
The 467th Group assigned twenty-four B-24s and crews, including *Witchcraft* flown by Lt. G.W. Reed and Crew #62, for the mission to Bohlen. The bomb loads varied: twelve B-24s were loaded with 10 x 500-lb. GPs; eleven planes loaded with 40 x 100-lb. GPs; and one ship was loaded with 8 x 500-lb. GPs.

The B-24s commenced take-off at 0845. Lt. Edward Hooton flew with Lt. Homer Y. Harris and Crew #29 from the 789th Squadron in B-24 41-29363, leading the first Squadron and flying high right on the 466th Group formations. Capt. Griffith R. Beatty flew with Lt. J.D. Swearingen and Crew #78 from the 791st Squadron in B-24 4294963, leading the second squadron flying high right on the 458th Group formations. Two of the Group planes returned early: one because of mechanical problems and the other due to a smoke bomb detonated in the bomb bay, giving the impression that the ship was on fire.

At the Wing IP, the first squadron failed to see any flares, took up the wrong heading, picked a target, and bombed Merseburg. One plane failed to bomb because of a rack malfunction. The second squadron bombed the target at Bohlen from 22,000 feet, and the results were rated excellent. Flak was moderate, but fairly accurate over the target, and four of the Group planes incurred minor damage, one of those being *Witchcraft*. Although twenty-four enemy fighters were seen, none were encountered. The B-24s had fighter support cover provided by P-38s, P-47s, and P-51s.

A flight time of eight hours thirty minutes is shown in Lt. Reed's flight log, whereas Group records reflect a small variation, showing a flight time of eight hours eleven minutes. Group records also show a total of 1,820 gallons were used to top up the fuel tanks in the "Witch" after the mission.

Citation No. 3, dated 1 July 1944, relating to 35571430 T/Sgt. William C. Willis, Radio Operator on Lt. A.B. Horner's Crew #34 (789th Squadron), and relating to Group Mission #26 to Bohlen, Germany, on May 12, 1944:

Bohlen, Germany, an aerial view of the target.

CITATION

The following named Enlisted Man is cited for outstanding performance of duty while serving as Radio Operator of a B-24 aircraft on a bombing mission to Germany 12 May 1944.

TECHNICAL SERGEANT WILLIAM C. WILLIS – 35571430

789TH Bombardment Squadron

While approaching the target on the bomb run, seven of ten 500-pound general purpose bombs were accidentally released, tearing out the left bomb bay door, fragments of which damaged the left vertical stabilizer and elevator and the No. 2 engine cowling. Appreciating the possible danger to the right vertical stabilizer and elevator, and the subsequent control of the aircraft if the three remaining bombs were released through the right bomb bay door, Sergeant Willis—without parachute or flak helmet—laid on the catwalk and held the right bomb bay door open with his feet. The three bombs were successfully released on the target with excellent results.

The exemplary conduct of Sergeant Willis and his loyal teamwork, courage and intelligence in arising to this emergency are within the finest tradition of the Army Air Forces and are deserving of high commendation.

By order of Col. SHOWER:
Signed: J.J. TORMA
Major, Air Corps
Adjutant.

Note: The catwalk was only ten inches wide and seventeen feet in length from the front to the rear end of the bomb bay. Squeezing along the catwalk from the nose section through the bomb bay to the rear of a B-24 was an arduous task on the ground. At 20,000 feet, with an empty bomb bay and the bay doors cracked open, a crewmember was well advised to

Photo of the catwalk in the bomb bay of a B-24 facing towards the flight deck.

think about every step. But when wearing a heavy flight suit, parachute harness, and carrying a portable oxygen bottle, the task of crossing on the catwalk could not have been an easy task.

Mission 23 – 13 May 1944 to Tutow, Germany
Group Mission #27 – Target – Luftwaffe Airfield
For the mission to Tutow, the Group assigned eighteen B-24s and their crewss, including *Witchcraft* flown by Lt. G.W. Reed and Crew #62.

Each loaded with 10 x 500-lb. GPs, the planes commenced take-off from Rackheath at 1014. Maj. Walter R. Smith flew with Lt. Douglas P. Volk and Crew #30 on B-24 42-52525 *Six Bits* and led the Group. Capt. Robert W. Doenges flew as Group Deputy lead with Lt. Edward K. Lominack and Crew #28 on B-24 41-29363—both crews and planes were from the 789th Squadron. One ship returned to base early due to an engine smoking after jettisoning its bomb load into the North Sea.

The B-24s had good fighter escort provided by P-38s, P-47s, and P-51s, and no enemy fighter aircraft were seen. Flak was fairly light, although reasonably accurate, causing damage to two of the B-24s.

The target was bombed from 17,000 feet and the results were rated just a little more than fair. Another good day for the Group, as it did not incur any aircraft losses or crew casualties.

Group records reveal the flight time was seven hours forty-six minutes. However, it is noted that the flight records of both Lts. Reed and Oder show a flight time of eight hours thirty minutes. Group records also reveal that *Witchcraft* needed 2,000 gallons after flying the mission.

Mission 24 – 19 May 1944 to Brunswick, Germany
Group Mission #28 – Target – Airfield at Wagram and Aircraft Assembly Plant
Twenty-four planes and crews, including *Witchcraft* flown by Lt. Elroy W. Beaney and Crew #70, were assigned for the mission to Brunswick.

The ships, each carrying six 1,000-lb. GPs, commenced take-off at 0850, with Lt.Col. A.F. Herzberg flying with Lt. Charles C. Russell and Crew #36 on B-24 41-29368 *Tailwind* leading the formations from the 96th Combat Wing to the IP; due to mechanical problems they had to turn back, and Maj. Fred E. Holdrege—flying in a PFF ship—took the lead position. Lt. Edward Hooton flew with Lt. Monefeldt and Crew #32 on B-24 42-52525 *Six Bits*, leading the second squadron. One of the Group B-24s made an early return to base due to some mechanical problem.

Dense contrails and high clouds made assembly very difficult. The second squadron was briefed to fly high right

Staff Sgt. Bob McEwen (TG) and the ball turret on *Witchcraft*, giving an idea of the limited space a BT gunner had.

Staff Sgt. Melvin Bland mowing the grass in front of "his" Nissen Hut.

Staff Sgt. Vernon Bundrock with his pet rabbit.

Staff Sgt. Bob McEwen's "quarters" in *Witchcraft*.

The Enlisted Men's Aero Club on the base at Rackheath.

Lt. George W. Reed, affectionately referred to as "Pappy" by his fellow crewmembers (but obviously not addressed as such).

Staff Sgt. Bob McEwen at Ascot, visiting his brother Glenn.

on the 467th Group lead, but lost them in the clouds and later attached themselves to a Group in the Second Combat Wing, bombing with that formation. The bombing was carried out by PFF from 21,000 feet and the results were not determined. Thirteen Me-109s attacked the second squadron, but caused very minor damage, and fourteen of the Group ships reported minor hits from the intense and fairly accurate flak. Two of the 467th Group gunners claimed two enemy planes destroyed and two damaged. P-38s, P-47s, and P-51s flew escort cover for the B-24s.

The flight time for Lt. Beaney and his crew in *Witchcraft* is shown in Group records as six hours thirty-three minutes. The records also show that her fuel tanks took 1,680 gallons.

Mission 25 – 23 May 1944 to Bourges, France
Group Mission #31 – Target – Airfield and Aircraft Assembly Plant

For the mission to Bourges, the Group assigned twenty-nine planes and crews, including *Witchcraft* flown by its original pilot, Lt. G.W. Reed, and Crew #62. The planes were loaded with a real mixture of ordnance, as one ship was loaded with 12 x 250-lb. GPs, three were each loaded with 18 x 250-lb. GPs, and the remaining twenty-five each carrying 24 x 250-lb. GPs. The B-24s commenced take-off from Rackheath at 0500.

Lt. Col. Allen F. Herzberg flew with Lt. Robert D. Sheehan and Crew #61 on B-24 42-95273, leading the formation, but at assembly, the crew experienced trouble with communications and relinquished the lead to Lt. Brandon, who flew with Lt. Richard J. Campbell and Crew #53 on B-24 42-95094 *Leading Lady*.

The target was bombed from 15,000 feet, and the results were rated very good. Good fighter escort was provided by P-38s, P-47s, and P-51s. No flak or enemy fighter aircraft were encountered.

Staff Sgt. Bob McEwen (left) with his brother, Capt. Glenn McEwen, sitting on a bridge over the Thames in London.

Lt. Elroy Beaney and Crew #70. Rear (L to R): Robert Sander (CP), Elroy Beaney (P), William Davies (B), and Morton Deutsch (N). Front (L to R): Robert Finch (BTG), Benjamin Meredith (TG), Joseph Perrault (ROG), Roy Rainwater (AEG), Carl Kleinert (NG), and George Leeper (TTG).

Group records indicate that on the mission, *Witchcraft*'s tanks were topped up with 1,800 gallons; they also show a flight time of seven hours one minute, whereas the flight records of both Lts. Reed and Oder show a small variation, recording it as six hours forty-five minutes.

Mission 26 – 25 May 1944 to Mulhouse, France
Group Mission #33 – Target – Railroad Marshalling Yards
Witchcraft, flown by Lt. E. Bryson and Crew #56, was one of twenty-four B-24s and crews assigned the mission to Mulhouse. The planes, each loaded with 10 x 500-lb. GPs, commenced lift off from Rackheath at 0520. The lead ship of each squadron also carried 2 x 100-lb. incendiary signal flares.

Capt. R.W. Doenges flew with Lt. L.H. Monefeldt and Crew #32 on B-24 42-50309 *Ten Of Us* from the 789th Squadron and led the first squadron. Capt. G.R. Beatty flew with Lt. C.W. Grace and Crew #77 on B-24 41-29375 *Lil' Peach* from the 791st Squadron and led the second squadron. The B-24s had good fighter support, provided by P-38s, P-47s, and P-51s.

The marshalling yards were bombed from 20,000 feet and the Group achieved excellent results.

The Group was fortunate again, as there was very little flak and no enemy fighter aircraft were seen.

Flight time for Lt. Bryson and his crew is shown in the records as seven hours twenty-seven minutes, and 2,100 gallons were used to top up the fuel tanks.

Note: Lt. A. Lyle Prichard—copilot on Lt. C. Grace's plane, in which Capt. Beatty led the second Squadron—made the following comments relating to mission #33:

> We led the Group on our ninth mission. It was a long one, about fifteen miles from the Swiss border at Mulhouse, France. The target was a coal and oil storage depot for trains. A perfect mission—no fighters, sparse flak, and we really plastered the target. I really don't mind missions like this, even if they are long and tiring.

Citation No. 1, 29 dated May 1944 – relating to crew members from the 789th and 791st Squadrons and Group Mission 33 on 25 May 1944, to Mulhouse, France.

CITATION

The following officers are cited for outstanding performance of duty while leading the 1st and 2nd Squadrons of the 467th Bombardment Group (H) on a bombing mission to France, 25 May 1944.

789th Bombardment Squadron (H)

Command Pilot CAPT	ROBERT W. DOENGES	0437390 AC
Pilot	1ST LT. LEONARD H. MONEFELDT	0681460 AC
Pilotage Navigator	1ST LT. BILL G. DECK	0673496 AC
Navigator	1ST LT. ROBERT P. LUKEMAN	0687873 AC
Bombardier	2ND LT. ANTON J. LOOMAN	0685804 AC
791st Bombardment Squadron (H)		
Command Pilot	CAPT. GRIFFIN R. BEATTY	0406509 AC
Pilot	1ST LT. CHARLES W. GRACE	0681060 AC
Pilotage Navigator	2ND LT. BRUCE W. OWEN	0809411 AC
Navigator	2ND LT. WILLIAM A. BUCHECKER	0688415 AC
Bombardier	1ST LT. ARTHUR R. KIRSIS	0685466 AC

The 789th Squadron lead crew led the second Group of the 96th Combat Wing on this combat mission. Supervised by CAPT. DOENGES as Command Pilot, 1ST LT. MONEFELDT piloted the aircraft to adhere as closely as possible to the briefed route, thus avoiding virtually all flak. 1ST LT. DECK, as pilotage navigator, ably directed the flight to the dead-reckoning navigator, 1ST LT. LUKEMAN. Easily finding the checkpoints for the bomb run, LT. LOOMAN released bombs from 22,000 feet on the target with excellent results.

Leading the second Squadron, the 791st Squadron lead crew virtually duplicated the successful efforts, with CAPT. BEATTY commanding the aircraft piloted by 1ST LT. GRACE. 2ND LT. OWEN and 2ND LT. BUCHECKER as pilotage navigator and dead-reckoning navigator, guided the bombardier, 1ST LT. KIRSIS, directly to the target, where bombs were released with excellent results.

Ninety-five percent of the two squadrons' bombs were within 2,000 feet of the aiming point, forming a terrific concentration of bombs on the military objective.

The leadership displayed by these Command Pilots and lead crew Officers climaxed three successive days, during which all the assigned Group aircraft were dispatched, dropped bombs on the assigned targets, and returned safely. The alertness, efficiency, and devotion to duty displayed by these Officers is deserving of the highest commendation.

Signed: J.J. TORMA
By order of Col. SHOWER
Major, Air Corps, Adjutant

Mission 27 – 27 May 1944 to Neunkirchen, Germany
Group Mission #34 – Target – Rail Locomotive Repair Depot

The Group assigned twenty-four B-24s, including *Witchcraft* flown by Lt. G.W. Reed and Crew #62, for the attack on the rail locomotive repair depot at Neunkirchen. The B-24s, each carrying 10 x 500-lb. semi-armor piercing bombs, commenced take-off at 0800.

The first squadron was led by Maj. Walter R. Smith, who flew with Lt. Richard J. Campbell and Crew #53 on B-24 42-95094 *Leading Lady* from the 790th Squadron; Maj. Garnet B. Palmer flew with Lt. Douglas B. Volk and Crew #30 in B-24 42-52525 *Six Bits* from the 789th Squadron and led the second squadron. P-38s, P-47s, and P-51s again gave the B-24s good fighter support. No flak or enemy fighters were seen.

Due to a good bomb run at 18,000 feet, the target was effectively destroyed.

The recorded flight time for *Witchcraft* and Lt. Reed and Crew #62 is shown as seven hours twenty-eight minutes in Group records, and that 1,650 gallons topped up her fuel tanks. The entry in Lt. Reed's flight record reveals a very minor variance, as it shows a flight time of seven hours thirty minutes.

Mission 28 – 28 May 1944 to Zeitz, Germany
Group Mission #35 – Target – Oil Refinery and Gas Generating Plant

For the rather long seven and a half hour mission to Zeitz, the Group assigned twenty-five B-24s and crew, including *Witchcraft* flown by Lt. George W. Reed and Crew #62. Each plane was loaded with 10 x 500-lb. GP bombs and take-off commenced at 1016.

Maj. Fred E. Holdrege flew with Lt. Robert D.Sheeham and Crew #61 from the 790th Squadron in B-24 42-95273, leading the first squadron and flying high right on the 458th Group. The second squadron was led by Lt. Robert S. Seiler, who flew with Lt. James D. Swearingen and Crew #78 from the 791st Squadron on B-24 42-94963, flying high right on the 466th Group.

The 791st Squadron's 42-52530 *Bug's Bunny*—flown by Lt. Wells L. Wescott and Crew #87 from the 791st Squadron—developed supercharger trouble and turned back to base, but dropped its bomb load on an airfield five miles north of Meppel on the way home. Another 467th Group B-24 made an early return to base due to a crewmember developing a problem.

Lt. Joseph G. Mulheran and Crew #60 from the 790th Squadron in B-24 42-52303 *Topper* took off late and failed to join the formation. However, he joined a formation of the 492nd Group and released his bombs on cue from the leader on an unidentified target near 51'00"N 11'30"E.

The target was bombed from 20,000 feet, and the results were rated excellent. Three enemy fighter aircraft (2 Me -109s and 1 FW-190) were seen, but none attacked the Group B-24s, perhaps due to the P-38s, P-47s, and P-51s giving good fighter cover for the B-24s. Flak was light and inaccurate.

The flight record of Lt. Reed and Group records show a flight time of seven hours thirty minutes. The quantity used to top up the fuel tanks on *Witchcraft* is unknown, but twenty of the B-24s, including *Witchcraft*, were refueled after landing back at base and an overall total of 45,440 gallons was used—an average of 2,270 per ship.

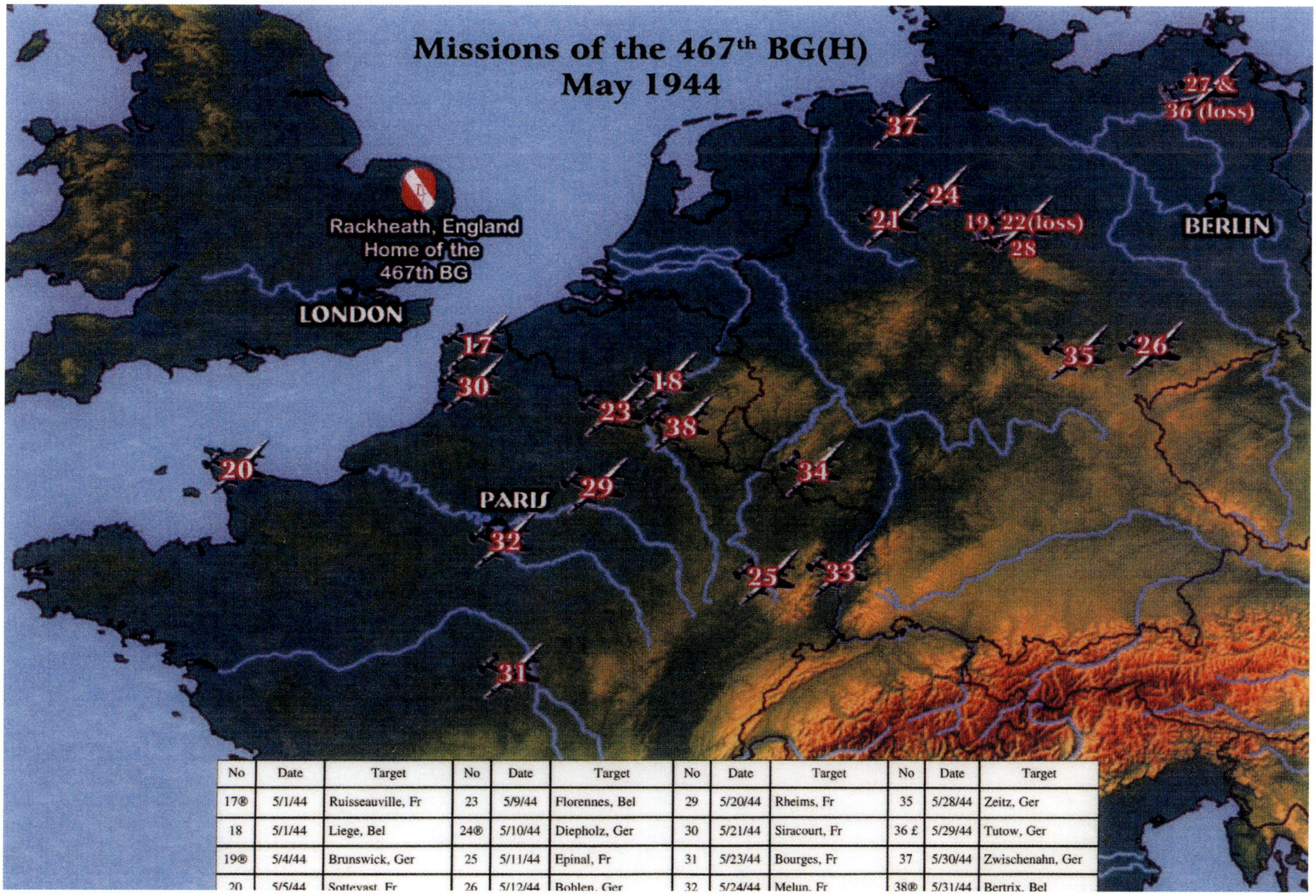

No	Date	Target	No	Date	Target	No	Date	Target	No	Date	Target
17®	5/1/44	Ruisseauville, Fr	23	5/9/44	Florennes, Bel	29	5/20/44	Rheims, Fr	35	5/28/44	Zeitz, Ger
18	5/1/44	Liege, Bel	24®	5/10/44	Diepholz, Ger	30	5/21/44	Siracourt, Fr	36 £	5/29/44	Tutow, Ger
19®	5/4/44	Brunswick, Ger	25	5/11/44	Epinal, Fr	31	5/23/44	Bourges, Fr	37	5/30/44	Zwischenahn, Ger
20	5/5/44	Sottevast, Fr	26	5/12/44	Bohlen, Ger	32	5/24/44	Melun, Fr	38®	5/31/44	Bertrix, Bel

467th Bombardment Group Combat Missions, May 1944.

Witchcraft flying on its twenty-eighth combat mission.

Mission 29 – 2 June 1944 to Stella-Plage, France
Group Mission #39 – Target – Coastal Gun Batteries
Witchcraft—flown by Lt. George W. Reed and Crew #62—was one of twenty-two aircraft and crew assigned by the Group for the mission to Stella-Plage. The planes, each carrying 4 x 2,000-lb. GPs, commenced take-off from Rackheath at 0859.

Maj. Garnet B. Palmer, flying in a Pathfinder Flare (PFF) ship, led the first squadron. Capt. G.R. Beatty—also flying in a PFF ship—led the second squadron.

The target was bombed from 20,000 feet by PFF, but due to 10/10 cloud cover, the results were unobserved. No flak or enemy fighter aircraft were encountered. P-38s gave good fighter support.

The flight logs for both Lts. Reed and Oder show a flight time of five hours thirty minutes, whereas Group records indicate five hours eleven minutes. The records also reveal that 1,350 gallons topped up the fuel tanks of *Witchcraft* following the mission.

Mission 30 – 3 June 1944 to Berck-sur-Mer, France
Group Mission #40 – Target – Coastal Gun Batteries
Lt. George W. Reed and Crew #62 in *Witchcraft* accompanied thirty-five other 467th Group planes and their crews to attack the coastal guns at Berck-sur-Mer.

The thirty-six B-24s, each loaded with 12 x 500-lb. GP bombs, commenced take-off from Rackheath at 1200. Maj. Wallace, flying in a PFF plane, led the first squadron and Capt. Doenges, also flying in a PFF ship, led the second.

The target was bombed from 18,000 feet through 10/10 cloud cover using Pathfinder flares, but due to the density of the clouds results were unobserved.

No flak or enemy fighter planes were encountered. Good fighter support for the bombers was provided by P-38s and P-47s.

Again, a slight variance on the flight time for *Witchcraft* and Crew #62, as the flight records of Lts. Reed and Oder show four hours fifteen minutes, compared to Group records showing a time of three hours fifty minutes. The records also reveal it took 1,135 gallons to top up *Witchcraft* following the mission.

Mission 31 – 6 June 1944 to Colleville, France
Group Mission #42 – Target – Coastal Gun Batteries (First D-Day Mission)
For the first D-Day mission, the Group assigned thirty-four airplanes, including *Witchcraft* flown by Lt. George Reed and Crew #62. The B-24s flew in formations of six ships and commenced take-off from Rackheath at 0250.

Lt. Col. Herzberg led the first squadron in a PFF ship and another PFF plane led the fourth squadron. P-47s and P-51s provided escort cover.

Lt. George Reed and his nine fellow crewmembers sitting on the grass adjoining hardstand #32, awaiting transport after having completed their first D-Day mission.

Landing craft and ships approaching the French coast as seen by the flight crews on D-Day.

Only sixteen of the Group planes reached the target and dropped an overall total of 260 x 100-lb. and 132 x 500-lb. GP bombs; the remaining eighteen airplanes returned to base due to adverse weather. The bombing was carried out by PFF from 15,000 feet, but due to cloud density the results were unobserved. No enemy aircraft or flak was encountered.

The flight time for Lt. Reed and Crew #62 in *Witchcraft* is shown in Group records as five hours fifty-eight minutes; fuel tanks were topped up with 1,325 gallons of fuel.

The following quotes from diaries of two 791st Squadron crew members reflect views and thoughts following the D-Day missions. In both instances, the entries were made immediately following the missions they flew that day.

The diary entry by former Staff Sgt. Radio Operator (Crew #84) Tony Bell reads:

> We took off at 0310. "INVASION." I saw hundreds of landing craft and a sea battle in the Channel. I am glad and proud to say I was over the beachhead before the landing forces. The world is going crazy with joy!
>
> To me it's joy, too, but hard days are ahead. For instance, I just landed 20 minutes ago and we're going to take off again! As Churchill said, "We will hit the enemy wherever and however we can." – and we will. We didn't fly again after all. [Tony was referring to a possibility of flying on the third D-Day mission. Although Tony's crew was not assigned, some eighteen crews that had already flown on the first D-Day mission were assigned and flew the third mission that day. -P.W]

Former 791st Squadron Crew #77 copilot Lt. A. Lyle Prichard recalled from the notes he made after flying the mission:

> We flew mission number thirteen over the Channel early today. . . Visibility was poor, but there were breaks in the clouds, so we could see the invasion fleet. There were thousands of ships—some dragging barrage balloons over them—moving across the Channel. Some LSTs (Landing Ship Tanks) had already unloaded troops into Higgens boats and they were nearly on the beaches. We went in at 6,500 feet and encountered no enemy opposition.
>
> Paratroopers were dropped during the night to capture crossroads, bridges, etc. The RAF and the 8th and 9th USAF put up every plane that would fly to pound the Germans. Allied battleships, cruisers, and destroyers of the Navy shelled the beaches and inland as far as they could reach. It is a real spectacle, something that cannot be imagined; you had to be there to believe it!
>
> Our Group flew three missions today, as did most of the divisions.
>
> As we lay on our cots tonight and reflect of the day's happenings, we cannot help but think of the men who hit the beaches from the boats today. Here we are safe in our little huts and they are fighting and clawing to hold on to those sandy beaches! Our hearts go out to them, because we are fully aware that thousands of them will not be with us tomorrow.

Mission 32 – 6 June 1944 to Pontaubault, France
Group Mission #44 – Target – Railroad Bridge
For the third D-Day mission, the 467th put up twenty-four planes, including *Witchcraft* flown by her original Crew #62 and Lt. George W. Reed. The B-24s were each loaded with 12 x 500-lb. GP bombs and commenced take-off at 1630.

Col. Albert J. Shower—similar to commanding officers of other Groups—had not been permitted to fly on combat missions immediately leading up to D-Day, but was finally permitted to fly on the third D-Day mission. Col. Shower led the first squadron and Capt. S.J. Neitzel led the second. Five planes returned to base because of bad weather and one plane returned early due to mechanical problems.

Eighteen of the Group's planes, plus two PFF ships, reached the target, where a 360° turn was made prior to the planes dropping their bomb loads from 15,000 feet. The bombing results were rated fair. No flak or enemy aircraft were seen, but Allied fighter aircraft were everywhere. P-47s and P-51s provided fighter escort for the B-24s.

A flight time of seven hours thirty minutes is shown in both Lts. Reed's and Oder's records after landing in darkness at a base near Kings Lynn, Norfolk, due to bad weather. No fuel figures are available.

Two photographs taken of *Witchcraft* being refuelled at an airfield near Kings Lynn, Norfolk. The personnel on the fuselage/wing are Tech Sgt. Robert DeKerf and a WAAF "flight line girl."

Mike Bailey's painting of *Witchcraft* on permanent display in the control tower at Rackheath.

Mission 33 – 8 June 1944 to Pontaubault, France
Group Mission #46 – Target – Railroad Bridge
Twenty-four aircraft and crew, including Lt. George W. Reed's Crew #62 in *Witchcraft*, were assigned to fly another mission to Pontaubault, having flown there only two days earlier. The planes, each loaded with 6 x 1,000-lb. GP bombs, commenced take-off from Rackheath at 0437.

Maj. Fred E. Holdrege led the first squadron and Maj. Garnet B. Palmer led the second. Two of the ships returned to base early: one because of personnel error and the other due to weather conditions.

The remaining twenty-two B-24s reached the target and dropped an overall total of 132 bombs by PFF at 15,700 feet. The bombing was unobserved, but was later rated as poor. No flak or enemy aircraft were seen.

A flight time of seven hours thirty minutes is shown for *Witchcraft* and Crew #62 in Lt. Reed's flight records, whereas Group records show a flight time of seven hours ten minutes. The records also indicate a total of 1,900 gallons were used to top up the fuel tanks in *Witchcraft*.

Mission 34 – 10 June 1944 to Chateaudun, France.
Group Mission #47 – Target – Airfield
The Group assigned twelve B-24s and crews—including Lt. George Reed and Crew #62 in *Witchcraft*—for the mission to Chateaudun. The B-24s, each carrying 52 x 100-lb. GP bombs, commenced take-off at 1037, with Maj. Walter R. Smith leading the formations.

All aircraft bombed the target using the GH system (a radar-guided bombing system used when the target was totally covered by cloud), but due to the 10/10 cloud coverage, the results were unobserved. Some light flak was seen over the target, but no enemy aircraft were encountered. Good fighter protection was provided by P-47s and P-51s.

A flight time of six hours is shown in Lt. Reed's flight records. The "Witch" was not refueled after the mission, but records show that for the nine B-24s that were refueled, an average of 1,700 gallons were used.

Mission 35 – 14 June 1944 to Beauvoir, France
Group Mission #51 – Target – German Military Installations
The Group assigned thirty-nine B-24s and crews, including *Witchcraft* flown by Lt. George W. Reed and Crew #62.

The B-24s, each carrying 10 x 500-lb. GPs, commenced take-off from Rackheath at 0342, with Maj. A.L. Wallace leading the first squadron, Capt. A.R. Garner the second, and Maj. G.B. Palmer the third.

All thirty-nine planes reached the target, which was bombed visually from 22,000 feet, although the visibility level was down to 20% due to heavy clouds covering the area. The bombing results were rated poor. Flak was moderate but reasonably accurate, and no German fighter planes were seen. The B-24s had good fighter support coverage by P-38s, P-47s, and P-51s.

A flight time of four hours fifteen minutes is shown in the flight logs of both Lts. Reed and Oder, whereas Group records have it as three hours forty-seven minutes. A total of 1,000 gallons were used to fill *Witchcraft*'s tanks at mission completion.

Mission 36 – 15 June 1944 to Evreux, France
Group Mission #52 – Target – Raid/Road Overpass at Evreux
The Group selected twenty-six B-24s and crews—including *Witchcraft*, flown by Lt. G.W. Reed and Crew #62—to attack either the primary target, which was the airfield at Evreux/Guyancourt; or the secondary target, which was the railway and road overpass at Evreux.

Bomb loads varied, as thirteen planes each carried 48 x 100-lb. GPs; twelve were loaded with 12 x 500-lb. GPs each; and one plane was loaded with 12 x 500-lb. GPs with delayed action fuses. The B-24s commenced take-off at 0430 with Lt. Col. Herxberg leading the first squadron and Capt. Beatty the second. Two of the B-24s made an early return due to mechanical problems.

The 467th Group squadrons had to make a 360° turn at the IP, as a squadron from the 95th Group came in and was immediately underneath the 467th as they made their bomb run. As the MPI could not be identified, it was decided that the 467th Group squadrons would bomb the secondary target, and the results were rated fair. Moderate but very accurate flak was encountered over the areas of Evreux and Paris—a piece of shrapnel from a flak burst made a hole in *Witchcraft*—but no enemy fighter aircraft were seen. Very good fighter support cover was provided by P-47s.

There is a slight variation in the flight time of six hours recorded by Lts. George Reed and John Oder in their flight logs, compared to the five hours thirty-seven minutes shown in Group records for *Witchcraft* and Crew #62. The records also reveal that 1,800 gallons were used to top up the fuel tanks in *Witchcraft*.

Lt. Edwin Helton's original Crew #55 at Wendover, Utah. Rear (L to R): Thomas Gensert (BTG), Robert Clark (TG), Ernest Booth (AEG), Frank Borchick (ROG), Stanley Brezowski (TTG), and Charles Knowles (NG). Front (L to R): Richard Ludka (B), Richard Hirsch (N), Maurice Nelson (CP), and Edwin Helton (P). Robert Clark, Ernest Booth, and Richard Hirsch did not fly with Crew #55 on Group Mission #60, but Tech Sgt. G. Rankin (AEG) and Staff Sgt. Carmine Margiasso (WG), who are not in the above photo, flew with Crew #55 that fateful day.

Mission 37 – 17 June 1944 to Guyancourt, France
Group Mission #53 – Target – Luftwaffe Airfield
The 467th assigned twenty-four ships and crews for this mission, including Lt. Sherman D. Martin and Crew #65 in *Witchcraft*. Each B-24 was loaded with 12 x 500-lb. GP bombs and the mission had a take-off starting at 0813.

Maj. Walter Smith flew with Lt. D.B. Volk and Crew #30 in B-24 42-95032 *Silver Chief* (789th Squadron) and led the first squadron. Maj. Fred E. Holdrege flew with Lt. Kenneth G. Ford and Crew #52 in 42-95057 *Angel* (790th Squadron) and led the second. Two planes from the 790th squadron developed mechanical problems and returned to base early.

All twenty-two aircraft reached the target and dropped their combined total load of 264 x 500-lb. bombs from 22,600 feet using GH, due to the target being obscured by heavy cloud. The results of the bombing, although unobserved, were rated good. No flak nor enemy aircraft were seen. P-38s, P-47s, and P-51s provided good fighter support.

A flight time of seven hours two minutes is shown for *Witchcraft* and Crew #65 in Group records, which also indicate that 2,350 gallons were pumped into her fuel tanks after the mission.

Mission 38 – 18 June 1944 to Bremerhaven/Wesermunde, Germany
Group Mission #55 – Target – Airfield at Bremerhaven
Secondary Target – Shipyards and Docks at Wesermunde
At 0531 hours, twenty-five B-24s and crews—including *Witchcraft*, flown by Lt. G.W. Reed and Crew #62—commenced take-off from Rackheath. The planes—each loaded with 40 x 100-lb. GP bombs for this long-haul mission—were led by Maj. A.L.Wallace, who flew with Lt. J.D. Swearingen and Crew #78 in B-24 42-94910 from the 791st Squadron.

Due to heavy overcast and bad weather over the target, the IP could not be located; consequently, the secondary target—shipyards and docks at Wesermunde—was bombed using PFF. Some hits were seen across the shipyards and within the dock area, but the results are unknown. While approaching and over the target area, the flak encountered was both intense and accurate; minor damage was caused to some of the B-24s, but no enemy aircraft were seen. Good fighter coverage was provided by P-51s.

The records reveal the flight time for Crew #62 and *Witchcraft* was seven hours eighteen minutes; following the mission, 2,000 gallons were used to top up her fuel tanks.

Mission 39 – 20 June 1944 to Ostermoor, Germany
Group Mission #58 – Target – Oil Refinery
For the first of the two missions flown on 20 June 1944, the Group put up twenty-six B-24s, including *Witchcraft* flown by Lt. G.W. Reed and Crew #62. The planes, each loaded with 12 x 500-lb. GP bombs, started take-off at 0440. Lt. R.S. Seiler flew with Lt. J.D. Swearingen and Crew #78 in B-24 42-94910 from the 791st Squadron, leading the first squadron; and Lt. E. Hooton flew with Lt. D.B. Volk and Crew #30 in B-24 42-95004 *The Honey Wagon* from the 789th Squadron, leading the second.

All twenty-six B-24s bombed the target from 22,000 feet, and the results were rated excellent. No enemy aircraft were seen. Although the flak was moderate and accurate, it did not cause the Group any serious aircraft damage or crew casualties. The fighter support provided by P-38s, P-47s, and P-51s was not very close to the B-24s and could only be regarded as fair.

The flight time for Crew #62 and *Witchcraft* is shown in the flight log of Lt. Reed as six hours thirty minutes, whereas Group records show six hours eleven minutes. Group records reveal 1,750 gallons were used to top up the fuel tanks of *Witchcraft* following the mission.

Mission 40 – 21 June 1944 to Berlin, Germany
Group Mission #60 – Target – Workshops at Genshagen
For the mission to Berlin, the Group assigned thirty-four B-24s and crew, including *Witchcraft* flown by Lt. G.W. Reed and Crew #62. The ships were loaded with an assortment of 500-lb. GP high explosive and 100-lb. IB and commenced take-off from Rackheath at 0443.

Col. Shower led the 96th Combat Wing and Second Bombardment Division on this mission. Several Group aircraft returned to base early due to mechanical problems. As the PFF flares failed on the bomb run, the target was bombed from 21,000 feet visually, through breaks in the clouds, and the results were officially rated as good. P-38s, P-47s, and P-51s provided good fighter cover. Only a few enemy aircraft were seen, but did not attack.

Over the target, the crews came up against moderate to intense anti-aircraft fire that was fairly accurate and caused the loss of two Group B-24s after the target was bombed. The first—42-52525 *Six Bits*, flown by Lt. Edward F. Rudowski and Crew #45 from the 789th Squadron—was badly damaged; the crew somehow managed to keep the plane airborne, but realized that it would be unable to make the flight back to England, so they headed for neutral Sweden and landed at Bulltofta (Malmo) Airport, where both crew and plane were interned (the B-24 was returned to England in May 1945).

The other airplane lost was B-24H 42-52497 *Osage Express*, flown by Lt. Edwin M. Helton and Crew #55 from the 790th Squadron. Lt. Helton's plane was last seen falling behind the reassembled formation and going down under control with an engine on fire. It was at first speculated that the crew had bailed out and was captured; unfortunately, it was not at all like that. All nine members of the crew lost their lives, but not due to the crash. In addition to the loss of two planes, the tail gunner of Lt. W. Shiner's Crew #38—Staff Sgt. Paul D. Luna—on B-24H 41-29385 *Double Trouble* (789th Squadron) was killed by flak; also, four members from other crews were seriously wounded by flak.

The flight time for *Witchcraft* in Lt. Reed's flight log is eight hours forty-five minutes; Group records show eight hours thirty-one minutes. Group records also show that 2,500 gallons were used to top up her tanks following the mission.

Note: What actually happened to Lt. Helton and his crew was officially verified through research by Walter Mundy for the Roll of Honor review committee of the Second Air Division Memorial. Walter has held the offices of president of both the Second Air Division and the 467th Bombardment Group Associations. He served with the 467th Group as a Staff Sergeant armorer gunner, and flew with Lt. Jack Howe's Crew #10 of the 788th Squadron. In the course of his research, Walter Mundy corresponded with the Army Total Personnel Command and the verification document he received is not a pleasant story.

"What Happened to Lt. EDWIN HELTON and his Fellow Crewmembers"

The crew-members from the 790th Squadron flying on B-24H 15 FO 42-52497 *Osage Express* on June 21, 1944, were:

1/Lt. Edwin M.Helton – Pilot	2/Lt. Maurice R.Nelson – Co-pilot
2/Lt. Richard J.Ludka – Bombardier	T/Sgt. Warren G.Rankin – Engineer
T/Sgt. Frank Borchick – Radio Operator	Staff Sgt. Thomas A. Gensert – B/T Gunner
Staff Sgt. Charles L.Knowles – Gunner	Staff Sgt. Carmine Margiasso – Gunner
Staff Sgt. Stanley E. Brzezowski – Tail Gunner	

Lt. Helton's B-24 was damaged by flak over the target and was last seen going down under control, with one engine on fire and one engine's propeller feathered. Reports indicate that the aircraft crashed on the west bank of the Muritz See, near the village of Klink, Germany. All nine members of the crew were rescued and captured.

Seven crew-members, except Lt. Helton and Lt. Ludka, were taken into the town of Waren, where they were turned over to the Security Police, who executed them and had them buried in a common grave in Poppentin, Germany. The remains of these seven were subsequently disinterred and sent to the US cemetery at St. Avold, France, where they were identified. German reports indicate that all seven had been shot in the head. Lt. Helton and Lt. Ludka were turned over to SS Police Commissioner Stempel in Fuerstenbert-Mecklenburg, where they were similarly executed and allegedly buried in Droegen/Stargard. The remains of Lts. Helton and Ludka have been determined to be unrecoverable. This wartime atrocity was investigated and The Gauleiter of Mecklenberg—one Friedrich Hildebrandt, the Nazi criminal who ordered the murders of these airmen—was tried as a war criminal and hanged. Other German SS Police and officials who participated in the atrocity are dead by suicide or were detained by the German police and prosecuted as war criminals.

Mission 41 – 23 June 1944 to Belloy-sur-Somme, France
Group Mission #61 – Target – V-Weapon Site

Thirty-three planes and crews, including *Witchcraft* piloted by Lt. George Reed and Crew #62, were assigned the mission to Belloy-sur-Somme. The B-24s, each carrying 20 x 250-lb. GP bombs, commenced lift-off from Rackheath at 0920, with Capt. R.W. Doenges, Capt. G.R. Beatty, and Lt. C.H. Brandon leading the first, second, and third squadrons, respectively; each squadron was comprised of eleven airplanes.

All thirty-three planes bombed the targets. The first squadron dropped bombs on the target at Belloy-sur-Somme; the second squadron bombed the site at Frissin; and the third dropped bombs on the target at Beaumetz-les-Aire. Because the targets were blanketed with 10/10 cloud coverage, the bombs were dropped using GH; as the bombing was unobserved, the results are unknown.

Light flak was seen over the target, but no enemy fighters were seen. P-51s gave good escort cover for the B-24s.

The flight time for *Witchcraft* and Crew #62 is shown in Lt. Reed's records as five hours fifteen minutes,

Witchcraft after flying on forty-two combat missions, thirty-eight of which were credited.

Photograph taken by Lt. John Oder (Copilot on George Reed's Crew #62) when he was flying in 4-29446 *Tangerine* on Group Mission #67 to Aschersleben, Germany, on 29 June 1944; the plane going down was 789th Squadron 41-110187 flown by Lt. W.H. Counts and Crew #40.

compared to the four hours fifty-three minutes shown in Group records. The records also show that 1,200 gallons were used to top up *Witchcraft* after the mission.

Mission 42 – 24 June 1944 to Belle Croix, France
Group Mission #63 – Target – V-Weapon Site
The 467th Group assigned twelve B-24s—including *Witchcraft*, flown by Lt. Leonard P. Vogt and Crew #63—for the mission to Belle Croix. The B-24s, each carrying 20 x 250-lb. GPs, commenced take-off at 0700. Lt. Charles Brandon flew with Lt. Richard Campbell and Crew #53 from the 790th Squadron in B-24H 42-95094 *Leading Lady* and led the Group ships. Very soon after taking off, two of the planes made an early return to base due to mechanical problems.

The remaining ten ships flew over the target, but did not drop any bombs, because the target was totally covered by 10/10 clouds and the squadron did not have a PFF ship. Fighter support coverage was fair. No enemy airplanes were seen and only light flak was encountered.

The flight time for Crew #63 and *Witchcraft*, and the quantity of fuel used, is unknown, but Group records indicate the average flight time for each of the ten planes that made it to the target was four hours fifty-eight minutes, and the average figure used for topping up the fuel tanks was 1,540 gallons. Note: Although the mission was given a "No Attack" rating, it was given a Credit rating.

Mission 43 – 1 July 1944 to Beaumetz-les-Aires, France
Group Mission #68 – Target – V-Weapon Site
Twenty-four B-24s, including *Witchcraft* flown by Lt. Travis S. Whitsel and Crew #73, were assigned to attack the V-Weapon site. Each plane was loaded with 25 x 250-lb. GPs, except for two ships each loaded with 12 x 500-lb. GPs fitted with long-delay fuses. The planes commenced take-off at 0800 and flew as two squadrons, each being led by a PFF ship.

Due to bad weather, the aircraft were recalled when they reached the Splasher Beacon 5 area. All aircraft returned to base with their bomb loads; the two carrying the long-delay fused bombs dropped theirs into the North Sea.

Group records show a flight time of three hours thirty-six minutes and 1,240 gallons were used by *Witchcraft*. The mission was not given a credit rating.

Removal of Ball Turrets from B-24s
The 467th was the first Group to remove a ball turret from a B-24. This came about after an

analysis of the number of rounds of ammunition fired by each of the gun locations revealed that the ball turret provided minimal, if any, defense against attacking aircraft. Removal of the ball turret meant the plane's weight was lightened approximately 2,100 pounds—plus the weight of the gunner—and the number of crew was reduced from ten to nine. The flying speed of the B-24 was increased, plus the fuel consumption was slightly improved. Additionally, the center of gravity of the plane was moved forward; thus, the B-24 was less tail heavy. By modifying government equipment without permission, Col. Shower violated Air Corps regulations, but all went well, as tests of the ball turret were considered very successful. The success was acknowledged and met full approval by "authorities in the higher

Witchcraft landing after completing another combat mission.

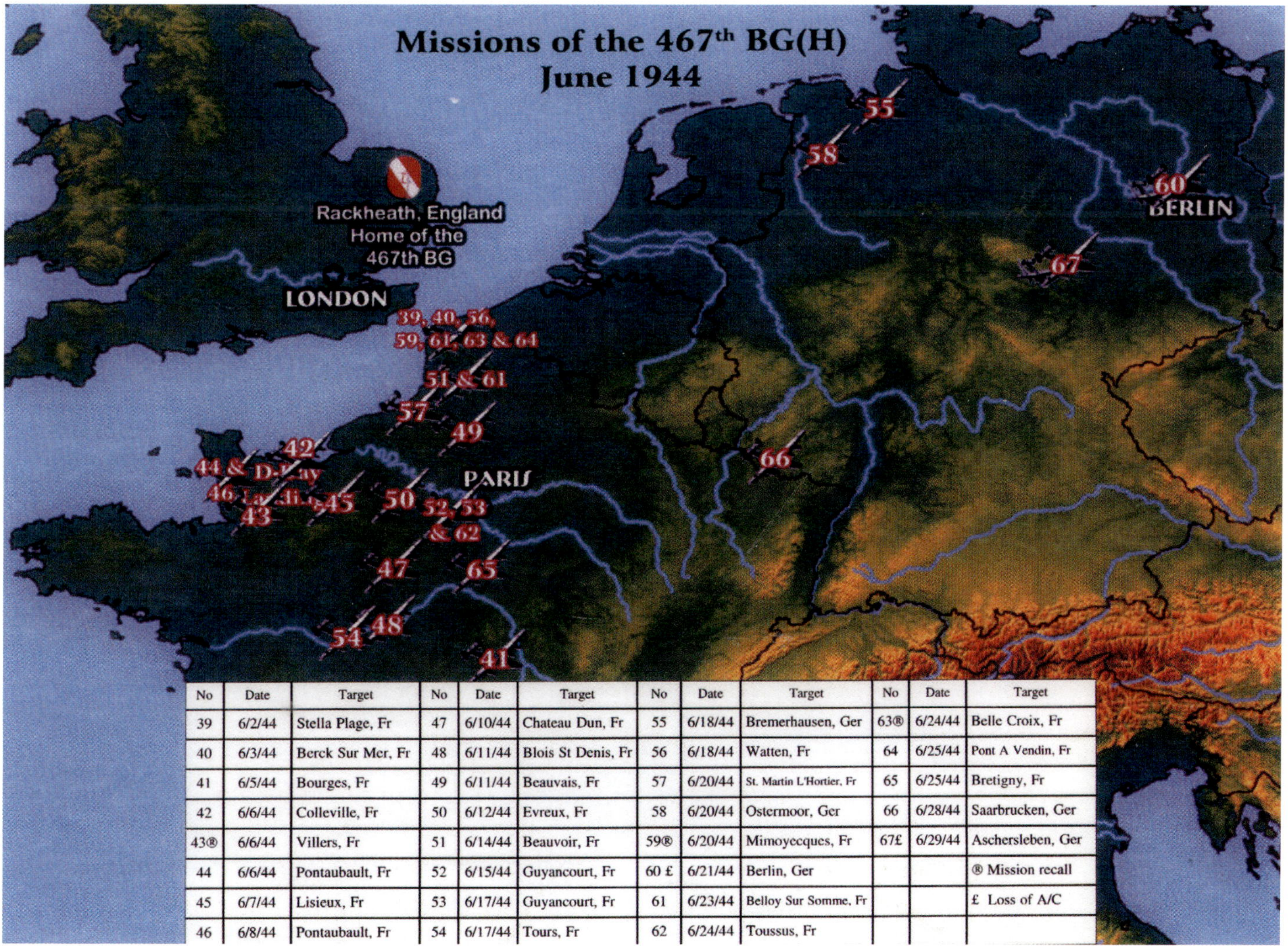

No	Date	Target	No	Date	Target
39	6/2/44	Stella Plage, Fr	47	6/10/44	Chateau Dun, Fr
40	6/3/44	Berck Sur Mer, Fr	48	6/11/44	Blois St Denis, Fr
41	6/5/44	Bourges, Fr	49	6/11/44	Beauvais, Fr
42	6/6/44	Colleville, Fr	50	6/12/44	Evreux, Fr
43®	6/6/44	Villers, Fr	51	6/14/44	Beauvoir, Fr
44	6/6/44	Pontaubault, Fr	52	6/15/44	Guyancourt, Fr
45	6/7/44	Lisieux, Fr	53	6/17/44	Guyancourt, Fr
46	6/8/44	Pontaubault, Fr	54	6/17/44	Tours, Fr

No	Date	Target	No	Date	Target
55	6/18/44	Bremerhausen, Ger	63®	6/24/44	Belle Croix, Fr
56	6/18/44	Watten, Fr	64	6/25/44	Pont A Vendin, Fr
57	6/20/44	St. Martin L'Hortier, Fr	65	6/25/44	Bretigny, Fr
58	6/20/44	Ostermoor, Ger	66	6/28/44	Saarbrucken, Ger
59®	6/20/44	Mimoyecques, Fr	67£	6/29/44	Aschersleben, Ger
60 £	6/21/44	Berlin, Ger			® Mission recall
61	6/23/44	Belloy Sur Somme, Fr			£ Loss of A/C
62	6/24/44	Toussus, Fr			

467th Bombardment Group Combat Missions, June 1944.

echelon." Consequently, all ball turrets on the 467th Group's B-24s were removed by the end of August. Other Groups of the Second Air Division realized the significance of the improvements and soon after carried out the same modifications.

Mission 44 – 2 July 1944 to Blanc Pignon Ferme, France
Group Mission #69 – Target – V-Weapon Sites
The Group assigned twenty-three B-24s and crew—including *Witchcraft* and Lt. Elroy W. Beaney and Crew #70—the mission to Blanc Pignon Ferme. Each plane was loaded with 20 x 250-lb. GPs and the lift-off from Rackheath commenced at 0920.

Maj. Wallace led the first squadron and Capt. Beatty the second, both flying in PFF ships equipped with GH equipment. Two aircraft returned to base early due to mechanical problems.

Twenty-one ships bombed the target by GH. Results were unobserved. Light and inaccurate flak was encountered, but no enemy aircraft were seen. Good fighter coverage was provided by P-51s.

The Group did not incur any aircraft loss or crew injuries.

A flight time of four hours forty-nine minutes is recorded in Group records for Lt. Beaney and Crew #70 in *Witchcraft*. The records also show that 1,500 gallons were pumped into her fuel tanks after mission completion and return to base.

Mission 45 – 6 July 1944 to Kiel, Germany
Group Mission #71 – Target – Naval Base and City of Kiel
For the mission to Kiel, the Group assigned thirty B-24s and crews, including *Witchcraft* flown by Lt. Richard E. Evans and Crew #58. The planes were loaded with a total of 174 x 500-lb. GP bombs and 174 x 500-lb. Incendiary bomb clusters and commenced take-off at 0602. Due to a mechanical problem, one of the Group's B-24s had to make an early return to base.

Lt. Col. A.F. Herzberg flew in a PFF ship leading the first squadron, and Capt. S.J. Neitzel flew with Capt. D.B. Volk in 42-50309 *Plow Jockey/Ten Of Us* from the 789th Squadron, leading the second.

Twenty-nine ships reached the target and dropped an overall total of 174 x 500-lb. Incendiary bombs and 162 x 500-lb. GP bombs. The bombing was visual and the results, although not observed, were rated poor. Excellent support for the B-24s was provided by P-51s. No enemy aircraft were seen in the area; ground anti-aircraft fire was meager prior to the IP, but nearer to the target, it was moderate to intense and fairly accurate.

The Group had a good day, with no aircraft losses or crew injuries, although several ships received minor flak damage.

Group records reveal the flight time for Lt. Evans and Crew #58 in *Witchcraft* was six hours fourteen minutes, and 1,900 gallons were used to top up her fuel tanks.

Mission 46 – 7 July 1944 to Lutzkendorf, Germany
Group Mission #72 – Target – Synthetic Oil Plant
The 467th Group assigned twenty-five B-24s and crews for the mission, including Lt. R.E. Evans and Crew #58 in *Witchcraft*. Thirteen of the planes, each loaded with 20 x 250-lb. GPs, and the remaining twelve, each loaded with 10 x 500-lb. GP bombs, commenced take-off at 0517. Maj. R. Smith flew with Capt. J.D. Swearingen in 42-94910 (791st Squadron), leading the first squadron;

Lt. Richard E. Evans and Crew #58. Rear (L to R): Edward Coltey, Richard Evans, and Harris Conway. Front (L to R): Eugene Bateman, Nathan Nelson, Lorran Wise, Garrett Allen, John Vinson, and Wesley Rawhauser.

the second squadron was led by Lt. Joseph G. Mulheran (790th Squadron) flying in B-24H 42-95094 *Leading Lady*.

All twenty-five aircraft reached the target, but due to a poor initial approach, they had to make a second run to the right of the target. The aircraft bombed visually and the results were rated very good. Three aircraft dropped their bombs on targets of opportunity. Fighter escort coverage provided by P-38s, P-47s, and P-51s was excellent, and no enemy fighter aircraft approached the squadrons. Very intense and accurate flak was encountered on route to and over the target area.

This was the fifth mission flown by the Group since the beginning of July without any lost planes or crew casualties, although some of the Group's B-24s sustained light flak damage.

Group records show a flight time of six hours forty-eight minutes for Lt. Evans's Crew #58 in *Witchcraft*. The records also reveal that it took 2,030 gallons to top up the fuel tanks after the mission.

Mission 47 – 8 July 1944 to Fismes, France
Group Mission #73 – Target – Railway Bridge
The Group put up twenty-six aircraft and crew to fly the mission, including *Witchcraft* flown by Lt. L.P. Vogt and Crew #63. The B-24s, each loaded with 8 x 1000-lb. GP bombs, commenced take-off from Rackheath at 0401.

Maj. Palmer flew with Capt. D.B. Volk in 42 50309 *Plow Jockey/Ten Of Us* (789th Squadron), leading the first squadron; and Capt. Garner, flying with Capt. L.H. Monefeldt in J42-51032, led the second. One plane made an early return to base due to a malfunction. The Wing was recalled due to bad weather after flying for nearly four hours. No bombs were dropped. Light, accurate flak was encountered, but no enemy aircraft were seen. On return to base, the fuel tanks in *Witchcraft* were topped up with 1,225 gallons and Group records show a flight time of three hours thirty-eight minutes.

Although recalled, the mission was given a credit rating, as the crews had flown over enemy territory.

Mission 48 – 12 July 1944 to Munich, Germany
Group Mission #75 – Target – Railway Marshalling Yards
For this long mission to Munich, the Group assigned thirty-six B-24s and crews, including *Witchcraft* flown by Lt. L.P. Vogt and Crew #63. The B-24s were loaded with a mix of GPs and Incendiaries; the bomb total load was 204 x 500-lb. GPs and 136 x 400-lb. Incendiaries fitted with 37-second fuses. The planes commenced take-off at 0910, with Capt. Garner flying with Lt. J. G. Mulheran and Crew #60 in 42 95154 (790th Squadron) leading the first squadron; and Capt. Seiler, flying with Lt. K.G. Ford and Crew #52 in B-24 42-52571 *Snooper* (790th Squadron), leading the second. Two ships made an early return to base: one because of mechanical failure and the other due to personnel error.

Thirty-four ships reached the target and dropped their bombs from 24,000 feet using PFF. The bombing was unobserved and the results are unknown. Good fighter coverage was provided for the Liberators by P-38s, P-47s, and P-51s. Heavy flak was encountered over the target area, but no enemy fighters were seen.

The Group lost two B-24s. The first was B-24H-15 FO 42-52512 *Baffl'ing Brat* from the 789th Squadron. The aircraft received heavy flak damage during the bomb run.

Lt. John E. Thompson and Crew #68. Rear (L to R): Kenneth Hurst (AEG); Milton Kinnaugh (B); and possibly Joseph Zbilowski (CP) or Robert Sprague (N). Front (L to R): Cruz Flores (?), Buel Rose (NG), Dennis Hook (ROG), William Pollard (TG), and John Barrum (BTG).

Lt. Fred R. Sullivan made a valiant attempt to fly his aircraft and Crew #49 to Switzerland, but the aircraft was too damaged to complete the flight. All of the crew safely abandoned the aircraft near Landac, Austria, but one crew member—Staff Sgt. Joseph R. Lund (Radio Operator)—was believed drowned after landing in a river; his body was never found. The remaining nine crew members were taken POW. The second aircraft lost was B-24H-15 FO 42-52559 *Miss Fortune* from the 790th Squadron, flown by Lt. Richard E. Evans and Crew #58. Due to a bad gasoline leakage problem, the aircraft was flown to Switzerland and landed on the airfield at Dubendorf, near Zurich. All nine crew members were interned.

Group records indicate the flight time for Lt. Vogt and Crew #63 in *Witchcraft* was eight hours thirty-five minutes. The records also reveal that 2,400 gallons were used to top up her fuel tanks following mission completion.

Mission 49 – 13 July 1944 to Saarbrucken, Germany
Group Mission #76 – Target – Rail Marshalling Yards
Thirteen B-24s and crews, including *Witchcraft* flown by Lt. John E. Thompson and Crew #68, were assigned to hit the railway yards at Saarbrucken. The B-24s, each loaded with 3 x 2000-lb. GP bombs and led by Capt. Robert W. Doenges, commenced take-off from Rackheath at 0510.

The bombing was carried out using PFF; although the results of the bombing were unobserved, they were rated moderate. Although flak was intense, it was not very accurate, and no enemy aircraft were encountered. Good fighter escort was provided by P-38s, P-47s, and P-51s.

The 467th had another good day, with no aircraft losses or casualties incurred.

Group records indicate a flight time of six hours fifty minutes for Lt. John Thompson and Crew #68 in *Witchcraft*; they also show that 1,875 gallons were used to top up her fuel tanks.

Mission 50 – 16 July 1944 to Saarbrucken, Germany
Group Mission #77 – Target – Railway Center
Witchcraft—flown by Lt. L.P. Vogt and Crew #63—was assigned as one of thirty-two aircraft and crew for this second mission to attack the rail marshalling yards at Saarbrucken. The planes, each carrying 12 x 500-lb. GPs, commenced take-off from Rackheath at 0517. Maj. W.R. Smith flew with Capt. J.D. Swearingen and Crew #78 (791st Squadron) in 42-94881, leading the Group's B-24s. Two aircraft returned to base early because of mechanical problems.

The remaining thirty B-24s reached the target and bombed using PFF. The results were rated good. Flak was moderate and inaccurate, and no enemy aircraft were seen. Good fighter coverage was given by P-38s, P-47s, and P-51s.

Group records show a flight time of six hours thirty-four minutes for Lt. Vogt and Crew #63 in *Witchcraft*, and 2,100 gallons were used to top up her fuel tanks after mission completion.

Mission 51 – 17 July 1944 to Haute Maisnel; Villers-l'Hopital, Bois de Queue Contessa, and Belloy-sur-Somme, France
Group Mission #78 – Target – V-Weapon Sites

Aerial photo of Eisenach, Germany, taken on the Group mission 20 July 1944.

The Group assigned thirty-six B-24s and crews for this mission, including *Witchcraft* flown by Lt. L.P. Vogt and Crew #63. The ships, each carrying 16 x 250-lb. GP bombs, commenced take-off from Rackheath at 1759. Lt. Charles W. Grace flew with Capt. J.D. Swearingen and Crew #78 (791st Squadron) leading the first squadron; the second squadron was led by Capt. Robert D. Sheehan and Crew #61 from the 790th Squadron. Col. Shower led the third squadron, and the fourth was led by Maj. Beaudry.

All thirty-six aircraft bombed the targets visually from 22,000 feet; the results were rated excellent at Villers-l'Hopital and Belloy-sur-Somme. They were rated fair at Haute Maisel and poor at Bois de Queue Contessa. Flak was moderate, but quite accurate, over the target, causing some minor damage to the Group's ships, but no enemy aircraft were encountered. Good fighter support cover was provided by P-38s, P-47s, and P-51s.

The Group had a good day, as no aircraft were lost and there were no crew injuries.

Group records show a flight time of three hours forty-nine minutes for Lt. Vogt and Crew #63 in *Witchcraft*. The records also reveal that 1,200 gallons were used to top up the fuel tanks.

Mission 52 – 18 July 1944 to Troarn, France.
Group Mission #79 – Target – German Troops West of the Village of Troarn

Witchcraft—flown by Lt. L.P. Vogt and Crew #63—was accompanied by thirty-two other 467th planes to Troarn. The mission was to support Allied ground troops. The B-24s, each loaded with 40 x 100-lb. M-1 fragmentation cluster bombs, commenced take-off from Rackheath at 0520.

Lt. Col. Allen Herzberg led the first of three squadrons; Capts. Neitzel and Beatty led the second and third squadrons. One B-24 made an early return to base due to mechanical failure.

The bombing was visual from 14,000 feet, and the results were rated good. Light, fairly accurate flak was encountered, but no enemy aircraft were seen. The crews reported they saw Allied P-38s, P-47s, P-51s, and Spitfires attacking targets within the area of Troarn.

Group records reveal the flight time for Lt.Vogt and Crew #63 was four hours forty-five minutes. They also show that 1,250 gallons were pumped into the fuel tanks of *Witchcraft* following landing.

Mission 53 – 19 July 1944 to Kempten, Germany
Group Mission #80 – Target – aircraft plant

Twenty-four Liberators and their crews—including *Witchcraft*, flown by Lt. L.P. Vogt and Crew #63—were assigned to attack the Me-109 airplane components plant at Kempten, Germany. Each carrying 10 x 500-lb. GP bombs, the B-24s commenced take-off at 0518, with Col. A.J. Shower flying in a PFF ship leading the Group's formations. One plane returned to base early because of mechanical failure.

The remaining twenty-three ships bombed the target from 18,000 feet visually, and the results were rated very good. Flak was meager, and although some enemy fighter activity was seen in the target area, no attack was made on the 467th. Good fighter support cover was provided by P-38s, P-47s, and P-51s.

Group records reveal a flight time of seven hours fifty-one minutes for *Witchcraft* and Lt. Vogt and Crew #63. They also show that when *Witchcraft*'s tanks were later topped up, some 2,250 gallons were used.

Mission 54 – 20 July 1944 to Eisenach, Germany.
Group Mission #81 – Target – Aero Engine Factory

To hit this target, the 467th put up thirty-one aircraft loaded with a total of 250 x 500-lb. GP and 480 x 100-lb. Incendiary bombs. *Witchcraft* was flown by Lt. Joseph N. Zbikowski and Crew #54. The Group formations, led by Maj. A.L. Wallace flying with Capt. J.D. Swearingen and Crew #78 in 42-94910 (791st Squadron) commenced take-off at 0815.

Twenty-one of the Group's ships bombed the target visually from 23,000 feet; the remaining ten bombed a target of opportunity. The bombing results were rated fair. Flak was moderate, and no enemy aircraft were encountered. The fighter protection coverage provided by P-38s, P-47s, and P-51s was good. No losses of aircraft or crew and no crew casualties incurred.

Group records reveal the flight time for *Witchcraft* and Lt. J. Zbikowski and Crew #54 was six hours forty-seven minutes, and 2,150 gallons were used to top her fuel tanks.

This mission was Lt. Lyle Prichard's twenty-second, and he flew as copilot with Crew #77 of the 791st Squadron. He well remembers some unusual happenings:

> Our new pilot, George Perry, was a transplanted Czechoslovakian; his real name was Zhizzy Pollock. He was a very well educated man and could speak seven languages fluently. He visited London the evening before this mission to broadcast on the radio to France and Germany on just what it feels like to bomb the heart of Europe. When he returned, we asked him if he told the Germans how damned scared we were up there. He winked and said, "Yes, I told them that there were so many American planes over Germany we were afraid of running into each other."
>
> We went on mission twenty-two to Eisenach, Germany, and the target was an airplane engine factory. Weather sometimes dictates one's fate. If clouds are high, you use more than the normal amount of fuel to get up over them. If you encounter higher than predicted winds, it will also affect the gas consumption. Today was a case of strong headwinds on the return trip and, as we were letting down for the English coast and had reached ten thousand feet, I flipped off the booster pumps. A couple of minutes later, number four engine quit, and then the other three faltered and stopped. I remember thinking, "Oh God, here we go again!" When you are way out over water and sinking like a rock, the thing to do is try and lighten the plane and get rid of loose items, so they don't fly around when you ditch in the water. I called the waist section and told them what to do. Out went flak vests, machine guns, belts of ammunition, and things like that. We were down to less than four thousand feet and falling when, as a last resort, after trying to get the engines restarted by going to full rich, etc., I flipped on the booster pumps. On came the engines—all four! What a sweet sound, what a surge of power, what a lift of spirits! We called for a straight-in approach, fired a couple flares, and dropped onto the runway with twenty-five gallons of fuel left; enough to not get us enthusiastic about going round again. I felt just great, but others—like the armament section and Maj. Wallace—kinda frowned on what we did. It took quite a lot of explaining to convince them about how the machine guns and ammo had disappeared.

Mission 55 – 24 July 1944 to Montreuil, France.
Group Mission #83 – Target – Support for Allied Troops in Montreuil Area
Thirty-eight B-24s and crew, including *Witchcraft* flown by Lt. L.P. Vogt and Crew #63, were assigned to support ground troops fighting in the Montreuil area. The B-24s, each loaded with 40 x 100-lb. M-I fragmentation cluster bombs, commenced take-off at 0900, with Col. Shower, flying with Capt. Leonard H. Monefeldt and Crew #32 in 42-50309 *Plow Jockey/Ten of Us* (789th Squadron), leading the Group formations.

Aerial view of Rackheath showing how effectively the accommodation sites were camouflaged by the surrounding woodlands.

467th Bombardment Group Operations Block at Rackheath.

Due to bad weather encountered when the planes reached the Montreuil and St. Lo areas, no bombs were dropped and the mission was recalled. Flak was moderate, but no fighter opposition was encountered.

No aircraft loss or damage, and no crew casualties were incurred.

To top up *Witchcraft*'s tanks after a flight time of five hours thirty-two minutes took 1,550 gallons of gasoline.

Note: As the crews flew over enemy-occupied territory, the mission was given a credit rating.

Mission 56 – 25 July 1944 to Montreuil, France
Group Mission #84 – Target – Aerial Support for Allied Ground Forces in Montreuil Area.

Thirty-seven B-24s—including *Witchcraft*, flown by Lt. L.P. Vogt and Crew #63—were assigned to provide air bombardment support for Allied ground troops around the Montreuil area, west of St. Lo, France. The B-24s, each carrying 40 x 100-lb. M-I fragmentation cluster bombs, commenced take-off from Rackheath at 0729.

Col. A.J. Shower again led the Group's aircraft and flew with Capt. L.H. Monefeldt and Crew #32 in 42-95094 *Leading Lady* (789th Squadron).

All aircraft reached the target and dropped a total of 1,416 bombs from 11,000 feet on various targets. The bombing results were rated very good. Flak varied between heavy and moderate, and was reasonably accurate—especially after leaving the target area—but was light over the target area and no enemy aircraft were seen. Good fighter support was provided on the five-hour mission by P-38s, P-47s, and P-51s.

Another good day for the Group, as no aircraft losses or crew casualties were incurred.

Group records reveal a flight time of five hours twenty-two minutes for Lt. Vogt's Crew #63 in *Witchcraft*, and it took 1,450 gallons to top up her fuel tanks after mission completion.

Gunner Staff Sgt. Paul V. Hatten of the 791st Squadron (Lt. Charles J. White's Crew #99), after flying the mission in 41-29388 *Slick Chick*, wrote the following in his diary:

> Mission 12 – We had the same crew as yesterday and returned to the German lines at Montreuil, France, west of St. Lo. We dropped fragmentation bombs on the Germans 1,500 yards from our own lines. Twelve bombs failed to release, which we brought back. Flak was light over the target and we were not hit. Hunt [Staff Sgt.Francis J. Hunt - Tail Gunner] saw one B-24 go down [not a 467th ship], and no one got out as far as he could see. We had good area cover by our fighters. Tuesday, July 25, 1944, from 0712 til 1205 at 12,000 ft.

Mission 57 – 29 July 1944 to Bremen, Germany
Group Mission #85 – Target – Oil Refinery
Thirty-four B-24s, including *Witchcraft* flown by Lt. John E. Thompson and Crew #68, were assigned to Bremen and loaded with a mix of 250-lb. GPs and 500-lb. Incendiary cluster bombs.

The B-24s commenced take-off at 0630, led by Maj. Garnet B. Palmer in a PFF ship, with Lt. Col. Schwart (from the 96th Combat Wing HQ) leading the second squadron with Capt. D.B. Volk and Crew #30 in 42-50309 *Plow Jockey* (789th Squadron).

One plane returned to base early because of mechanical problems. Thirty-two of the Group's ships dropped a total of 536 x 250-lb. GPs and 88 x 500-lb. IB Incendiary cluster bombs on the target by PFF from 23,000 ft., and one aircraft dropped bombs on a target of opportunity. As the bombing was unobserved, the results are unknown. Flak was heavy and intense, but not accurate, and no enemy aircraft were seen. Good fighter support was provided by P-51s.

Bombs being delivered and unloaded at the bomb storage area on the north side of the airfield.

Another good day for the Group, as it did not sustain any aircraft losses or crew casualties.

Group records show neither a flight time for *Witchcraft* and Lt. Thompson and Crew #68 nor the gallons of fuel used to top-up the fuel tanks, but the records reveal overall average figures of six hours seven minutes for the flight time and 1,730 gallons of fuel used by each plane.

Mission 58 – 2 August 1944 to Haut Maisnil, France
Group Mission #88 – Target – V-Weapon Sites
The 467th assigned twenty-four B-24s and their crews, including *Witchcraft* flown by Lt. L.P. Vogt and Crew #63, to fly to Haut Maisnil. The Group's planes, each loaded with 24 x 250-lb. GPs, commenced take-off from Rackheath at 1550 and were led by Capt. Doenges, flying in a GH radar-equipped PFF plane. One aircraft returned to base early due to equipment failure.

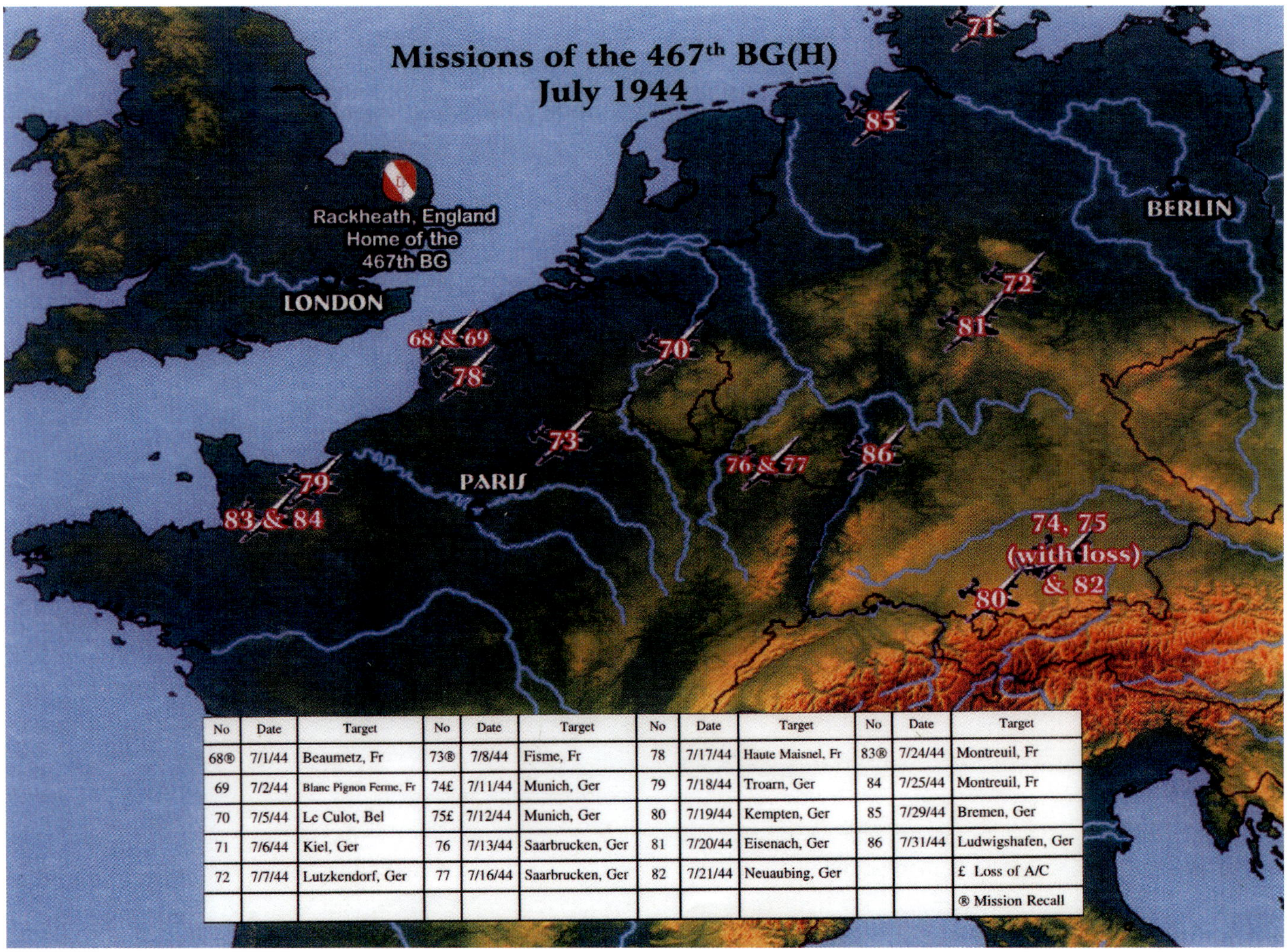

No	Date	Target	No	Date	Target	No	Date	Target	No	Date	Target
68®	7/1/44	Beaumetz, Fr	73®	7/8/44	Fisme, Fr	78	7/17/44	Haute Maisnel, Fr	83®	7/24/44	Montreuil, Fr
69	7/2/44	Blanc Pignon Ferme, Fr	74£	7/11/44	Munich, Ger	79	7/18/44	Troarn, Ger	84	7/25/44	Montreuil, Fr
70	7/5/44	Le Culot, Bel	75£	7/12/44	Munich, Ger	80	7/19/44	Kempten, Ger	85	7/29/44	Bremen, Ger
71	7/6/44	Kiel, Ger	76	7/13/44	Saarbrucken, Ger	81	7/20/44	Eisenach, Ger	86	7/31/44	Ludwigshafen, Ger
72	7/7/44	Lutzkendorf, Ger	77	7/16/44	Saarbrucken, Ger	82	7/21/44	Neuaubing, Ger			£ Loss of A/C
											® Mission Recall

467th Bombardment Group Combat Missions, July 1944.

The 467th plaster the airfield at Clastres in France on 8 August 1944. Shower

Bombing of the airfield at Clastres, France, on 8 August 1944.

Twelve of the planes dropped their bombs from 21,000 feet; the remaining eleven planes did not drop their bombs due to GH equipment failure. The bombing was rated as poor. Meager flak was encountered, but no enemy aircraft were sighted. Good fighter protection support for the B-24s was provided by P-51s.

Group records reveal that the flight time for *Witchcraft* and Lt. L.P. Vogt and Crew #63 was five hours; records also show 1,700 gallons were pumped into the fuel tanks following the mission.

Mission 59 – 3 August 1944 to Lille, France
Group Mission #89 – Target – Gasoline/Oil Storage Plant
Thirty-three aircraft and crew, including *Witchcraft* flown by Lt. L.P. Vogt and Crew #63, were assigned to the mission to Lille. The planes, each loaded with 24 x 250-lb. GP bombs, lifted off from Rackheath at 1630. Maj. Fred E. Holdrege flew with Capt. A.R. Garner and Crew #53 in H42-95094 *Leading Lady*, leading the Group formations. Due to mechanical problems, two of the Group's B-24s made an early return to base.

The target was bombed from 22,500 feet by twenty of the 467th planes, and the results were rated fair. Eleven ships failed to drop bombs due to the target obscured by cloud. Flak was moderate, but became intense and accurate over the target area, causing damage to some of the Group B-24s, but no enemy fighters were seen. The fighter protection provided by P-51s was good.

The Group lost one aircraft: B-24H 42-52424 *Jack The Ripper II*, from the 791st Squadron. The plane crash-landed at the RAF airfield at Manston, Kent; four of the crew members lost their lives and four were injured.

A flight time of four hours seventeen minutes is shown in Group records for Lt. L.P. Vogt and Crew #63 in *Witchcraft*, and the fuel tanks were topped up with 1,325 gallons after return to base.

In his autobiography, the author's friend, Paul Hatten—a former Staff Sgt. Ball Turret Gunner on Lt. Charles J. White's Crew #98, of the 791st Squadron—refers to superstition and missions. Paul wrote:

> August 3, 1944 – Our 14th mission. We were not aware that superstition could possibly affect a mission, but thanks to me, it did. My lovely wife gave me a cameo ring prior to my entering the service that I wore at all times. We were preparing *Topper* as usual with flak suits, etc., when I noticed the set had fallen from my ring. I casually mentioned it to the rest of the crew, and without any conversation, we were crawling on our hands and knees in the grass to no avail. Just to prove a point, I guess, as we encountered intense accurate flak at the target area, quite a bit of which found our plane. We dropped our bombs on oil storage tanks at Lille, France, and limped back to England. When Lt. White departed from the plane, he came to me, put his arm around my neck, and said, "Please don't wear any more rings." I answered, "Yes Sir."

Mission 60 – 4 August 1944 to Rostock, Germany
Group Mission #90 – Target – Heinkel Aircraft Assembly Plant
Witchcraft, flown by Lt. Howard W. Johnson and Crew #69, was one of twenty-five B-24s and crews assigned the mission to Rostock. Twenty-three planes were each loaded with 10 x 500-lb. GP bombs, and the remaining two with 10 x 500-lb. GPs with long-delay fuses. The

Group's planes, led by Maj. Wallace in a PFF ship, took off from Rackheath at 1010. Three aircraft returned to base early due to mechanical problems.

Twenty-two aircraft bombed the target from 23,000 feet visually, and the results were rated good. Light flak was encountered to and from the target, but became moderate over the target. Although enemy fighter aircraft were reported, they did not approach the Group. Good fighter support for the B-24s was provided by P-51s.

A good day for the 467th, as it did not incur any aircraft loss or crew fatalities or injuries.

Following return to base, the fuel tanks in *Witchcraft* were topped up with 2,475 gallons of gasoline; Group records also reveal that the flight time for Lt. Johnson and Crew #69 was seven hours two minutes.

Mission 61 – 5 August 1944 to Brunswick, Germany
Group Mission #91 – Target – Aircraft Assembly Plant and Wagram Airfield
The Group assigned twenty-four planes—including *Witchcraft*, flown by Lt. L.P. Vogt and Crew #63—for the mission to Brunswick with a scheduled take-off time starting at 0832.

Maj. Emil E. Beaudry led the first squadron and Capt. Robert S. Seiler led the second.

Each of the first squadron aircraft carried 52 x 100-lb. GP bombs, and the planes of the second squadron each carried 12 x 500-lb. GPs.

B-24H 41-29388 *Slick Chick*, flown by Lt. Charles J. White and Crew #98 (791st Squadron), developed an engine problem and had to leave the second squadron formation when it was in the vicinity of the German coastline. As a last resort, Lt. C. White dropped his bombs on the island of Borkum, hitting a warehouse before flying back to base.

The remaining twenty-three aircraft bombed the target visually from 22,000 feet; the results were rated excellent. Light but accurate flak was encountered over the target area, but no German fighters were seen. Good fighter escort was provided by P-51s.

Unfortunately, it was a disastrous day for the Group, as it lost two B-24s over Germany to severe flak damage; of the nineteen crewmen on board, fourteen were KIA and five became POWs.

Brief details of the losses portray a very sad picture. The first ship to go down was 41-29363 from the 789th Squadron, flown by Lt. Willard A. Langenfeld and Crew #35. The plane was hit by flak soon after leaving the target. All ten crew members bailed out near Minden, Germany. Pilot Lt. Langenfeld, Copilot Lt. Charles E. Whitacre, and Ball Turret Gunner Staff Sgt. John A. Vittitoe were the only crew members that survived and were made POWs. Lt. Whitacre was of the opinion that the other seven crew members were murdered by hostile German civilians upon reaching the ground after safely bailing out.

The second plane lost was Lt. David E. Love's 42-95162 *Perils of Pauline*, from the 790th Squadron. *Perils of Pauline* had sustained severe flak damage and dropped out of formation. The ship finally went into a spin, and only two crew members—Pilot Lt. Love and Engineer Staff Sgt. John D. Collins—bailed out; they soon became POWs. Unfortunately, seven members of Lt. Love's Crew #70 lost their lives. The Radio Operator fell out of the bomb bay prior to the instruction to bail out and the bombardier is thought to have hit a propeller after bailing out of the airplane's nose. The copilot bailed out, but slipped through his unfastened parachute, and the remaining four members of the crew went down with the ship.

Group records do not show any individual aircraft flight times or fuel consumption figures following mission completion, but the average flight time was seven hours one minute and the fuel consumption per plane was 2,110 gallons.

Mission 62 – 7 August 1944 to Ghent, Belgium.
Group Mission #93 – Target – Oil Storage Depot
Twenty planes and crews, including *Witchcraft* flown by Lt. L.P. Vogt and Crew #63, were assigned the mission to Ghent. Bomb loads varied, as some were loaded with 250-lb. GPs and some with 500-lb. GPs. Capt. Robert Seiler, flying with Capt. George Tormoen and Crew #85 in 42-94910, led the Group formations, which commenced lift-off from Rackheath at 0940. Lt. Charles J. Leyes's ship—42-52303 *Topper* from the 791st Squadron—developed a mechanical problem and returned to base early.

The remaining nineteen B-24s reached the target, but due to very bad weather, only the first squadron of nine planes dropped bombs from 12,000 feet at the MPI; the remaining ten ships returned to base with their bombs. The bombing result was rated excellent. Flak over the target area was meager, and no enemy aircraft were seen. The B-24s had good fighter escort provided by P-51s.

All was going very well for the Group until 42-52565 *My Ideal*, flown by Lt. Harold R. Chilver and Crew #41 from the 789th Squadron, reached the base with their bomb load still on board. The propeller on #1 engine was feathered and, as the aircraft circled the field before making its landing approach, it stalled, clipped some of the trees on Eleven Acre Plantation, and crashed in a field about half a mile from the base. The crash occurred near Norwich Road and about mid-point between Station Road and Honeycombe Road, Salhouse (Field #2863 on the O.S. Map.) Although injured, Air Gunner Sgt. Ray L. Finch was thrown clear of the wrecked aircraft and was the only survivor; the remaining eight crew members lost their lives.

Group records show a flight time of four hours twenty-two minutes for Lt. Vogt and Crew #63 in *Witchcraft*; they also show that 1,500 gallons were used to top up the "Witch's" fuel tanks following the mission.

Group Citation No: 5 – Dated September 7, 1944.

CITATION

The following Officers are cited for outstanding performance of duty while leading the 1st Squadron of the 467th Bombardment Group (H) on a bombing mission to Belgium, 7 August 1944:

CAPT. ROBERT S. SEILER	0677898 Command Pilot
CAPT. GEORGE E. TORMOEN	0743218 Pilot
1ST LT. JOHN K. GILE	0731163 Bombardier
1ST LT. DAVID B. MAZER	0695683 Pilotage Navigator
1ST LT. HERBERT M. DUNNING	0688426 Navigator

When middle clouds forced the formation down to 12,000 feet, the Officers of this lead crew displayed exceptional skill and teamwork to achieve successful the mission on a day other formations were unable to bomb their assigned targets because of restricted visibility. This squadron lead crew, leading eight other B-24 aircraft, was the only formation in the Group to bomb, and the result of "very good" was the highest score of the Division for the day.

The alertness, efficiency, and devotion to duty displayed by these Officers are deserving of the highest commendation.

By order of Col. SHOWER: Signed: G.W.DARNELL

Major, Air Corps -- Adjutant

Mission 63 – 8 August 1944 to Clastres, France
Group Mission #94 – Target – Airfield
Nineteen B-24s and their crewss, including Lt. Robert L. McKenzie and Crew #58 in *Witchcraft*, were assigned the mission to Clastres. Ten of the planes, including *Witchcraft*, were each loaded with 12 x 500-lb. GP bombs, and each of the remaining nine were loaded with 68 x 100-lb. GPs. The Group B-24s, led by Col. A.J. Shower flying with Capt. D.B. Volk and Crew #30 in 42-50309 *Plow Jockey/Ten Ov Us* (789th Squadron) commenced take-off at 1010.

All nineteen ships bombed the target visually from 20,500 feet, and buildings and runways on the airfield were hit. The results were rated excellent. Moderate to heavy flak was encountered over the target, but no enemy aircraft were seen. P-47s and P-51s provided good fighter support for the B-24s.

It was another good day for the Group, as no crew losses or injuries occurred and no aircraft were lost, although some ships received minor flak damage.

Group records reveal a flight time of four hours twenty-two minutes for Lt. Bob McKenzie and Crew #58 in *Witchcraft*. The records also show that a total of 1,195 gallons were used to top up the fuel tanks following mission completion.

Mission 64 – 9 August 1944 to Saarbrucken, Germany
Group Mission #95 – Target – Railway Center
For the mission to Saarbrucken, the Group assigned twenty-four B-24s and their crews, including *Witchcraft* flown by Lt. L.P. Vogt and Crew #63. The B-24s, each carrying 10 x 500-lb. M17 Incendiary bombs, commenced take-off at 0710, with Maj. Fred E. Holdrege leading the first squadron and Capt. Griffin R. Beatty leading the second. One B-24 made an early return to base due to mechanical problems.

Bombs were dropped on the target from 18,000 feet by PFF, and the results were rated fair. Moderate but accurate flak was encountered and no German fighter aircraft were seen. Good fighter coverage was given by P-38s, P-47s, and P-51s.

An excellent day for the Group, as there was no loss of crew or aircraft and no crew injuries were incurred.

Group records reveal a flight time of five hours twenty-nine minutes for *Witchcraft* and Lt. Vogt and Crew #63, and 1,800 gallons were used to top up her fuel tanks.

Lt. Robert McKenzie's Crew #58. Rear (L to R): Richard Garver (B), Robert McKenzie (P), William Fryer (CP), and Norman Zeichick (N). Front (L to R): Gail Derr (AE), William Wells (WG), Joseph Nogan (E), J. Fred Segalia (RO), and Curtiss Williams (TG).

Photograph of *Witchcraft* taken 11 August 1944, on completion of sixty credited combat missions.

Mission 65 – 11 August 1944 to Strasbourg, Germany
Group Mission #96 – Target – Railway Marshalling Yards
Twenty-four planes, each loaded with 12 x 500-lb. GP—including *Witchcraft*, flown by Lt. L.P. Vogt and Crew #63—commenced take-off from Rackheath at 1120 to fly this long-haul mission. Maj. Wallace flew as Command Pilot of the lead squadron in Capt. Robert Sheehan's PFF ship, and Capt. Richard Campbell led the second squadron. Two of the ships returned to base early due to mechanical problems.

The target was bombed visually from 21,000 feet by twenty-one planes; one aircraft did not drop its bombs due to a malfunction. The bombing results were rated very good. Moderate and accurate flak was encountered, but no enemy aircraft were seen. Excellent fighter support was provided by P-51s.

No losses of any kind were incurred by the Group.

A flight time of six hours twenty-one minutes is shown in Group records for *Witchcraft*, Lt. Vogt, and Crew #63. The records also reveal that 1,950 gallons were used to top up the fuel tanks.

Mission 66 – 12 August 1944 to Mourmelon-le-Grande, France.
Group Mission #97 – Target – Airfield
Twenty-six B-24s, including *Witchcraft* flown by Lt. James K. Newhouse and Crew #57, were assigned. The planes, each loaded with 12 x 500-lb. GP bombs, commenced lift-off from Rackheath at 0500. Maj. Beaudry flew as Command Pilot, leading the first squadron with Capt. L.H. Monefeldt and Crew #32 in 42-95032 *Silver Chief* (789th Squadron), and Capt. Neitzel led the second squadron with Capt. J.E. Swearingen and Crew #78 in 42-94910 (791st Squadron).

Master Sgt. Joe Ramirez and his ground crew team with *Witchcraft* on completion of sixty credited strikes.

467th Group B-24s bombing the airfield at Dole-Taveaux, France, on 14 August 1944.

All twenty-six ships bombed the target visually from 26,000 ft; the results were rated fair. Flak was moderate and inaccurate, and no enemy aircraft were seen. Good fighter cover for the B-24s was provided by P-51s. Another good mission for the 467th, with no aircraft losses or crew fatalities or injuries incurred.

Group records show a flight time of six hours fifty-nine minutes for Lt. Newhouse and Crew #57 in *Witchcraft*. The records also show that 2,035 gallons were used to top up her fuel tanks.

Mission 67 – 13 August1944 to Area on Western Side of Seine River, France Group Mission #98 – Target – Bridges and Crossroads

To attack the several targets assigned, consisting of road junctions, bridges, and ferries west of the Seine River in France, the 467th assigned twenty-seven B-24s and crew, including *Witchcraft* flown by Lt. Carl E. Epting and Crew #67. The planes, each carrying 48 x 100-lb. GP bombs, commenced take-off from Rackheath at 1025. The first squadron was led by Maj. Holdrege, flying with Capt. Garner and Crew #53 in 42-95094 *Leading Lady* from the 790th Squadron. Lt. Edward Hooton flew with Capt. Douglas B. Volk and Crew #30 in 42-50309 *Plow Jockey/Ten Ov Us* (789th Squadron), leading the second squadron. One B-24 made an early return to base due to mechanical problems.

The remaining twenty-six planes reached the target, but one ship—42-52530 *Bugs Bunny*—received direct flak hits in the bomb bay and right wing just after bombs away; it fell out of control before breaking up. 41-29388 *Slick Chick*, flown by Lt. Charles J. White and Crew #98 (791st Squadron), had to leave the formation due to its wing being damaged by a piece of the disintegrating *Bugs Bunny*. The remaining twenty-four planes bombed the selected targets from 17,500ft and the results were judged fair. Flak was moderate but accurate before the planes reached the IP, but no enemy planes were seen. Good fighter support for the B-24s was provided by P-51s.

Group records reveal a flight time of four hours 30 minutes for *Witchcraft* and Lt. Epton and crew. The records also show that 1,525 gallons were used to top up the fuel tanks following mission completion. 467th Group losses were: one B-24 lost, eight crew members KIA, two crew members taken POW, and two crewmen flying in other aircraft were lightly injured.

Bugs Bunny was hit by flak in the bomb bay, nose, and right wing immediately after bombs away. The crew in the plane flying immediately behind witnessed a huge red fireball. The plane broke in two, with the nose section pitching upwards, and then it went into a spin. Pilot Lt. Leyes and Copilot Lt. Myles Coolidge were both blown clear of the ship when the cockpit disintegrated. Leyes was able to hang onto his chute harness in spite of not being fastened in it. Both Lt. Leyes and Lt. Coolidge were taken POW; the remaining eight crew members were KIA when the plane disintegrated.

Sgt. Paul V. Hatten flew this mission with Lt. Charles White and Crew #98 in *Slick Chick*, and their airplane was immediately behind *Bugs Bunny*. On return from the mission, Paul made the following entry in his diary:

> 17th Mission – We had a ten man crew, with Lt. Downing as Bombardier and Lt. R.L.Trantor as our new Copilot. We carried 48 x 100-lb. demolition bombs to the German lines in France. Our seven-ship squadron was supposed to bomb road intersections at Bougnetot and Berville, but we ran into very accurate but moderate flak five minutes before the IP. Lt. Leyes's plane, just in front of us, got a flak hit in the bomb bay and the plane broke in two. A piece of their plane caught in the leading edge of our wing and we were forced to leave the formation. We dropped our bombs in the Channel on our return trip home. We had a large flak hole in the left wing. I saw one chute from Lt. Leyes's plane and there were reports of two others. The enlisted men were in our hut and we were all good friends. Aug. 13, 1944 from 1037 till 1524 at 17,000ft.

Mission 68 – 14 August 1944 to Dole-Tavaux, France
Group Mission #99 – Target – Airfield
Twenty-four B-24s and crews, including *Witchcraft* flown by Lt. L.P. Vogt and Crew #63, were assigned the mission to attack the airfield at Dole-Tavaux. The B-24s, each loaded with 48 x 100-lb. GP bombs, commenced take-off at 0710. Maj. Wallace flew with Capt. D.B. Volk and Crew #30 in 42-51032 (789th Squadron), leading the first squadron. The second squadron was led by Lt. J.G. Mulheran and Crew #60 (790th) in 42-52571 *Snooper*.

The newly formed 788th Squadron (2nd establishment) participated; it was their first combat mission with the 467th.

All twenty-four planes bombed the target visually from 20,000ft. Results were rated excellent. No flak or enemy aircraft were encountered, and the B-24s were given good fighter coverage by P-51s.

The Group did not incur losses or injuries of any kind.

Group records reveal the flight time for Lt. Vogt and Crew #63 was seven hours twenty minutes, and 2,350 gallons were used to top up the "Witch's" tanks.

Mission 69 – 15 August 1944 to Vechta, Germany.
Group Mission #100 – Target – Airfield

The 467th Bombardment Group's "war weary" monitor ship, P-47D-25 RE 42-26393 *Little Pete 2*. Generally flown by either the Group Commanding Officer, Col. Albert J. Shower, or his deputy, Lt. Col. James J. Mahoney.

The Group assigned twenty-four B-24s and crews, including *Witchcraft* flown by Lt. L.P. Vogt and Crew #63. The planes were each loaded with 4 x 1,000-lb. GPs and 4 x 500-lb. Incendiary bomb clusters, and commenced take-off at 0900, with Lt. Col. Herzberg flying with Capt. Hanna in a PFF ship leading the first squadron. The second squadron was led by Capt. Seiler, with Capt. Swearingen and Crew #78 in 42-94881 from the 791st Squadron.

All twenty-four planes bombed the target by PFF from 20,500ft, and the results were reported as very good. Fairly good fighter cover support for the B-24s was provided by P-38s and P-51s. No flak was encountered, but some bursts were seen at a distance before reaching the target; although no enemy aircraft attacked, some were seen attacking bombers from other Groups.

Another good day for the 467th on their 100th mission, as no crew or aircraft losses occurred.

Group records indicate the flight time for Lt. Vogt and Crew #63 in *Witchcraft* was five hours twenty-seven minutes, and it took 1,550 gallons to top up her fuel tanks.

Mission 70 – 16 August 1944 to Magdeburg, Germany
Group Mission #101 – Target – Junkers Aircraft Engine Factory

The 467th assigned thirty-six planes—including *Witchcraft*—for the mission to Magdeburg; again, the "Witch" was flown by Lt. L.P. Vogt and Crew #63. Each plane was loaded with 12 x 500-lb. Incendiary cluster bombs, 12 x 500-lb. GPs, or a mixture of 12 x 500-lb. Incendiaries and 500-lb. GPs. The B-24s flew in a three-squadron formation and commenced take-off at 0700, with Lt. Col. Walter Smith leading the Group formations. Two of the B-24s had to make an early return to base due to mechanical problems.

The remaining thirty-four ships reached the target and dropped a total of 249 x 500-lb. GP bombs and 144 x 500-lb. Incendiary clusters from 22,000ft. The results were rated poor for the second squadron, good for the third squadron, and very good for the first squadron. B-24J 401-CF 42-50481, flown by Lt. G.H. Miller and Crew #13 from the 788th Squadron, received a direct hit by flak over the target, causing the ship to break in two just aft of the rear bomb bay. None of the crew members were able to vacate the airplane and all ten men were KIA. Moderate flak was encountered over the Dutch coast and there was intense and accurate flak over the target area. Enemy fighter aircraft seen in the distance did not approach the 467th Group. P-38s and P-51s provided good fighter support for the B-24s.

A flight time of six hours two minutes is shown in Group records for Lt. Vogt, Crew #63, and *Witchcraft*; records also indicate that 2,100 gallons were used to top up the fuel tanks.

Mission 71 – 18 August 1944 to Woippy, France
Group Mission #102 – Target – Aero-Engine Works

Witchcraft, flown by Lt. Joseph W. Cravens and Crew #62, was included in the thirty-seven B-24s and crews assigned for the mission to Woippy. Twenty-five of the B-24s were each loaded with 12 x 500-lb. GP bombs and the remaining twelve were each loaded with 48 x 100-lb. Incendiaries. The B-24s commenced take-off at 1040.

Col. A.J. Shower, flying with Capt. Arthur P. Garner and Crew #53 in 42-95094 *Leading Lady* (790th Squadron) led the Group formations.

All thirty-seven B-24s reached the target and dropped a total of 299 x 500-lb. GPs and 576 x 100-lb. Incendiaries from 18,000ft. The results were rated excellent. Although there was no flak over the target, the crews faced light flak after leaving the area; no enemy aircraft were seen. Good fighter support was provided by P-38s and P-51s.

The Group lost 42-50439 *Broad and High*, flown by Lt. Roger L. Leister and Crew #8 from the 788th Squadron. *Broad and High* crash-landed at Kirby Bedon—only about five miles from base—during the return flight due to severe battle damage and a shortage of fuel. Four crew members lost their lives, and three of the five surviving crew members were seriously wounded; the remaining two were lightly injured. That day, Lt. Leister was flying his eleventh combat mission, but just his second with the 467th, as he was transferred to Rackheath from North Pickenham when the 859th Squadron of the 492nd Group became the second established 788th Squadron on August 12th.

Group records show a flight time of eight hours fourteen minutes for *Witchcraft* and Lt. Cravens and Crew #62, and that 1,980 gallons were used to top up the fuel tanks.

The author and his wife Jill have a personal link that revolves around the mission on 18 August 1944. Although Jill was only eight years old and living with her parents in Strumpshaw at that time, she well remembers that particular early evening, when her dad arrived home at the end of his working day. The first words he said to her mother were: "Annie, there is an American bomber down near Kirby Bedon Church." In more recent years, I realized the significance of her dad's words, but it was only after I discovered that Jill's grandparents, Mr. William and Mrs.Alice Payne, lived in Kirby Bedon for the greater part of their lifetime. Furthermore, they lived in a cottage reasonably close to the village church at the time of the crash of Lt. Roger Leister's *Broad and High*. It was through research of details relating to this incident that I then discovered that Jill's dad was born in Kirby Bedon and lived there with his parents throughout his childhood until 1928, until he left home in his late teens to join the Merchant Navy. I now fully appreciate that on that particular evening, he was concerned about the safety of his parents, and hence his mention of the crash. Literally, it was through that unfortunate plane crash the author learned the details about his wife's late grandparents, and many years later formed friendships with persons associated directly and indirectly with *Broad and High*.

Mission 72 – 24 August 1944 to Misburg, Germany.
Group Mission #103 – Target – Oil Refinery
Thirty-seven planes—including *Witchcraft*, flown by Lt. L.P. Vogt and Crew #63—were assigned the mission to Misburg. The B-24s, each loaded with 500-lb. GP and 350-lb. Leaflet bombs, commenced take-off from Rackheath at 0730 and were led by Lt. Col. A.F. Herzberg flying in a PFF ship with Capt. L.J. Hanna and Crew #76 (791st Squadron). Lt. Addison B. Manning and Crew #88 (791st Squadron)—also in a PFF ship—flew as Deputy Group Lead.

All of the thirty-seven ships bombed the target, dropping a total of 399 x 500-lb. GP and 10 x 350-lb. Leaflet bombs; the results were rated very good. Heavy flak was encountered on the flight to and at the target, but remarkably, there was no flak on the return flight. No enemy aircraft were seen. On the return flight, 42-52394 *Palace Meat Market/Scrapper* (791st Squadron) developed mechanical problems and the crew—Lt. Paul A. DeBlois and Crew #90—had to make an emergency landing at Woodbridge, Suffolk. The remaining thirty-six planes returned safely to Rackheath.

Another good mission for the Group, as no crew casualties or aircraft losses were incurred.

Group records reveal that the flight time for *Witchcraft* and Lt. Vogt and Crew #63 was six hours forty-one minutes. Records also show that 1,900 gallons were used to top up the fuel tanks in the "Witch" after mission completion.

Mission 73 – 25 August 1944 to Lubeck, Germany
Group Mission #104 – Target – Dornier aircraft plant
Witchcraft, flown by Lt. L.P. Vogt and Crew #63, was one of the thirty-six planes and crews assigned to fly the mission to Lubeck, attacking the Dornier Aircraft factory. Each of the B-24s was loaded with 500-lb. GP, 500-lb. XG 20, and 500-lb. G25 Leaflets, and commenced take-off from Rackheath at 0730.

Lt. Col. Walter Smith led the Group formations, flying in a PFF ship with Capt. L.J. Hanna and Crew #76 from the 791st Squadron. Due to a mechanical problem, one ship had to make an early return to base.

Thirty-four planes bombed the target from 22,000ft, dropping 324 x 500-lb. GPs, 5 x 500-lb. XG 20, and 5 x 500-lb. G25 Leaflets; for some reason, one plane dropped 10 x 500-lb. GPs on a target of opportunity. The bombing results were rated very good. Heavy but inaccurate flak was encountered on the way to the target. A dogfight involving twenty-five fighters was seen, but no enemy fighters approached the 467th Group.

The Group lost 41-29420 *Belle Of The East*, flown by Lt. Craig W. Harrington and Crew #84 from the 791st Squadron. The aircraft had engine problems on the return flight and the crew bailed out following an engine cut out; the plane crashed at Belton, Suffolk. Three of the crew members sustained minor injuries.

Group records reveal that 2,000 gallons topped the tanks of *Witchcraft*, and that the flight time for Lt. Vogt and Crew #63 was seven hours thirty-six minutes.

Mission 74 – 26 August 1944 to Dulmen, Germany.
Group Mission #105 – Target – Luftwaffe Fuel Depot
Twenty-four B-24s and their crewss, including *Witchcraft*, again flown by Lt. L.P. Vogt and Crew #63, were assigned the mission to Dulmen. The planes, carrying a total of 552 x 250-lb. GP and 10 x 300-lb. TI G26 bombs, commenced lift-off at 0945.

The Group formations were led by Lt. Col. James J. Mahoney, flying with Lt. Marvin M. Paul and Crew #4 in 42-50675 *Bold Venture III* (788th Squadron).

All twenty-four ships bombed the target, and the results were rated excellent for the first squadron and poor for the second squadron. Flak was encountered en route to the target and became heavy but inaccurate over the target area; two enemy aircraft were seen, but did not approach the Group.

Another good day for the 467th, as it did not incur any aircraft losses or crew casualties.

Group records show the flight time for Lt. L.P. Vogt and Crew #63 in *Witchcraft* was four hours fifty minutes; records also show it took 1,475 gallons to top up the fuel tanks.

Mission 75 – 27 August 1944 to Finow/Oranienburg, Germany.
Group Mission #106 – Target – aircraft plant and Airfield
The 467th assigned thirty-five aircraft and crew—including *Witchcraft*, flown by Lt. L.P. Vogt and Crew #63—for the mission to Oranienburg. Each B-24 was loaded with 500-lb. GP and 100-lb. incendiary bombs. Capt. Robert D. Sheehan and Crew #61 (790th Squadron) flew in a PFF ship, leading the Group formations. Two B-24s had to make an early return to base due to aircraft mechanical problems.

While flying over Denmark to the target, the aircraft were recalled because of bad weather over northern

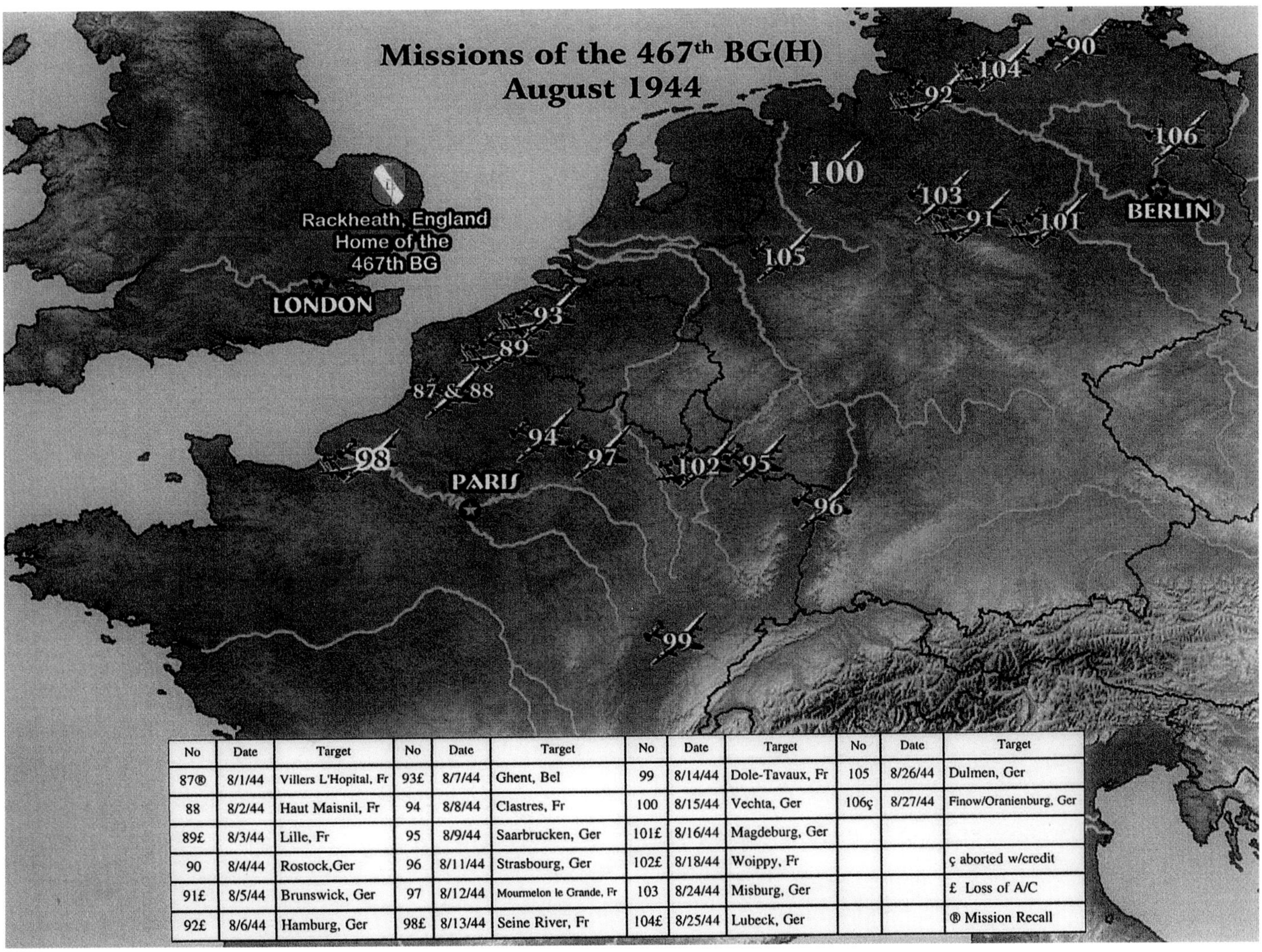

No	Date	Target	No	Date	Target	No	Date	Target	No	Date	Target
87®	8/1/44	Villers L'Hopital, Fr	93£	8/7/44	Ghent, Bel	99	8/14/44	Dole-Tavaux, Fr	105	8/26/44	Dulmen, Ger
88	8/2/44	Haut Maisnil, Fr	94	8/8/44	Clastres, Fr	100	8/15/44	Vechta, Ger	106ç	8/27/44	Finow/Oranienburg, Ger
89£	8/3/44	Lille, Fr	95	8/9/44	Saarbrucken, Ger	101£	8/16/44	Magdeburg, Ger			
90	8/4/44	Rostock,Ger	96	8/11/44	Strasbourg, Ger	102£	8/18/44	Woippy, Fr			ç aborted w/credit
91£	8/5/44	Brunswick, Ger	97	8/12/44	Mourmelon le Grande, Fr	103	8/24/44	Misburg, Ger			£ Loss of A/C
92£	8/6/44	Hamburg, Ger	98£	8/13/44	Seine River, Fr	104£	8/25/44	Lubeck, Ger			® Mission Recall

467th Bombardment Group Combat Missions, August 1944.

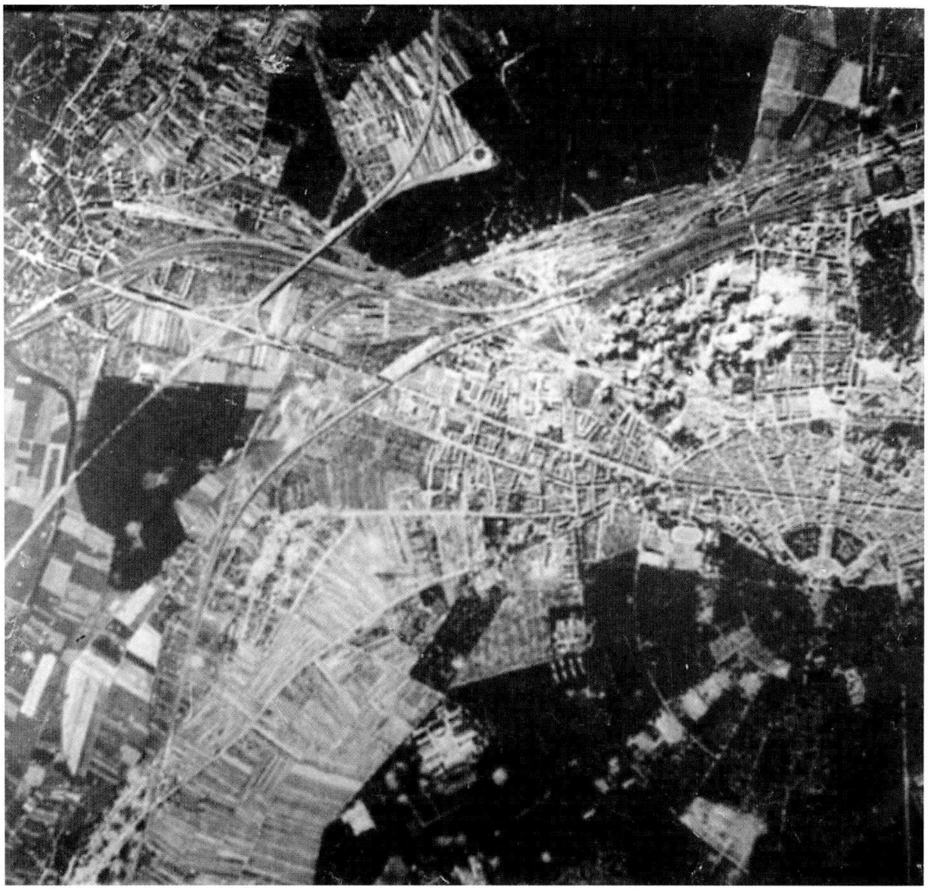

Photo taken of Karlsruhe, Germany, on 8 September 1944, Group Mission #109.

Germany; all of the ships and their crews returned to base safely after being airborne for nearly six hours. Although the aircraft were recalled, the crews received credit for the mission, having flown over enemy-occupied Europe.

The flight time for *Witchcraft* and Lt. Vogt and Crew #63 was five hours forty-six minutes, and the fuel tanks were topped up with 1,700 gallons.

Mission 76 – 8 September 1944 to Karlsruhe, Germany
Group Mission #109 – Target – Railway Marshalling Yards
Thirty-seven planes and crew—including *Witchcraft*, flown by Lt. S.T. Gray and Crew #64—were assigned the mission to Karlsruhe. The B-24s, each loaded with 6 x 1000-lb. GP bombs, commenced lift-off from Rackheath at 0730. Capt. L.J. Hanna and Crew #76 (791st Squadron) flew the Group PFF lead ship and led the Group formations. One plane made an early return to base due to a mechanical problem.

Inclement weather caused some problems for the formations while assembling and necessitated the ships climb to 26,200ft—where it was -43.6°F—to get above the clouds soon after crossing the French coastline. Fortunately, the cloud cover broke up on the approach to the target and bombs were dropped from 21,000ft. The results were rated good. The flak was moderate and reasonably accurate over the target, but only caused minor damage to some of the 467th aircraft. No enemy aircraft were seen. The weather conditions overall were bad throughout this eight and three quarter hour mission. Good fighter support for the Group was provided by P-51s.

No crew casualties or aircraft losses were incurred by the Group, but one plane from the 788th Squadron—42-95234 *Everythin's Jake*, flown by Lt. Billy Williams and Crew #22—was forced to make an emergency landing on an Allied airfield in France.

Group records show the flight time for Lt. Gray and Crew #64 in *Witchcraft* was eight hours thirty-three minutes, and a total of 2,250 gallons was used to top up the fuel tanks.

Mission 77 – 9 September 1944 to Mainz and Wurmz, Germany.
Group Mission #110 – Target – Railway Marshalling Yards
Thirty-seven B-24s and their crews—including *Witchcraft*, flown by Lt. S.T. Gray and Crew #64—were assigned for this mission to Mainz. The B-24s, each loaded with 6 x 1000-lb. GP bombs, commenced take-off from Rackheath at 0700.

Lt. Col. W.R. Smith led the Group, flying with Capt. L.J. Hanna and Crew #76 (791st Squadron) in a PFF ship. Capt. K.G. Ford and Crew #52 (790th Squadron) and Capt. W.J. Grundmann with Crew #33 (789th) flew as Squadron Lead pilots.

The formation that attacked the yards at Mainz achieved a good bombing rating; the formation that attacked the yards at Wurmz, led by Lt. Col. Smith,

The bomb-damaged runway at Clastres airfield.

achieved an excellent bombing rating. Flak was moderate but reasonably accurate and no enemy aircraft were seen. Very good fighter support was provided by P-51s.

The Group did not incur any aircraft losses or crew casualties, although a few of the ships received minor flak damage.

Group records show the flight time for *Witchcraft* and Lt. Gray and Crew #64 was six hours thirty-three minutes, and it took 1,900 gallons to top up the fuel tanks.

Mission 78 – 10 September 1944 to Ulm, Germany
Group Mission #111 – Target – Railway Marshalling Yards
Witchcraft, flown by Lt. Edwin B. Lackens and Crew #71, was included in the twenty-four planes and crew assigned for the mission to attack the rail marshalling yards at Ulm. The planes, each loaded with 10 x 500-lb. GP bombs, commenced take-off at 0805.

Col. A.J. Shower flew as Command Pilot and led the 96th Combat Wing on this mission. Capt. Carl W. Johnson and Crew #1 (788th Squadron) flew the PFF ship that led the 467th Group aircraft, and Lt. Travis S. Whitsel and Crew #73 in 42-51354 (791st Squadron) flew as Squadron Lead.

The bombing by PFF at 20,000ft was unobserved and the results are unknown. No flak was over the target, but some reasonably heavy flak was encountered on the return flight as the ships flew over Stuttgart and Karlsruhe. Good fighter support was provided by P-51s.

On the return flight, two of the Group's B-24s landed away from base for refueling, returning to Rackheath later that afternoon; otherwise, the remaining twenty-two planes returned to base safely and no crew casualties were incurred.

Flight time for Lt. Lackens's Crew #71 in *Witchcraft* is shown as seven hours twenty-five minutes. The records also show that 1,900 gallons filled *Witchcraft*'s tanks.

Witchcraft did not fly on any further combat missions until 3 October 1944, as from 12 September to 29 September, the 467th's crews were assigned to ferry gasoline to General Patton's US 3rd Army in France. During those "Trucking Flights," the 467th's crews shipped 646,079 gallons of 80-octane fuel to the 3rd Army. Despite the highly dangerous load carried on these trucking missions, the crews were not given any credit rating, as they did not fly over enemy-occupied territory, albeit flying quite close to it.

Mission 79 – 3 October 1944 to Gaggenau, Germany
Group Mission #113 – Target – Industrial Sites
Twelve planes and crews, including *Witchcraft* flown by Lt. S.T. Gray and Crew #64, were assigned by the 467th for the mission to Gaggenau. Loaded with 10 x 500-lb. IB cluster bombs each, the B-24s commenced take-off at 0705.

Col. A. J. Shower flew as Command Pilot and led the 96th Combat Wing; Lt. Donald C. Tibbetts and Crew #29 in 44-10488 *Massilon Tiger* (789th Squadron) flew the deputy lead ship.

All planes bombed the target visually from 23,000ft, and the results were rated good. There was moderate flak over the target area and some enemy aircraft were seen. No aircraft were lost by the Group and no crew casualties were incurred.

Lt. Col. James J. Mahoney, Deputy Commanding Officer of the 467th Bombardment Group. He was twenty-seven years of age when he flew *Little Pete 2* to Clastres, France.

Lt. S.T Gray and his fellow flight crewmembers. Rear (L to R): S. Arnold (Crew Chief), James Buck (N), Henry Meyer (CP), and S.T. Gray Jr. (CP). Front (L to R): Clarence Togarini (RO), Warren O'Neal (Gr), Edmund Laczynski (Gr), Allen Francis (TG), and James Eberline (NG).

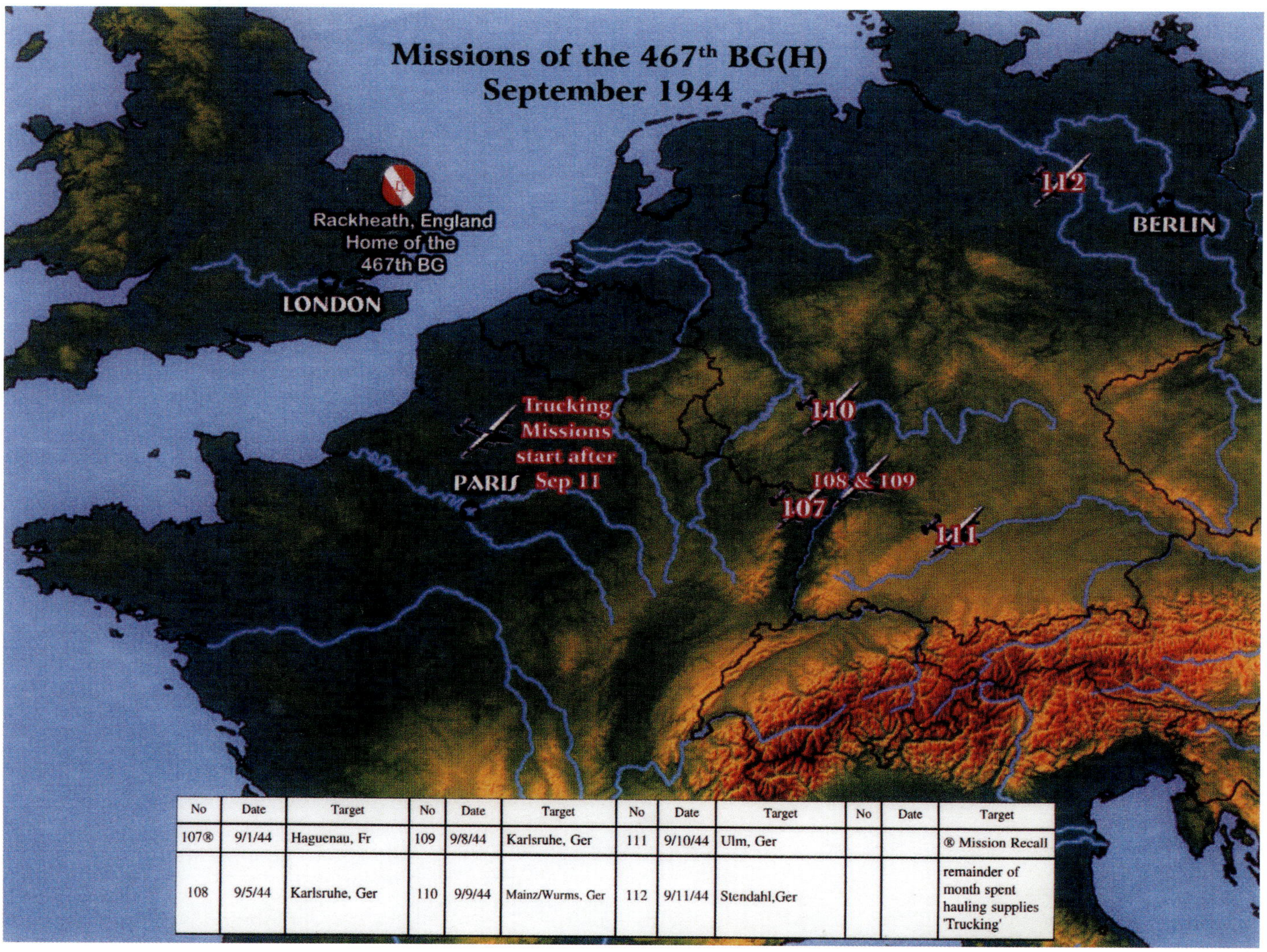

No	Date	Target	No	Date	Target	No	Date	Target	No	Date	Target
107®	9/1/44	Haguenau, Fr	109	9/8/44	Karlsruhe, Ger	111	9/10/44	Ulm, Ger			® Mission Recall
108	9/5/44	Karlsruhe, Ger	110	9/9/44	Mainz/Wurms, Ger	112	9/11/44	Stendahl,Ger			remainder of month spent hauling supplies 'Trucking'

467th Bombardment Group Combat Missions, September 1944.

Group records reveal the flight time for *Witchcraft*, Lt. S.T. Gray, and Crew #64 was seven hours twenty-nine minutes, and 1,900 gallons were pumped into the fuel tanks. Note: The mission was apparently to support the warning given to Germany that if they failed to cease fighting, fire bomb attacks would be carried out on various targets.

Mission 80 – 5 October 1944 to Paderborn-Lippstadt-Herford, Germany
Group Mission #114 – Target – Airdrome.
The Group assigned twenty-six planes and crews—including *Witchcraft*, flown by Lt. S.T. Gray and Crew #64—and each B-24 was loaded with 12 x 500-lb. GP bombs. Capt. L.J. Hanna and Crew #76, flying the Group's PPF lead ship 42-51154 *Silver Dollar* (791st Squadron), led the Group B-24s. Two aircraft returned to base early because of mechanical problems.

The bombing results were officially reported as good. Flak was very light, and some enemy aircraft were reported seen in the distance. P-51s provided very good fighter support.

Another good day for the Group, as it did not incur any crew casualties or aircraft losses.

A flight time of five hours twenty-two minutes is shown in Group records for *Witchcraft* and Lt. S.T. Gray and Crew #64. The records also reveal that it took 1,800 gallons to top up the fuel tanks.

Mission 81 – 6 October 1944 to Wenzendorf-Stade, Germany.
Group Mission #115 – Target – Jet-Aircraft Parts Factory
Lt. S.T. Gray and Crew #64 flew *Witchcraft*, along with twenty-nine other B-24s and crews. The B-24s, each carrying 12 x 500-lb. GPs, were led by Maj. Garnett B. Palmer, commencing take-off at 0815. All ships bombed the target from 20,000ft, and the results were rated fair. No flak or enemy fighter aircraft were encountered, although heavy flak was seen in the distance in the Hamburg area, which was being attacked by other groups. P-47s gave good fighter protection.

No crew casualties or planes were reported lost by the Group.

A flight time of six hours seventeen minutes is shown in Group records for Lt. S.T. Gray and Crew #64 in *Witchcraft*. Records also reveal that 1,825 gallons were used by the "Witch."

Mission 82 – 7 October 1944 to Magdeburg, Germany
Group Mission #116 – Target – Krupps Munitions Works
Thirty-eight planes—including *Witchcraft*, flown by Lt. Maynard M. Ungerer and Crew #63—were assigned by the Group and each B-24 was loaded with 6 x 1,000-lb. GP bombs.

Three planes had to make an early return to base due to mechanical problems. However, the remaining thirty-five B-24s bombed the target visually from 23,000ft and the results were rated excellent. Over the target area, the crews encountered heavy and reasonably accurate flak; a number of Group B-24s received minor flak damage.

The Group lost no aircraft and no crew fatalities were incurred, but Lt. Harvey P. Pettitt (791st Squadron)—flying H42-95224 *Lonely Heart*—was seriously injured by flak.

Group records show a flight time of six hours twenty-eight minutes for Lt. M.M. Ungerer and Crew #63 in *Witchcraft*, and 1,925 gallons were used to top up the tanks after mission completion.

Mission 83 – 9 October 1944 to Coblenz, Germany
Group Mission #117 – Target – Railway Marshalling Yards
For this mission, the 467th assigned twenty-eight planes and crews, including *Witchcraft* flown by Lt. Carl E. Epting and Crew #67. The B-24s, each loaded with 20 x 250-lb. GP bombs, commenced take-off at 0950. One aircraft returned to base early due to mechanical malfunction.

The target was bombed from 21,000ft using PFF and the results are unknown. Flak over the target was moderate and inaccurate.

The Group did not incur any aircraft or crew losses.

Group records reveal the flight time for Lt. Epting and Crew #67 in *Witchcraft* was five hours forty-one minutes. Also, the records reveal that 1,700 gallons were used to top up the fuel tanks.

Mission 84 – 14 October 1944 to Cologne, Germany.
Group Mission #119 – Target – Railway Marshalling Yards
For this mission, the Group assigned thirty-six aircraft and crews, including *Witchcraft* flown by Lt. C.E. Epting

and Crew #67. The bomb loads carried were mixed, with some planes loaded with 250-lb. GPs, some with 500-lb. IB incendiaries, and some with both types of bombs. Soon after take-off (time unknown), the crews flew in a continuous overcast up to 20,000ft before it became reasonably clear; flying in the overcast caused problems during the squadron assembly. Four ships returned to base early due to various reasons.

The remaining thirty-two B-24s bombed the target using PFF, but the results are unknown. Flak was intense and reasonably accurate, causing considerable damage to fourteen of the planes. German fighter aircraft were encountered, but were unable to make any real effective passes.

Lt. John Smith—Bombardier on Lt. Billy Williams's Crew #22 flying 42-5073 from the 788th Squadron—was KIA by flak shrapnel.

B-24H-15 FO 42-52507 *Miss Judy* (789th Squadron) developed an engine fire and severe vibration over western Germany, and all nine crew members bailed out. Eight of them became POWs, but sadly, the ninth crewmember—pilot Lt. Donald J. Hudson—was KIA. It is rumored that Lt. Hudson was shot and killed while hanging from a tree in his parachute.

Lt. Robert J. Curran, Navigator on Lt. Boyd L. Woodis's Crew #72 (790th Squadron), fell through the nose wheel door of 42-110171 *Prowler* and became a POW. Not at all a very good day for the 467th Group.

Group records do not show individual flight times for any of the crews, nor individual figures for the quantity used when the fuel tanks were topped. Only an overall average flight time of six hours sixteen minutes and an average fuel consumption figure of 1,740 gallons are provided.

Mission 85 – 22 October 1944 to Hamm, Germany.
Group Mission #123 – Target – Railway Marshalling Yards

At 1109, twenty-nine 467th Group planes—including *Witchcraft*, flown by Lt. S.T. Gray and Crew #64—commenced take-off. The B-24s were loaded with either 20 x 250-lb. GPs, 10 x 500-lb. M-17 Incendiaries, or a mixture of both.

All twenty-nine ships bombed the target from 23,000ft using PFF, but as the bombing was unobserved, the results are unknown. Moderate but inaccurate flak was encountered over the target area, but no enemy aircraft were seen.

Col. Albert J. Shower in the cockpit of *Little Pete 2*. Col. Shower held the unique distinction of being the only U.S. 8AF Bombardment Group Commanding Officer who brought his men to the United Kingdom, flew on combat missions with them, and following cessation of hostilities in Europe, took his men back to the US.

Photograph of Cologne Cathedral showing the damage to the immediate surrounding area by the bombing attacks.

Good fighter protection for the B-24s was provided by the accompanying P-51s.

No plane losses or crew injuries were incurred by the Group.

The flight time for Lt. Gray and his fellow crew members in *Witchcraft* was five hours eight minutes and the gasoline used by the "Witch" was 1,450 gallons.

Mission 86 – 25 October 1944 to Neumunster, Germany
Group Mission #124 – Target – Airfield and Aircraft Repair Center

At 0950, twenty-nine B-24s—including *Witchcraft*, flown by Lt. A.E. Rothchild and Crew #68—were assigned by the 467th this mission. The planes, loaded with various types of bombs ranging from 20 x 250-lb. GPs, to 10 x 500-lb. GPs, and 10 x 500-lb. M-17 incendiary cluster bombs—and some with a mix of GP and incendiaries—headed north for Cromer and over the North Sea to assemble at 10,000ft. Capt. James E. Swearingen with Crew #78 in 42-94910 and Lt. Donald C. Tibbetts with Crew #77 in 42-50599 led the Group formations.

The target, some thirty miles north of Hamburg, was bombed from 20,000ft through 10/10 cloud cover by Pathfinder Force radar system. Results achieved by the bombing are unknown. No flak was over the target area, but light and inaccurate flak was encountered to and from the target; no enemy aircraft were seen. The B-24s had good fighter protection provided by P-51s.

A good day for the 467th, as no aircraft were lost and no crew casualties were incurred.

The flight time for Lt. Rothchild and Crew #68 in *Witchcraft* is shown as five hours forty-eight minutes. Records also show that *Witchcraft* was topped up with 1,600 gallons of gasoline.

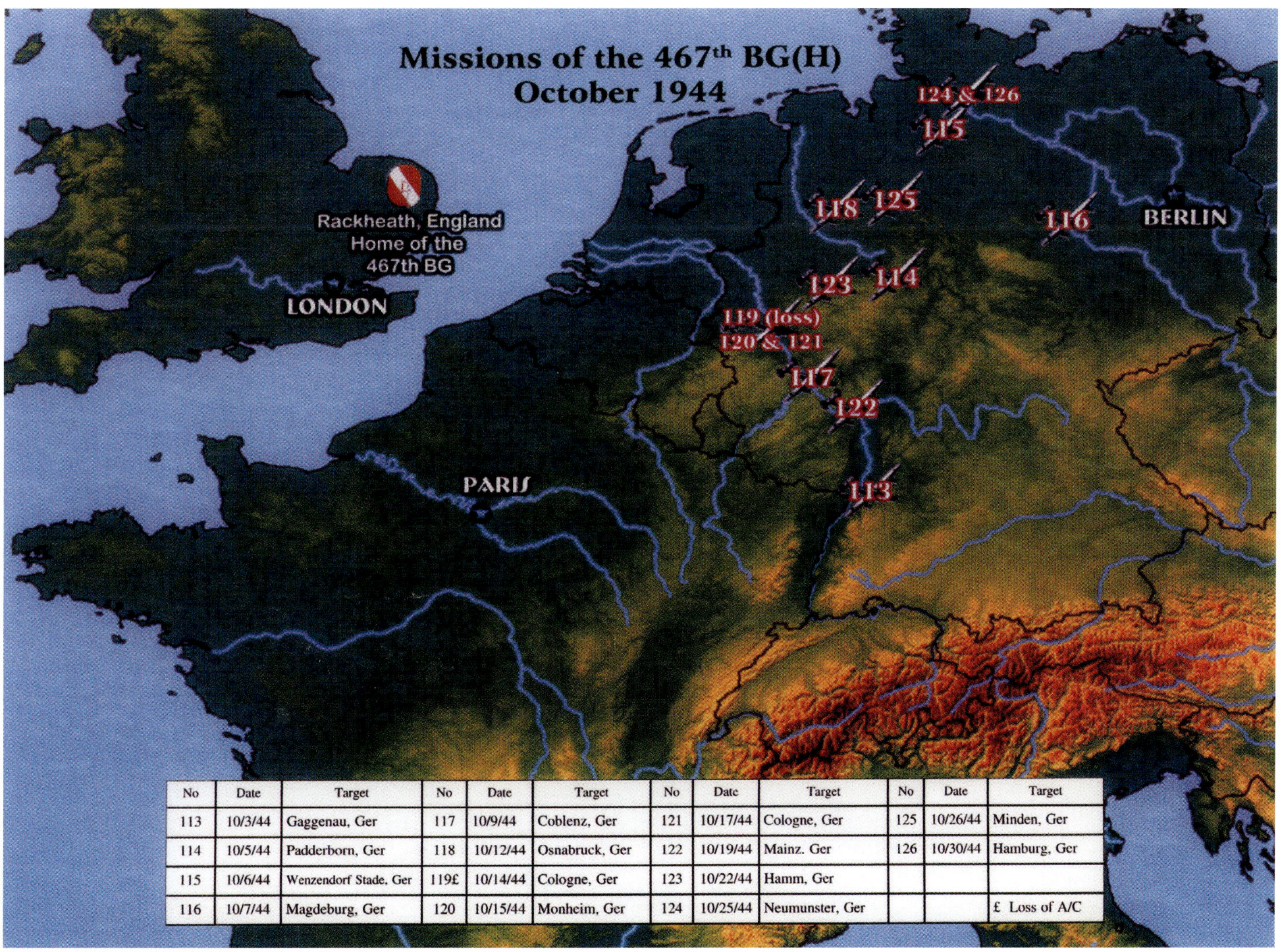

No	Date	Target	No	Date	Target	No	Date	Target	No	Date	Target
113	10/3/44	Gaggenau, Ger	117	10/9/44	Coblenz, Ger	121	10/17/44	Cologne, Ger	125	10/26/44	Minden, Ger
114	10/5/44	Padderborn, Ger	118	10/12/44	Osnabruck, Ger	122	10/19/44	Mainz. Ger	126	10/30/44	Hamburg, Ger
115	10/6/44	Wenzendorf Stade, Ger	119£	10/14/44	Cologne, Ger	123	10/22/44	Hamm, Ger			
116	10/7/44	Magdeburg, Ger	120	10/15/44	Monheim, Ger	124	10/25/44	Neumunster, Ger			£ Loss of A/C

467th Bombardment Group Combat Missions, September 1944.

Photograph taken during a crew briefing.

Mission 87 – 2 November 1944 to Bielefeld, Germany
Group Mission #127 – Target – Railway Marshalling Yards
Unfortunately, very few details of the mission to Bielefeld are available.

Group records reveal the participating B-24s were each loaded with either 20 x 250-lb. GPs, 10x 500-lb. Incendiaries, or a combination of both. The assigned planes and their crews commenced take-off at 0900 and assembled at 19,000ft over Buncher 15, close to the airfield. The assembly was delayed for several minutes due to the lead ship's abort due to mechanical problems.

The target was bombed visually and the results rated as very good. No flak was over the target area, but heavy and inaccurate flak was encountered over Osnabruck. No enemy aircraft were seen. Excellent fighter support was provided by P-47s.

No crew casualties or aircraft losses were incurred.

The flight time for *Witchcraft* and Lt. Nolan G. Patton and Crew #71 was in the region of five hours forty-five minutes (using the recorded flight time for Lt. Henry K. Close and Crew #33 from the 789th Squadron).

Note: The Eighth Air Force Band and its eighty-five musicians made the only Second Air Division base appearance when it played at Rackheath during the early part of the month. Such a prestigious function on the 467th Group's base was rated highly by the Second Air Division's "Top Brass."

Mission 88 – 4 November 1944 to Misburg, Germany
Group Mission #128 – Target – Oil Refinery
The 467th assigned thirty-eight ships—including *Witchcraft*, flown by Lt. S.T. Gray and Crew #64—for this mission. The B-24s—most of which were loaded with 12 x 500-lb. GPs, although some were loaded with 500-lb. IBs—commenced take-off at 0840. Maj. Robert W. Doenges flew with Lt. Addison B. Manning and Crew #88 in the Group PFF ship 42-50949 (791st Squadron), leading the Group formations. Due to heavy overcast, the B-24s had to climb to 11,000ft to assemble over "Splasher Beacon 5." Two of the planes made an early return to base because of mechanical problems.

As there was 6/10th cloud cover over the area, the target was bombed by PFF from 25,000ft. The bombing was unobserved and the results were later rated as poor. Flak over the target was fairly accurate and appeared to be from 105mm high-velocity anti-aircraft guns, which caused damage to some of the Group aircraft. Flak was also encountered over Dummer Lake as the planes were on their homebound flight. No enemy fighters were encountered and P-51s provided good fighter support.

A good day for the 467th Group, as no aircraft were lost, but sadly, Staff Sgt. Willard T.Woods was KIA and Sgt. Truman S. Thompson was seriously injured; both were waist gunners from Crew #23 flying in 44-40120 *That's All Brother* (788th Squadron).

Group records reveal that *Witchcraft* was not refueled following completion of this mission, probably due to scheduled service. The average for each of the thirty-four aircraft that were refueled is shown as 1,775 gallons, and an average flight time of six hours one minute was recorded.

Mission 89 – 9 November 1944 to Metz, France
Group Mission #131 – Target – Tactical Targets-Transportation
The Group assigned twenty-eight aircraft—including *Witchcraft*, flown by Lt. S.T. Gray and Crew #64—for this mission. No details are available relating to the take-off time or the bomb loads carried.

The target was bombed by PFF and was unobserved; the results are unknown.

The Group did not incur any aircraft losses or crew casualties.

Group records show a flight time of five hours fifty-four minutes for Lt. S.T. Gray and Crew #64 in *Witchcraft*;

records also reveal that a total of 1,650 gallons topped off the tanks.

Mission 90 – 10 November 1944 to Hanau, Germany
Group Mission #132 – Target – Railway Marshalling Yards
Witchcraft, flown by Lt. S.T. Gray and Crew #64, was included in the twenty-seven ships and crew assigned by the Group for this long-haul mission. The planes, each loaded with 40 x 100-lb. GP bombs, commenced lift-off at 0840.

Col. Albert J. Shower led the 96th Combat Wing's planes and the route was via Calais into Belgium, just south of Brussels and Liege, then straight through the Ruhr Valley south of Coblenz to Hanau.

Although the crews were warned at the briefing that it could be a rough mission through the Ruhr Valley south of Coblenz to the target, fortunately, the crews did not encounter any flak.

The target was bombed using PFF from 21,000ft unobserved and the results are unknown.

B-24H-15 FO 42-52571 *Snooper*, flown by Lt. Maynard M. Ungerer and Crew #63 (790th Squadron), was lost. Soon after leaving the target, "571" was seen with its No. 2 engine propeller feathered and losing altitude until out of sight. The last sighting of the plane was by aircraft from the 93rd Bomb Group when it was about thirty-five miles southwest of Brussels and attempting to make radio calls on Channel B for fighter protection. After being told they were "over friendly territory" no further contact could be made with the crew, and it was presumed that *Snooper*, along with her nine-man crew, went down over the North Sea. All nine crew members are listed as KIA.

A flight time of seven hours twenty-four minutes is shown for Lt. S.T. Gray and Crew #64 in *Witchcraft*. Records also show that 2,000 gallons were used to fill the "Witch's" tanks.

Mission 91 – 11 November 1944 to Bottrop, Germany.
Group Mission #133 – Target – Synthetic Oil Plant
The 467th put up seventeen planes, including *Witchcraft* flown by Lt. S.T. Gray and Crew #64, to attack the synthetic oil refinery plant at Bottrop.

The B-24s—some loaded with 24 x 250-lb. GPs and others with 12 x 500-lb. incendiary bombs—commenced take-off at 0900. Maj. Fred E. Holdrege led the Group's squadrons. One plane made an early return to base.

The target was bombed from 23,000ft using PFF; as the bombing was unobserved, the results are unknown. Flak was light and very inaccurate over the target, but flak encountered over the Dutch coast was reasonably accurate and caused minor damage to some of the Group's B-24s.

No planes were lost and no crew casualties were incurred.

Records reveal that *Witchcraft*'s fuel tanks were topped up with 1,550 gallons and a flight time of five hours eight minutes was recorded for Lt. Gray and Crew #64.

Mission 92 – 16 November 1944 to Eschweiler, Germany
Group Mission #134 – Target – German Army Installations and Gun Emplacements
Thirty-four planes and crews—including *Witchcraft*, flown by Lt. Lester O. Graham and Crew #66—commenced take-off from Rackheath at 1015. Thirty-three of the aircraft each carried 20 x 260-lb. fragmentation bombs and one plane carried a number of bombs, plus a load of leaflets. Maj. Albert L. Wallace flew in JSH 42-50949 with Lt. James W. Littleford and Crew #79 (791st Squadron), leading the formations. Capt. Charles W. Grace and Crew #97 flying 42-95094 *Leading Lady* (791st Squadron) flew Deputy Group Lead. Lt. Charles H. Brandon with Lt. Maurice B. Cramer and Crew #81 in 42-51282 (791st) led the third squadron. Lt. Frank S. Watson and Crew #44 flying in 44-10488 *Massilon Tiger* (789th) led the fourth squadron, due to Capt. William J. Grundmann and Crew #89 in 42-95032 *Silver Chief* (791st Squadron) having to abort the Lead position. Soon after take-off, the crews ran into really bad weather, with a cloud ceiling of zero and a visibility range of 2,000ft, but remarkably, at 5,000ft conditions were clear. Three of the B-24s made an early return to base due to the inclement weather.

Two aircraft of the remaining thirty-one B-24s that reached the target were unable to attack due to mechanical failure. Bombing of the selected targets (Tactical Targets selected were in support of the beginning of "Operation Queen"), which were reasonably close to the US Ninth Army lines, was by PFF lead ship GH from 21,000ft; the results were later reported and confirmed as good, and more effective than expected. Flak was meager, but reasonably accurate over the selected target area, and no enemy aircraft were encountered. Good fighter protection was provided for the B-24s.

Due to Rackheath being closed by the bad weather, the planes were diverted to the RAF airfield at Sandtoft, West Yorkshire. The crews were transported to another RAF base about fifteen miles away at Lindholme, where they were accommodated. Their stay at Lindholme was extended to two or three days due to the adverse weather that later closed in that area of Yorkshire. Following a two-day stopover at Lindholme, some of the crew members were taken on a six-hour truck ride back to Rackheath. The remaining crew members flew back to Rackheath with the aircraft the day after, following an enjoyable three-day stay with their Royal Air Force hosts.

Except for minor flak damage to two or three of the Group planes, no crew casualties were incurred and no aircraft were lost.

As all thirty-one B-24s landed at the RAF airfield at Sandtoft, Yorkshire, there are no official records relating to flight times nor gasoline consumption, but the average flight time for the mission was in the region of five hours twenty-eight minutes. Flight times were recorded in the diaries of Staff Sgt. Paul V. Hatten of the 788th Squadron and Staff Sgt. Albert J. Steffen of the 789th Squadron: Paul's diary shows a flight time of five hours twenty-six minutes and Albert's five hours thirty minutes.

The former RAF WWII airfield at Sandtoft, Yorkshire—now a private airfield.

Mission 93 – 21 November 1944 to Harburg, Germany
Group Mission #135 – Target – Synthetic Oil Plants
For the mission, the Group put up twenty-nine planes, including *Witchcraft* flown by Lt. S.T. Gray and Crew #64. Each B-24 was loaded with 12 x 500-lb. GP bombs.

The operation was a "96th Wing" mission; the 467th Group, flying "low right" in the Wing, was led by Maj. John J. Taylor, with Lt. Addison B. Manning and Crew #88 in JSH 42-50949 from the 791st Squadron. Lt. Aubrey E. Rothchild led the second squadron with Lt. William J. Grundmann and Crew #89 in 42-95154 (791st Squadron), and Capt. George E. Tormoen and Crew #85 in 42-94910 (791st) led the third squadron. The 467th commenced lift-off from Rackheath at 0830.

All twenty-nine ships visually bombed the target just south of Hamburg from 21,000ft, and the results were rated excellent. Initially, the target was going to be bombed by H2X; it was just about as the "Mickey" operator in the Lead ship—Lt. James W. Holt—was all set to give the word for bombs away when Lt. Charley J. Good (Bombardier) found he could make a visual correction, and in just forty-five seconds he was able to adjust his bombsight. Lt. Good had his bombing pattern mentioned in the Second Air Bombardment publication, referred to as "Best Hit of the Week."

Lt. Lester O. Graham and Crew #66. Rear (L to R): Lester Graham (P), John Rewey (C/P), George Frazer (B), and Bernard Weltmann (N). Front (L to R): John Doling (E), Carl Johnson (WG), Roland Renaud (R/O), Albert Steffen (TG), Chester York (NG), and Lyman Weigle (WG).

Light flak was encountered en route, but became very intense and accurate over the target, then became moderate after leaving the target. No enemy fighter planes were encountered by the Group, although some reports mentioned enemy fighters were seen. Good protection was provided by P-47s.

The Group did not lose any aircraft, although thirteen out of the twenty-nine aircraft sustained heavy flak damage. Fortunately, the Group did not incur any crew losses or injuries.

The flight time for *Witchcraft* and Lt. S.T. Gray and Crew #64 is shown in Group records as six hours fifty-two minutes; records also reveal that 1,930 gallons were used to top up the fuel tanks in the "Witch."

Group Citation No: 8 – 9 December 1944

CITATION

The following named Officers and Enlisted Men are cited for outstanding performance of duty on a bombing mission to Germany, 21 November 1944:

MAJOR JOHN J. TAYLOR	0421636 AC	Command Pilot
CAPT. ADDISON B. MANNING	0397536 AC	Pilot
1ST LT. CHARLEY J. GOOD	0550168 AC	Bombardier
1ST LT. LOREN L. ROUSH	0708823 AC	Navigator
1ST LT. EVERETT R. STEVENS	0699265 AC	Navigator
1ST LT. JAMES W. HOLT	0702920 AC	Navigator
T/SGT. PETER SKOLL	35535032	Engineer
T/SGT. ALLEN C. WHITEHEAD	33526180	Radio Operator
S/SGT. JULIUS G. GAVIN	34615301	Gunner
S/SGT. HENRY A. BROWN	16122349	Gunner
S/SGT. HENRY G. SIMON	33421882	Tail Gunner

This lead crew, leading a Group formation to attack a vital synthetic oil refinery target at Harburg/Hamburg, distinguished itself by extraordinary teamwork to destroy an enemy installation with devastating effect.

Despite 9-10 cloud cover and ground haze, this crew capitalized on a break in the clouds for a 45-second bomb run, the only completely visual bombing performed that day by Second Bombardment Division aircraft. Although the intervalometer setting was 150 feet, the lead squadron's bombs fell with 20 per cent within 1,000 feet and 70 per cent within 2,000 feet of the mean point of impact, forming a fairly tight pattern. Roads, buildings, docks, oil refineries, and loading sidings were destroyed and damaged by the bombs, which blanketed the MPI. The second and third squadrons, dropping on the Group lead, contributed to the excellence of the bombing, which put the enemy installation out of commission.

The coordination, crew teamwork, and leadership displayed by these Officers and Enlisted Men are within the finest traditions of the Army Air Forces and are deserving of high commendation.

By order of Col. SHOWER G.W. DARNELL
Major, Air Corps,
Adjutant

Mission 94 – 25 November 1944 to Bingen, Germany
Group Mission #136 – Target – Railway Marshalling Yards
Lt. Carl E. Epting and Crew #67 were assigned to *Witchcraft* on the mission, along with twenty-six other 467th B-24s. The ships, each loaded with 10 x 500-lb. GPs and 2 x 500-lb. incendiary bombs, commenced take-off from Rackheath at 0845.

Lt. Col. Walter Smith led the Group formations and Maj. Palmer flew as Deputy Lead. Following take-off, and due to inclement weather around the base, the planes assembled at 21,000ft over "Splasher Beacon 11," to the southwest of London and a few miles north of Portsmouth, in southern England. One B-24 made an early return to base. The weather en route to the target was reasonably good.

The target was bombed from 21,000ft by PFF with GH, and the results were rated poor. There was very little flak over the target area, but after the target was bombed and the Group ships were leaving the target area, the flak became more intense; it was especially heavy and fairly accurate over the Aachen area.

The Group did not lose any aircraft, although one B-24 landed in Belgium with a seriously wounded crewmember.

The weather at Rackheath started to close in just as the Group aircraft commenced landing procedures, but the crews managed to get their planes down, although two or three of them ran off the runway due to dense fog.

Witchcraft was not refueled following the mission due to scheduled service. However, the average flight time and fuel consumption are shown in Group records as six hours fourteen minutes and 1,745 gallons, respectively.

Mission 95 – 4 December 1944 to Bebra, Germany
Group Mission #140 – Target – Railway Marshalling Yards
Thirty-six B-24s—including *Witchcraft*, flown by Lt. S.T. Gray and Crew #64—were assigned for the mission. The B-24s, loaded with 8 x 500-lb. GPs and 2 x 500-lb. M-17 incendiary cluster bombs, commenced take-off at 0745.

Col. A.J. Shower flew with Lt. Donald C. Tibbetts and Crew #77 (791st Squadron) in JSH42-56950, leading the formations from several Groups of the 2nd Air Division. The B-24s from the various Groups and Wings formed up over Cromer at 0935.

GH was used to bomb the target from 22,000ft, and the bombing was unobserved. There was no flak to or over the target area, and the only flak seen was at a considerable distance, when the aircraft were making their way homebound. No enemy aircraft were encountered. Good fighter protection was provided by P-47s and P-51s.

No crew casualties or aircraft losses were incurred by the 467th.

Group records reveal the flight time for *Witchcraft* and Lt. Gray and Crew #64 was seven hours seventeen

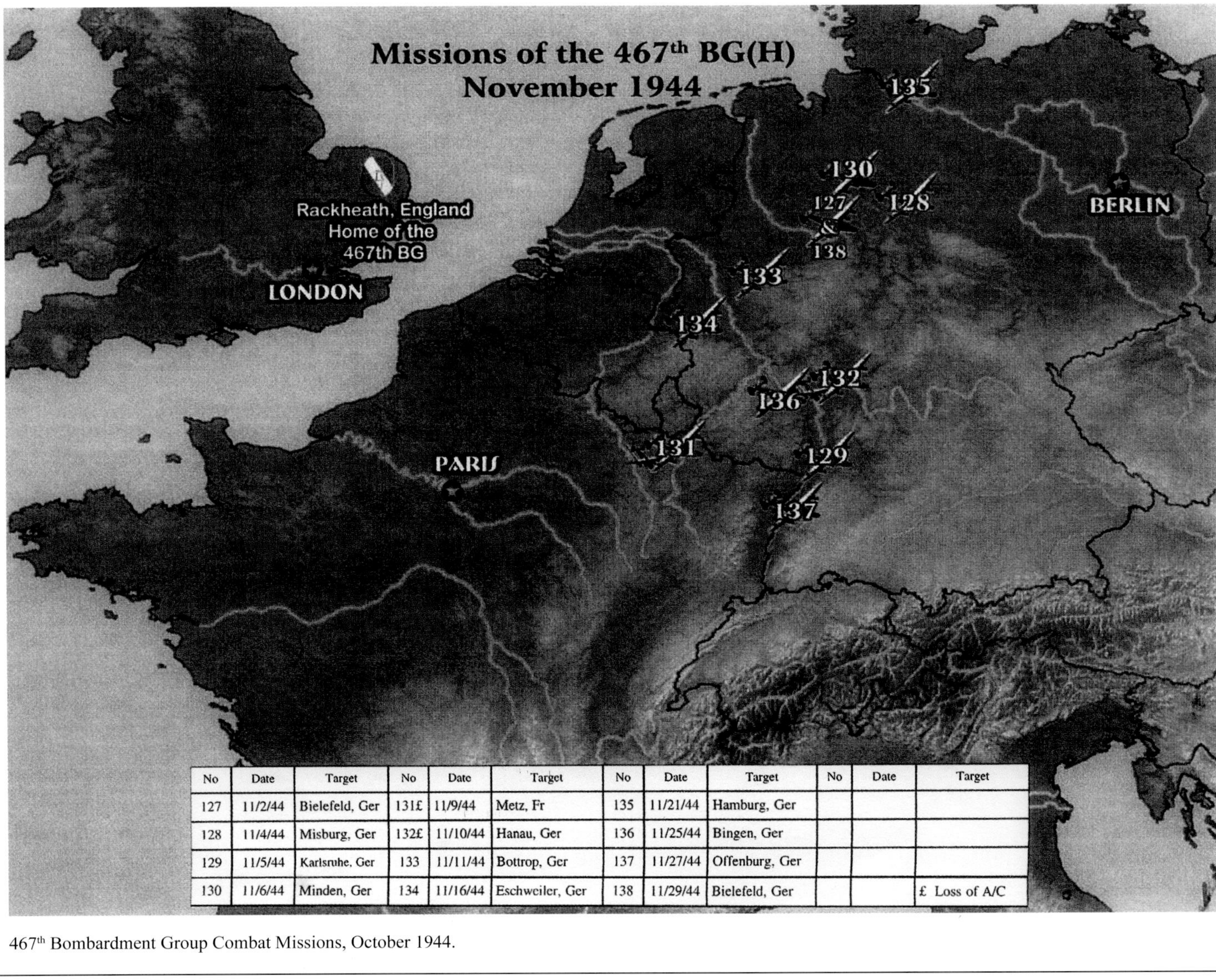

No	Date	Target	No	Date	Target	No	Date	Target	No	Date	Target
127	11/2/44	Bielefeld, Ger	131£	11/9/44	Metz, Fr	135	11/21/44	Hamburg, Ger			
128	11/4/44	Misburg, Ger	132£	11/10/44	Hanau, Ger	136	11/25/44	Bingen, Ger			
129	11/5/44	Karlsruhe, Ger	133	11/11/44	Bottrop, Ger	137	11/27/44	Offenburg, Ger			
130	11/6/44	Minden, Ger	134	11/16/44	Eschweiler, Ger	138	11/29/44	Bielefeld, Ger			£ Loss of A/C

467th Bombardment Group Combat Missions, October 1944.

minutes, and 2,000 gallons were used to fill the fuel tanks in the "Witch."

Mission 96 – 6 December 1944 to Bielefeld, Germany
Group Mission #141 – Target – Railway Marshalling Yards
The 467th Group assigned nineteen aircraft—including *Witchcraft*, flown by Lt. S.T. Gray and Crew #64—for the mission. Capt. Richard J. Campbell, flying with Capt. Leonard H. Monefeldt in 42-95094 *Leading Lady* (791st Squadron), led the Group B-24s. The planes, each loaded with 8 x 1,000-lb. GPs, commenced lift-off from Rackheath at 0900.

The target was bombed from 19,500ft by PFF, and the results were rated poor. No flak was encountered, other than light flak as the crews flew over the Dutch coastline en route to the target, and no enemy fighter aircraft were seen.

The Group did not incur any loss of crew or aircraft, and no crew members were injured.

Group records show a flight time of six hours twenty-five minutes for Lt. Gray and Crew #64 in *Witchcraft*. Records also show that 1,600 gallons topped her fuel tanks.

Mission 97 – 10 December 1944 to Bingen, Germany
Group Mission #142 – Target – Railway Marshalling Yards
Eighteen planes and crew—including *Witchcraft*, flown by Lt. S.T. Gray and Crew #64—were assigned to fly this mission. The B-24s, each carrying a mixture of 100-lb. GPs, 500-lb. M-17 IBs, and 100-lb. M-47 bombs commenced take-off at 0705. One plane made an early return to base due to a mechanical malfunction.

The target was bombed from 22,000ft using GH and, as the bombing was unobserved, the results are unknown. Light, inaccurate flak was encountered as the planes commenced their bomb run, but no enemy aircraft were encountered. Good fighter support was provided by P-47s and P-51s.

The Group did not incur any crew casualties nor lose any aircraft, but B-24H 42-94931 *Sacktime* from the 789th Squadron started to develop engine problems while assembling over "Splasher Beacon 5"; Pilot Lt. Henry K. Close and his Crew #33 continued to fly the mission. The plane's #4 engine was losing oil pressure and when over the target it was reading twenty pounds. Immediately after bombing the target #2 engine developed problems and #3 engine began to lose a lot of oil. Just before reaching Ostend and the North Sea, Lt. Close had to feather #4 propeller, as the engine would not hold its revolutions, and then #2 engine started to cut out and #3 was covered in oil. Lt. Close contacted Group formation and turned back, landing at the diversion field at Le Culot, Belgium. The B-24 was repaired and returned to Rackheath, next flying on mission #146 on December 24th.

The entry in Group records for this mission reveals that the flight time for Lt. Gray and Crew #64 in *Witchcraft* was five hours forty-nine minutes and 1,675 gallons were used to top up the fuel tanks.

It is most unusual for Ground Crew Staff to be cited, but for devotion to duty on 10 December 1944, four enlisted men received a well-deserved mention in Citation No: 1, dated 5 January 1945.

Group Citation No:1 – 5 January 1945

CITATION

The following named Enlisted Men of the 788th Bombardment Squadron (H) are hereby cited for outstanding devotion to duty, 10 December 1944:

Sgt. Howard M Smith	38141935
Sgt. Joe O. Bartolacci	37518338
Sgt. George W. Cromer	33536856
Sgt. Thomas J. Ford	36212430

Number three booster pump went out on pre-flight on B-24H 42-94986. With the crew chief absent on pass, Sergeants Cromer and Smith were in charge of the aircraft, which was due to fly on a combat mission that day. They called the refuelers, Sergeants Ford and Bartolacci, who set up a fuel transfer pump to drain the number three fuel tank.

While the tank was being drained, Sergeants Cromer and Smith procured a new booster pump, rigged up lights, and collected tools for the early morning task. As soon as the tank was dry, they removed the defective pump and installed a new one. Because of the closeness of the work, the men could not wear gloves, the lack of which made the work extremely difficult during the early-morning coldness, but the efficiency of the men was not impaired.

After the new pump was installed, the refuelers serviced the tank, and the aircraft was ready for the combat mission. The change took two hours and ten minutes, which normally requires about four hours.

The devotion to duty displayed by these men in readying the aircraft for a combat mission exemplifies the finest traditions of the Ground Personnel of the Army Air Forces and is deserving of the highest commendation.

By order of Col. SHOWER: G.W. DARNELL.
Major, Air Corps,
Adjutant

Mission 98 – 11 December 1944 to Hanau, Germany
Group Mission #143 – Target – Railway Marshalling Yards
For the mission to Hanau, the Group assigned forty-seven aircraft and crews, including *Witchcraft* flown by Lt. Joseph Severance and Crew #71. At this time, forty-seven planes was the highest number the Group had assigned to fly a combat mission. The ships, each loaded with 6 x 1,000-lb. GP bombs, commenced take-off from Rackheath at 0835. One B-24 made an early return to base due to a mechanical problem.

Light flak was encountered en route to and over the target area, but no enemy aircraft were seen. The target was bombed by PFF from 22,000ft; the bombing was unobserved and the results are unknown. Good fighter support and escort for the B-24s was provided by P-47s and P-51s.

Another good mission for the 467th, as it did not incur any crew casualties nor aircraft losses.

The flight time for Capt. Severance and Crew #71 in *Witchcraft* is shown in Group records as six hours fifty minutes. The records also show that 2,065 gallons were used to top up the "Witch's" tanks.

Former pilot Lt. John (Jack) B. Brinson remembers this seven-hour mission quite well. The cold, icy weather was far from ideal for flying, and the ground personnel were extra busy on that cold and damp English morning, getting more than the usual number of aircraft ready for take-off. Also, it was Jack's first combat mission, and that day he flew as copilot with Capt. Joseph Severance in *Witchcraft*.

Mission 99 – 18 December 1944 to Coblenz, Germany
Group Mission #145 – Target – Railway Marshalling Yards
Thirty-eight B-24s and crews—including *Witchcraft*, flown by Lt. George E. Loveless and Crew #61—were assigned this mission. The planes, each loaded with 12 x 500-lb. GP bombs, commenced take-off from Rackheath in the early hours of the morning.

Soon after the crews reached the continent, they were recalled to base due to inclement weather over western Europe.

Group records reveal the flight time for Lt. G.E. Loveless and Crew #61in *Witchcraft* was four hours twenty-six minutes, and that 1,625 gallons topped up the fuel tanks. The mission was not given a credit rating.

Mission 100 – 24 December 1944 to Gerolstein-Daun-Ober, Germany
Group Mission #146 – Target – Communication Centers – (Railway Marshalling Yards – Rail and Road Bridges)

Capt. Joe Severance and Crew #71 (L to R): Joseph Severance (P), John Brinson (C/P), Lonnie White (N), Gordon Sokoll (B), Francis Blackwell, Edward Wilson, Charles Wilcox, Leon Moquin, Joseph Abernathy, and James Crowell.

The 467th put up the highest number of aircraft ever to fly this mission. A total of sixty-two ships, including *Witchcraft* flown by Lt. Robert A. Meyers and Crew #62, were assigned. That number also included the Group assembly ship 41-29393 *Pete The P.O.M Inspector II* (formerly *Shoo Shoo Baby*) as a combat plane, flown by Lt. Blackwell C. Dunnam, along with some members of his Crew #83. Only two B-24s remained at base due to unavailability for operational use. Each of the sixty-one combat B-24s was loaded with 24 x 250-lb. GP bombs; the assembly ship carried 16 x 250-lb. GPs.

The B-24s commenced take-off from Rackheath at 1015, led by Col. Albert J. Shower with Capt. A.B. Manning and Crew #88 in JSH42-50949.

Maj. Fred E. Holdrege flew with Lt. Clarence W. Schulze and Crew #84 in JSH42-51491 as Deputy Group Lead and also led the first squadron. The six remaining squadrons were led by Lt.Travis S. Whitsel (2nd); Lt.Troy E. Wild with Capt. Malcolm B. Sturgis (3rd); Lt. Donald C. Tibbetts (4th); Lt.James W. Littleford with Capt. Robert S. Seiler (5th); Lt.James D. Hudson (6th); and Lt. Ralph H. Elliott with Capt. John E. Conley (7th). The ships assembled into their formations at 11,000ft over "Splasher Beacon 5" at 1156. One plane had to make an early return to base due to mechanical problems.

The weather was very clear and enabled visual bombing from 22,000ft; the results were rated very good. Some flak was encountered, and although enemy aircraft—including one jet fighter—were seen, and some of which attacked B-24s from other Groups, none approached the 467th. P-47s and P-51s provided excellent fighter coverage.

The 467th did not incur any aircraft losses and there were no crew injuries; sadly, a member of Lt. William S. Sullivan's Crew #36, flying 42-99971 *Battlin' Baby*, was KIA. The fatality occurred when the plane was about three miles northeast of Norwich and losing altitude. Sgt. Denver C. Loberg (Waist Gunner) was in the bomb bay, preparing to salvo bombs, and fell with the bombs when the plane was at about 500ft. (It is probable the airplane developed some major problem and was making an early return to base, as records indicate a total flight time of only four hours thirty minutes. The average for the mission was six hours thriteen minutes, and the next two shortest flight times by planes that completed the mission were five hours thirteen minutes and five hours thirty-three minutes.)

Group records reveal a flight time of six hours seven minutes for Lt. Meyers and Crew #62 in *Witchcraft*, and the plane had 2,400 gallons pumped into its fuel tanks.

Note: The mission flown by the 8th Air Force on Sunday, 24 December 1944, was the largest force of heavy bombers ever flown on a single mission. Over 2,000 heavy bombers and 900 fighters participated when the weather finally broke that Christmas Eve day. It is reputed and difficult to envisage that heavy bombers were flying over the German frontier as the tail of the "Air Armada" was just leaving England. This mission was important, and the turning point for the Allied Forces in winning the Battle of the Bulge.

Mission 101 – 25 December 1944 to Gerolstein Hallschlag, Schwabisch-Hall, Germany
Group Mission #147 – Target – Rail and Road Centers west of the Rhine

Lt. Blackwell "Blackie" Dunnam (Crew #83, 791st Squadron) at Casper, Wyoming. Standing (L to R): William Surface (E), Melvin Gillette (RO), Adrian Giguere (Gr), J. Thompson (Gr), Raymond Winden (Gr), and Robert Moran (Gr). Kneeling (L to R): J. Kish (B), Blackwell Dunnam (P), Carl Brasier (CP), and Lewis Blanich (N). W. Surface, J. Thompson, and J. Kish were grounded due to health problems.

Witchcraft, flown by Lt. John W. Rice and Crew #52, was one of twenty-nine planes assigned by the Group for this mission. Most of the aircraft were loaded with 6 x 500-lb. GP and 6 x 500-lb. incendiary cluster bombs, and take-off commenced at 0845.

The target was bombed visually and the results were rated poor. Heavy flak was not intense, but some of the bursts were reasonably accurate and caused varying degrees of damage to B-24s. The Group had P-51s escorting them for most of the flight to the target. However, soon after bombing the target and turning for the homebound flight—the ships were over the vicinity of St. Vith, Belgium—the formation of 788th Squadron B-24s was attacked by German fighter planes.

Not a good day at all for the 467th, as it lost three aircraft from the 788th Squadron: one plane went down over enemy-held territory; another crash-landed at St. Trond, Belgium; and the third plane was abandoned over France. Although unmanned, it flew over England, finally crashing at Vowchurch, Hereford, on the Welsh border, when the tanks were empty. The crew casualties/losses this day totaled nine KIA, seven POWs, and two SIA (seriously injured in action).

The first aircraft lost by the Group during this mission was FO 42-95220, flown by Lt. William W. Truxes and Crew #14. Enemy fighters attacked the B-24 when it was flying over the St. Vith (Belgium) area. Number three engine on the plane was hit and soon after was on fire; the flames spread throughout the right wing and fuselage and the plane exploded. The Pilot, Copilot, and Radio Operator bailed while over enemy territory and were taken POW by the German military. The remaining seven crew members lost their lives, either in the crash or when the plane exploded.

FO 42-94963, flown by Lt. Martin Sefca and Crew #23, was the second plane lost. Having sustained severe battle damage, the B-24 crash-landed on an airfield at St. Trond, Belgium. Without any flaps to reduce landing speed, the plane ran out of runway and crashed into a parked B-24, breaking in half at the bomb bay and starting to burn. The Pilot and Copilot were trapped in their seats and did not survive, despite heroic attempts made to rescue them; fortunately, all of the other crew members were able to vacate the B-24.

The third plane lost that day was FO 42-50675 *Bold Venture III*, flown by Lt. Paul Ehrlich and Crew #9. What actually happened to *Bold Venture III* is a remarkable story, and is best told as written in the statements by two members of the crew that were flying the aircraft that day. Staff Sgt. Leo F. Feeney (Tail Gunner) wrote:

> A short time after we left the target (still getting flak), I noticed a burst of flak. Within five minutes after the burst, we were attacked by enemy fighter planes. During the attack, I had a little trouble with one of my guns. Just after this, I saw two chutes about a thousand feet below and back of us. At that time, the plane lurched up and to the left, and I called the pilot and told him to get back into formation. I did not pay much attention to it when he did not answer, because everything seemed to be under control. Next, the navigator told him to take a 270 degree heading, and still no answer. The bombardier then went to the flight deck and found no one there. It is my belief that the two chutes I saw were those of the four men that left our plane. The bombardier then notified us of the situation and told us to stand by. The bombardier and pilotage-navigator then used the autopilot, which the pilot had set up before leaving the ship. With a 270 degree heading they got from the navigator, we managed to get into friendly territory and abandon the plane.

Lt. John Beyer (Bombardier) wrote:

> The mission was uneventful until about halfway down the bomb run, when the ship sustained flak damage on the tail section. The pilots then complained that the rudder control was stiff, and later on, from their conversations, I gathered they had no rudder control. The bomb run was successfully completed and the rally was under way when enemy fighters (FW-190s and Me-109s) attacked our squadron. Almost immediately #2 propeller ran away and there was a series of short rings on the alarm bell. The navigator and I removed our flak suits and put on our chest pack parachutes. In doing so, our intercom connection was severed for several minutes. In the meantime, #2 engine had been

feathered and the ship was flying along normally. However, we helped the Pilotage Navigator out of the nose turret and helped him remove his flak suit and adjust his chute. Noticing that we had left the formation, the navigator gave the pilot a heading to fly. It was then we learned that the pilots had bailed out. The Pilotage Navigator (Lt. Challenger Whitham) went up to the flight deck and I followed him. We discovered that the pilot, copilot, radio operator, and engineer had bailed out through the bomb bay, the doors of which were still open. The ship was flying on C-1 autopilot and was making a slow circle to the left, at the time heading back to Germany. Lt. Whitham used the control knob to turn the plane to a heading of 270 degrees and I went up to the nose to engage the secondary clutch on the bombsight so the autopilot would hold a steady heading. Returning to the flight deck, I got into the copilot's seat. By that time, the ship had almost reached a heading of 270 degrees. The remote-reading compasses were out, so the navigator used the sun as a guide and we used the gyro compass and the ball compass above the instrument panel. A few adjustments were necessary on the C-1, as we were losing altitude at about 500ft per minute, which I corrected. We encountered flak and I made some slow turns as evasive action. In the meantime, we contacted the gunners in the waist, who had not heard the alarm bell, and told them what the situation was: we intended to fly into France and bail out when certain we were far from the battle lines. After flying about 30-35 minutes, the navigator said we were deep enough into friendly territory to bail out. We instructed the gunners to bail out through the bomb bays so we could be certain everyone got out of the ship safely. We bailed out in this order: Navigator Lt. Ryan; Left Waist Gunner Staff Sgt. Pearson; Tail Gunner Staff Sgt. Feeney; Pilotage Navigator Lt. Whitham; Right Waist Gunner Staff Sgt. Salen; and Bombardier Lt. Beyer. We landed several miles south of Vallenciennes. To the best of our knowledge the Pilot, Copilot, Radio Operator, and Engineer bailed out approximately ten miles north of St. Vith or in that vicinity [it was over Le Quesnoy, France]. P-51s escorted us shortly after we were hit until we bailed out. Lt. Whitham tried to contact them, but had no success. When we had an opportunity to speak to the Gunners when we were on the ground, they said the waist filled with smoke after #2 engine was hit and that they thought the engine must have been on fire.

The four crew members that bailed out of *Bold Venture III* over the Le Quesnoy area were 1/Lt. Paul Ehrlich, Pilot; 2/Lt. Fred J. Killmeyer, Copilot; T/Sgt. Roy L. Yarnell, Engineer; and T/Sgt. Frank Sanders, Radio Operator. They were taken POW by the German Military. Two of the six men that bailed out over the Vallenciennes area (Lt. Challenger Whitham and Staff Sgt. John V. Salen) were SIA: Lt. Whitham broke his ankle and Staff Sgt. Salen severely sprained his ankle when they hit the ground after bailing out; they were hospitalized in Belgium. The remaining four that bailed out were flown back to England about one week later in a B-17.

Bold Venture III continued its flight on autopilot on the last course heading set by Lt. Whitham before he bailed out. The battered plane headed back across northwest France, the English Channel, and flew over at least five counties of England before the gasoline ran out and the engines stopped. The "eerie ghost flight" came to a stop when the plane crashed on the common at Vowchurch, Herefordshire, on the Welsh border. The plane was salvaged for parts 26 December 1944, at Madley, Herefordshire.

Group records reveal the flight time on this mission for Lt. Rice and Crew #52 in *Witchcraft* was five hours eleven minutes and that 1,850 gallons topped off the fuel tanks.

Mission 102 – 27 December 1944 to Neunkirchen, Germany.
Group Mission #149 – Target – Railway Marshall Yards
Eighteen planes—including *Witchcraft*, flown by Lt. John K. Ross and Crew #63—were assigned by the Group for the mission. The B-24s, each carrying 20 x 250-lb. GP explosive and 2 x 500-lb. M-17 incendiary bombs, commenced take-off at 0900 and were led by Lt. Col. Walter Smith, who also led the 96th Combat Wing.

All eighteen of the 467th Group's ships bombed the target from 22,000ft, and the results were rated poor. No losses of aircraft or crew.

Group records show that Lt. Ross and Crew #63 in *Witchcraft* had a flight time of six hours twenty minutes, and that the plane used 1,700 gallons.

Mission 103 – 28 December 1944 to Neunkirchen, Germany
Group Mission #150 – Target – Railway Marshalling Yards

For the return mission to hit the railroad yards at Neunkirchen, the Group put up twenty-eight B-24s, each carrying 20 x 250-lb. GPs and 2 x 500-lb. IBs. *Witchcraft*, flown by Lt. Learned W. Barry and Crew #55, was assigned to fly this mission.

After crossing the European coastline, the crews encountered undercast that extended all the way to the IP and then reappeared over the target area; consequently, bombs were dropped by PFF from 23,000ft. The bombing was unobserved and the results are unknown. Flak was moderate and reasonably accurate, causing some minor damage to a few of the ships. No enemy fighter aircraft were seen. Very good fighter protection was provided by P-47s and P-51s.

No crew casualties or aircraft losses were incurred.

Before reaching the target, an engine on *Witchcraft* developed a problem and had to be shut down, but Lt. Barry and crew carried on and bombed the target. On the homebound flight, soon after leaving the target, a second engine on *Witchcraft* started to overheat and Lt. Barry and crew headed for the RAF Station at Manston, Kent, where they made an emergency landing. No fuel or flight time for *Witchcraft* is available, however, Group records reveal the average for each of the twenty-seven B-24s

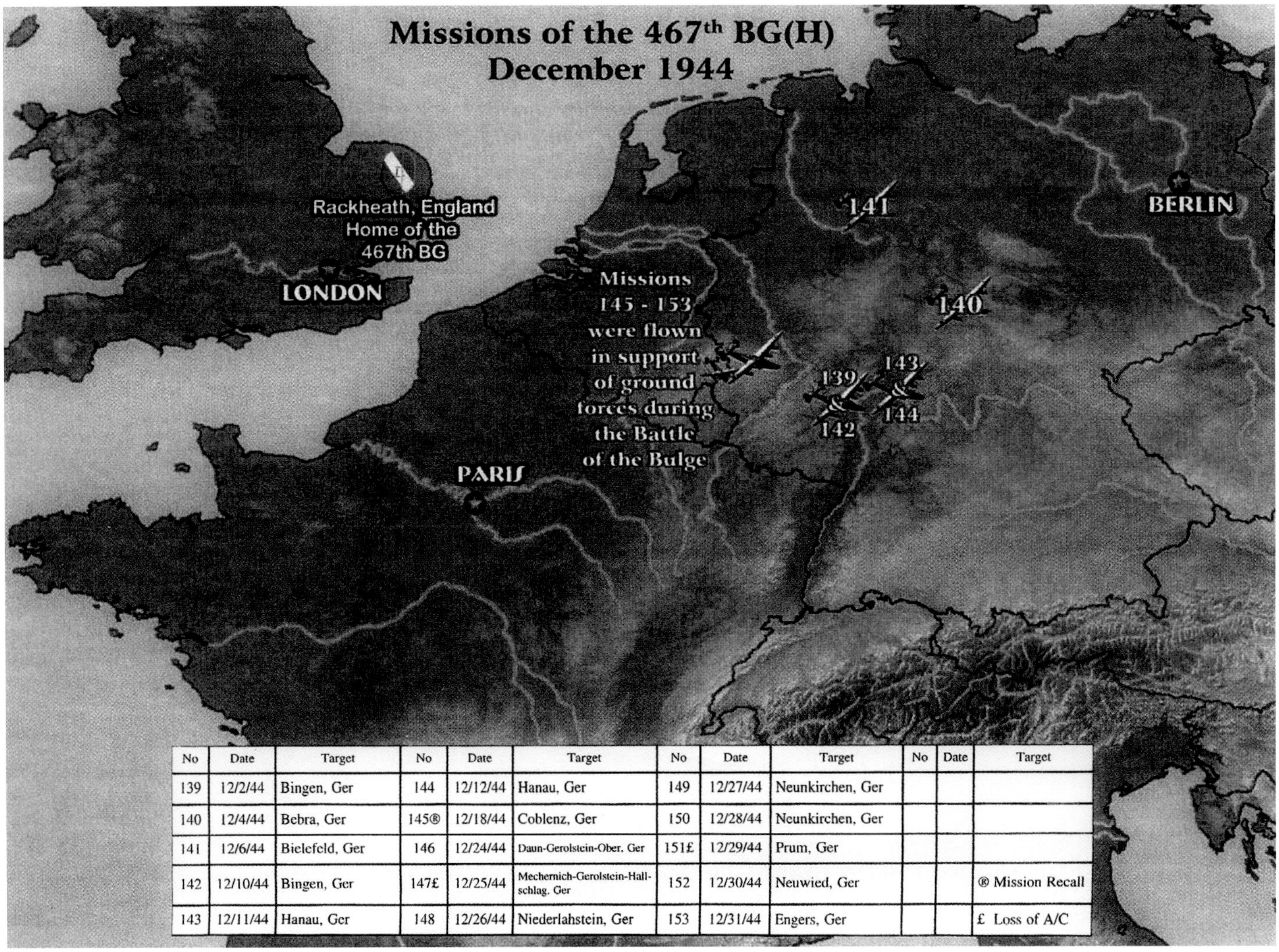

No	Date	Target	No	Date	Target	No	Date	Target	No	Date	Target
139	12/2/44	Bingen, Ger	144	12/12/44	Hanau, Ger	149	12/27/44	Neunkirchen, Ger			
140	12/4/44	Bebra, Ger	145®	12/18/44	Coblenz, Ger	150	12/28/44	Neunkirchen, Ger			
141	12/6/44	Bielefeld, Ger	146	12/24/44	Daun-Gerolstein-Ober. Ger	151£	12/29/44	Prum, Ger			
142	12/10/44	Bingen, Ger	147£	12/25/44	Mechernich-Gerolstein-Hall-schlag. Ger	152	12/30/44	Neuwied, Ger			® Mission Recall
143	12/11/44	Hanau, Ger	148	12/26/44	Niederlahstein, Ger	153	12/31/44	Engers, Ger			£ Loss of A/C

467th Bombardment Group Combat Missions, December 1944.

The former RAF station at Manston, Kent, and now Kent International Airport.

that returned to Rackheath was 1,685 gallons and an average flight time six hours three minutes.

This mission was the ninety-seventh credited mission for *Witchcraft*, and in all probability, Col. Shower had hopes that she would be the first B-24 to achieve 100 credited missions with no abort.

Mission 104 – 7 January 1945 to Rastatt, Germany
Group Mission #158 – Target – Railway Marshalling Yards
The Group assigned twenty-nine B-24s and crew—including *Witchcraft*, flown by Lt. Geza G. Laszlo and Crew #60—for the seven hour mission. Each Liberator was loaded with 20 x 250-lb. GP and 2 x 500-lb. M-17 incendiary bombs.

Due to weather conditions, the aircraft had to struggle to climb to 23,000ft; the weather and heavy contrails caused the formations to get separated. Nevertheless, all twenty-nine planes reached the target. The undercast was 10/10, but over the target thinned out slightly to 7/10. The undercast prevented bombing visually and GH was used. The results were rated fair. Flak over the target area was meager but reasonably accurate, and no enemy fighter planes were seen.

The Group did not incur any aircraft or crew losses. Group records show a flight time of seven hours four minutes for Lt. Laszlo and Crew #60 in *Witchcraft*; they also show 2,150 gallons were used to top up the "Witch's" fuel tanks.

Mission 105 – 10 January 1945 to Schonberg, Germany
Group Mission #159 – Target – Railway Bridge
Nineteen planes—including *Witchcraft*, flown by Lt. John W. Rice and Crew #52—were assigned; each of the B-24s were loaded with 6 x 1,000-lb. GP bombs.

All aircraft bombed the target through heavy undercast using H2X. The bombing was unobserved and the results are unknown.

No crew casualties or aircraft losses were incurred.

Group records reveal the flight time for Lt. Rice and Crew #52 in *Witchcraft* was five hours forty-five minutes. Records also reveal 2,100 gallons topped up the fuel tanks.

Mission 106 – 14 January 1945 to Hallendorf, Germany
Group Mission #161 – Target – Industrial Target (Steelworks)
The 467th assigned thirty planes, including *Witchcraft* flown by Lt. G.G. Laszlo and Crew #60. The ships were each loaded with 6 x 1,000-lb. GP bombs and commenced take-off at 0900. One plane made an early return to base due to mechanical problems.

Weather conditions were mostly clear on the flight to the target and some flak was encountered.

Twenty-nine planes bombed the target visually from 23,200ft, and the results were rated excellent. Flak over the target area was heavy and fairly accurate, causing minor damage to some planes. Some enemy fighter aircraft were seen but did not attack the Group.

B-24H 42-52737 *The Shaft* (788th Squadron) developed a gasoline leak all the way to the target and was low on fuel soon after bombing the target. The plane left the formation and was escorted by a P-51 fighter until it landed at the P-47 fighter base at Le Culot.

Another good mission for the 467th, as no aircraft were lost and no crew casualties were incurred.

On completion of this mission, the 467th Group set and held a record for the Second Air Division when 42-52534 *Witchcraft* (790th Squadron) completed 100 credited missions without ever aborting due to mechanical or crew problems.

Group records show a flight time of six hours thirty-five minutes for Lt. Laszlo and Crew #60 in *Witchcraft*. The records also show that the fuel tanks in *Witchcraft* were topped with 1,600 gallons.

Mission 107 – 16 January 1945 to Dresden, Germany
Group Mission #162 – Target – Railway Marshalling Yards
Witchcraft, flown by Lt. G.G. Laszlo and Crew #60, was included in the thirty planes assigned by the 467th to fly the long-haul mission to Dresden. The B-24s, each

Lt. Geza Lazlo and his fellow Crew #60. Master Sgt. Dewey Dunbar—Crew Chief of B-24J-140 CO 42110171 *Prowler* and standing in the center—is flanked on the left by James Crosswell (N) and Mathew Nemeyer (CP) and on the right by Geza Lazlo (P) and Robert Stone (B).

790th Squadron Commanding Officer Major Fred E. Holdrege congratulating Master Sgt. Joe Ramirez on 14 January 1945, following the completion of 100 credited combat missions by *Witchcraft*.

A Nissen hut on the base at Rackheath appropriately named to celebrate the 100th credited combat mission by *Witchcraft*.

General Kepner making a presentation to Staff Sgt. George Dong on 14 January 1945.

Crew Chief Master Sgt. Joe Ramirez painting the hundredth "bomb strike" on *Witchcraft*.

General Kepner making a presentation to Sgt. Ray Betcher on 14 January 1945.

Master Sgt. Joe Ramirez photographed alongside "his" airplane on 14 January 1945.

467th senior officers photographed with *Witchcraft* on 14 January 1945, to commemorate the special occasion.

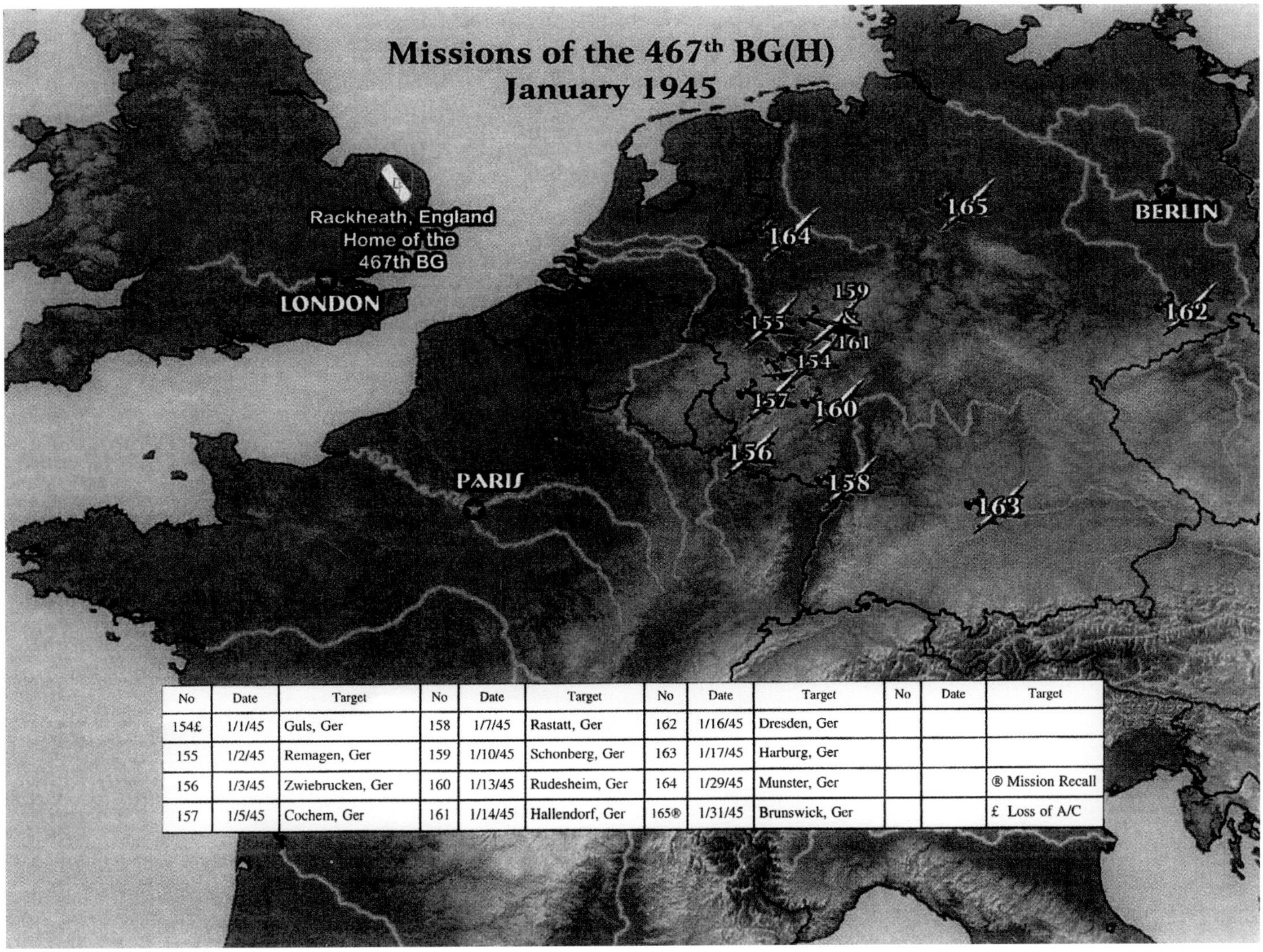

No	Date	Target	No	Date	Target	No	Date	Target	No	Date	Target
154£	1/1/45	Guls, Ger	158	1/7/45	Rastatt, Ger	162	1/16/45	Dresden, Ger			
155	1/2/45	Remagen, Ger	159	1/10/45	Schonberg, Ger	163	1/17/45	Harburg, Ger			
156	1/3/45	Zwiebrucken, Ger	160	1/13/45	Rudesheim, Ger	164	1/29/45	Munster, Ger			® Mission Recall
157	1/5/45	Cochem, Ger	161	1/14/45	Hallendorf, Ger	165®	1/31/45	Brunswick, Ger			£ Loss of A/C

467th Bombardment Group Combat Missions, January 1945.

carrying 10 x 500-lb. GP bombs, commenced take-off from Rackheath at 0800. One B-24 made an early return to base due to a mechanical problem.

Flak was meager as the aircraft crossed the line of battle in western Germany. The route to the target was directly on line for Berlin, and that course was held until the airplanes were fifty miles from the German capital, when the course was changed and the formations headed directly for Dresden. Although heavy flak was seen from a distance in the Berlin area, the crew did not encounter any flak over the target and no German fighter aircraft were seen.

The target was bombed visually from 24,000ft and the results were reported as good. A couple of the B-24s landed in France due to aircraft fuel gauges reading low: one landed at Orlick airfield, about six miles from Paris; and the other at an airfield at Merville, about twenty-two miles to the west of Lille. No other problems were encountered until the crews reached the base at Rackheath; the crews discovered it was closed in by heavy fog. Consequently, they were diverted to an RAF airfield in Yorkshire. The diversion entailed a further one and a half hours flying time in addition to the eight and one quarter already flown. The gasoline levels in the fuel tanks were somewhat critical, but fortunately, the remaining B-24s arrived at the RAF field.

The Group did not incur any crew injuries or casualties, and no aircraft losses.

Flight time and fuel consumption figures are unavailable due to the diversion to Yorkshire, but the flight time was probably in the region of nine hours or slightly more, and the fuel used was in the region of 2,600 gallons.

Mission 108 – 29 January 1945 to Munster, Germany
Group Mission #164 – Target – Railway Marshalling Yards
The Group assigned thirty-seven B-24s and crew—including *Witchcraft*, flown by Lt. James W. McFarland and Crew #73—for the mission to Munster. From the records, it appears that all of the aircraft reached the target and each plane dropped 6 x 1,000-lb. GPs from 23,000ft by "Mickey" (Micro-H radar) equipment. Fortunately for the crews, no flak was encountered over the target area, as a problem arose with the radar equipment, resulting in the planes having to make a 360° turn and a second bomb run over the target. The bombing was unobserved and the results are unknown.

A good mission for the Group, as there was no loss of aircraft and no crew casualties were incurred.

Group records show a flight time of five hours thirty-four minutes for Lt. McFarland and Crew #73 in *Witchcraft*, and 1,500 gallons were used to fill her tanks.

Despite severe, wintry conditions, the 467th still flew twelve combat missions during January.

Mission 109 – 3 February 1945 to Magdeburg, Germany
Group Mission #166 – Target – Primary – Synthetic Oil Plant
– Secondary – Railway Marshalling Yards
Thirty-nine B-24s—including 42-52534 *Witchcraft*, flown by Lt. Nolan G. Patton and Crew #70—were assigned for the mission. The planes, some of which were loaded with 10 x 500-lb. GP bombs and others with a combination of 500-lb. IBs and GP bombs, commenced take-off from Rackheath at 0815.

The oil refinery was a critical 8th Air Force target, although the Group aircraft missed it, as most of the bombs dropped by PFF from 22,500ft fell onto surrounding farmland. Weather conditions over the target area were marginal and the flak was moderate to intense, but no enemy aircraft were seen.

No aircraft were lost on the mission, but one crewmember was wounded.

The flight time for Lt. Patton and Crew #70 in *Witchcraft* is recorded as six hours fifty-five minutes. No gallon figures are shown in Group records for individual B-24s, but records reveal an overall average for each of the thirty-nine planes was 1,889 gallons.

This mission did achieve something that has lasted over the years. It was a combination of the results by the 467th on this mission of 3 February and the words used by Col. Shower in his description as to how he reviewed the mission results that the name "Rackheath Aggies" came about. Lt. William N. Scott—Copilot on Lt.Jacobsen's Crew #49 from the 789th Squadron—recalls the critique held that evening and has mentioned it in his diary *cum* booklet *A Pilot Remembers World War II – 1941-1945*:

> After each mission there was a critique. The officers of the crew would clean up, put on Class As, and have dinner. Then, Col. Shower and his senior officers would critique each phase of our performance, from takeoff to landing. On the evening of February 3rd, the Col. wasn't pleased with us. Since we had wasted our bombs on some farmer's field, the Col. labeled us "The Rackheath Agricultural Society." There was a ripple of embarrassed laughter. He advised us he was going to send us back to Magdeburg as often as required until we got it right. That was the end of our laughter. The rest of the personnel on the airfield soon heard about our new name. From then on we were called the "Rackheath Aggies."

Additionally, former Crew #49 Bombardier Lt. John Shirk wrote on completion of the mission: ". . .At the critique held that evening, Col. Shower called us the '467th Group Agricultural Society' because the bombing was pretty much just like plowing!"

Mission 110 – 6 February 1945 to Magdeburg, Germany
Group Mission #167 – Target – Railway Marshalling Yards
For this long-haul mission to Magdeburg, the Group assigned thirty-nine aircraft, including *Witchcraft* flown by Lt. J.W. Rice and Crew #52. The ships, each carrying 10 x 500-lb. GP bombs, commenced take-off at 0800. One B-24 made an early return to base due to a mechanical problem.

The weather was poor and the target was covered by 10/10 cloud. Bombs were dropped through the clouds from 23,300ft using PFF. The bombing was unobserved and the results are unknown. Flak was meager and inaccurate over the target area and no enemy aircraft were seen. On the homebound flight, the lead navigator appeared to use the wrong flight course and took the formations over Munster and Osnabruck, where the flak was both heavy and accurate, resulting in some minor damage to some of the Group's planes.

A reasonably good day for the 467th Group, as it did not incur any loss of crew members or planes, although one crewmember was wounded.

Group records reveal it took about 1,900 gallons to top up the fuel tanks in *Witchcraft*. The flight time for *Witchcraft* and Lt. Rice and Crew #52 is shown as seven hours twelve minutes.

Mission 111 – 14 February 1945 to Magdeburg, Germany
Group Mission #171 – Target – Railway Marshalling Yards
Witchcraft, flown by Lt. Cleason D. Barker and Crew #69, was one of the twenty-nine planes and crews assigned to attack Magdeburg for the fourth time. The B-24s, each loaded with 4 x 1000-lb. GP and 2 x 500-lb. M-17 incendiary bombs, commenced lift-off from Rackheath at 0930.

The target was bombed by PFF from 22,500ft and the results are unknown, as the bombing was unobserved. Flak over the target area was heavy but inaccurate.

Another mission completed without the Group sustaining any crew casualties or aircraft losses.

Although generally the mission went well, it was not quite so with Lt. M.R. Davis and Crew #57, flying in 42-95057 *Angel*. The propeller on No. 3 engine had to be feathered and Lt. Davis had to salvo the bomb load. The G-Box and compass were both out, which presented difficulties for the navigator when attempting to establish the course to return to base. The crew encountered flak over several places, but was fortunate the plane did not receive even minor damage, as they flew for quite a long time alone.

The flight time for Lt. Barker and Crew #69 in *Witchcraft* is shown in the records as five hours fifty-five minutes. No figures are available for refueling the "Witch," but an overall average for each of the twenty-six that had their tanks topped up was 1,776 gallons.

Mission 112 – 15 February 1945 to Magdeburg, Germany
Group Mission #172 – Target – Synthetic Oil Plant
Twenty-nine B-24s—including *Witchcraft*, flown by J.W. Rice and Crew #52—were assigned to fly the Group's fifth combat mission to Magdeburg. The majority of the ships were loaded with 12 x 500-lb. GP bombs and a few were loaded with a mix of GP and incendiary bombs; they commenced take-off at 0730. One aircraft was forced to make an early return to base due to engine failure.

The crews encountered undercast over the mainland of Europe immediately after flying over the Zuider Zee. The clouds had not dispersed when the planes reached the target and bombs were dropped from 24,000ft by PFF; the results were unobserved, but from all reports, it would appear that the target was hit.

The mission was the seventh flown by the Group in the first fifteen days of February, and five out of those seven missions were six and a half to seven hour long-haul missions to Magdeburg. Up to that date, no aircraft had been lost during February and the only casualties were two crew members wounded on the first two missions made on the third and sixth of the month.

Group records reveal that *Witchcraft* had 2,190 gallons pumped into its tanks following return to base and a flight time of six hours twenty-five minutes for Lt. Rice and Crew #52.

Main entrance site at Rackheath airfield, winter 1944-45.

Mission 113 –16 February 1945 to Osnabruck, Germany
Group Mission #173 – Target – Railway Marshalling Yards
Twenty-nine airplanes were assigned

to fly this mission, including *Witchcraft* flown by Lt. J.W. Rice and Crew #52. The B-24s, each loaded with 12 x 500-lb. GP bombs, commenced take-off at 0930.

Although weather reports indicated conditions over Europe were poor, it was decided the mission could be flown.

Flak over the target area was moderate but very accurate, and appeared to be fired from large caliber anti-aircraft guns, causing varying degrees of damage to the ships; no enemy aircraft were seen. Bombs were dropped on the target from 23,500ft using H2X and the results were rated fair.

The Group lost 42-95080 *Super Wolf*, flown by 2/Lt. John D. Mulligan and Crew #53 from the 790th Squadron. During the return flight, the aircraft was badly damaged by flak. The entire crew bailed out and the plane crashed at Valthe, Netherlands. Nine of the crew members were taken POW; one crewmember (Sgt. Walter M. Sies, Engineer) was KIA due to parachute failure. There were no other casualties.

Group records show a flight time of five hours thirty minutes for Lt. Rice and Crew #52 in *Witchcraft*. There are no records available relating to fuel consumption.

Mission 114 – 17 February 1945 to Aschaffenburg, Germany
Group Mission #X (the mission not given a number) – Target – Aircraft Components Plant

The Group assigned thirty-nine planes, including *Witchcraft* flown by Lt. J.W. Rice and Crew #52. The B-24s, each carrying 12 x 500-lb. GP bombs, commenced take-off at 0915.

Due to reports of bad weather over the North Sea and Europe, the mission was scrubbed and the crews were recalled while the Group was forming up.

The Group lost B-24J-145 CO 44-40068 *Umbriago*, flown by Lt. Leon F. Porter and Crew #13 from the 788th Squadron; the entire nine-man crew was listed KIA. It was presumed that severe icing on the ship probably forced it down into the North Sea. Other crews reported severe icing conditions and having to use excessive power settings to maintain altitude.

No flight times or fuel consumption figures are available, and the mission was not given a credit rating.

Mission 115 – 19 February 1945 to Meschede, Germany
Group Mission #174 – Target – Jet Aircraft Components Factory

Witchcraft, flown by Lt. J.W. Rice and Crew #52, was included in the thirty-nine ships assigned to fly this mission to Meschede. The planes, each carrying either 12 x 500-lb. GP bombs or 6 x 500-lb. GPs and 6 x 500-lb. M-17 IBs, commenced take-off from Rackheath at 1030.

Col. Albert J. Shower flew as Second Air Division leader with Capt. Troy E. Wild and Crew #78 in LSH 44-49591 (791st Squadron), leading the Group B-24s. Maj. John T. Conley flew with Lt. Ralph H. Elliott and Crew #95 (791st Squadron) in LSH 44-49340 as Deputy Second Air Division leader.

Very little flak was encountered en route to the target, but over Meschede the flak was meager and inaccurate, and no enemy fighter aircraft were seen. Excellent support was provided by P-51s. The target was bombed from 18,600ft through heavy 10/10 undercast by GH and the results were rated excellent.

The Group did not incur any crew casualties or aircraft losses.

Group records reveal the flight time for Lt. Rice and Crew #52 in *Witchcraft* was six hours twenty-four minutes, and that 1,975 gallons were used to top-up the fuel tanks in the "Witch."

Mission 116 – 21 February 1945 to Nurnberg, Germany
Group Mission #175 – Target – Railway Marshalling Yards

The 467th put up thirty-nine aircraft—including *Witchcraft*, flown by Lt. C.D. Barker and Crew #69—for the mission to Nurnberg. Thirty-six planes loaded with 10 x 500-lb. GPs and the three Lead ships each loaded with 4 x 500-lb. GPs commenced take-off at 0800. One plane developed mechanical problems and made an early return to base.

The target was covered by 10/10 undercast and was bombed from 21,000ft by PFF. The bombing was unobserved and the results are unknown.

Flak was encountered over the front lines and also as they were leaving the target, but no enemy aircraft were seen. Good fighter escort cover was provided by P-51s.

JSH 44-48852, flown by Lt. Blackwell C. Dunnam and Crew #83, received major flak damage and landed at Woodbridge, where it underwent repairs from 22 February to 15 March; otherwise no aircraft losses were suffered by the Group, but one crewmember was wounded.

The flight time for Lt. Barker and Crew #69 in *Witchcraft* is unknown, as the plane landed away from base. The average flight time for the mission was six hours eighteen minutes and the average fuel consumption was 2,124 gallons.

Former pilot 1/Lt. Blackwell (Blackie) Dunnam (Crew #83 from the 791st Squadron) flew on the mission as Group Deputy Lead in JSH-20 FO 44-48852. "Blackie" wrote:

> One of our most difficult missions occurred 21 February 1945, when our target was Nurnburg, Germany. We were the Group Deputy Lead that day, and a newly-assigned Capt. from Patterson Field, Dayton, Ohio, was flying in the Copilot seat. Well into Germany, our Group found itself several miles to the left of the main stream of aircraft of the Eighth Air Force. Suddenly, directly in front of the Lead ship appeared four bursts of anti-aircraft [flak] shells. The Germans had our altitude perfectly, and I was certain the next round was going to be up someone's tailpipe. The Lead ship started a left hand turn about this time, which I had to follow reluctantly, because this placed us directly in line for the next burst, which came close enough to tear out a part of the windshield and most of the instrument panel while knocking out one of our starboard engines and the oxygen system that supplied all the personnel in the nose section. Gasoline was pouring into the bomb bay, which had been badly damaged, and to top it off, a flash fire occurred through the aircraft, singeing everyone's eyebrows. For some unknown reason, the nose gear decided to extend itself and lock in the landing position. This left the wheel well door open for more unwanted ventilation. Hydraulic fluid was over everyone in the waist area. We could no longer stay with the Group and were fighting to keep the remaining starboard engine operating while trying to assess the condition of the crew and moving those without oxygen to the flight deck.
>
> The Engineer was able to eliminate the fuel leakage into the bomb bay area and we were able to stabilize the remaining starboard engine. Upon a thorough check of the crew, no one appeared to be seriously injured. With the windshield partly gone, the flight deck felt like being in the eye of a tornado, making it extremely difficult for the Navigator to function, as well as the Copilot and myself. Frost bite was becoming a big worry, along with enemy fighters that were out looking for stray bombers. We had to head home while still maintaining altitude the best we could, because we were still in enemy territory and worried about more flak.
>
> The aircraft was losing altitude; we would have liked jettison our bombs over enemy territory, but found out this was not possible due to some damage to the bomb racks caused by the flak. After several difficult hours, we managed to bring the Channel in view and accelerated our descent into a relatively warmer environment. When we were several hundred feet above the Channel, I asked Gunners Bob Moran and Ray Winden and the Engineer if there was any possibility they could unshackle the 500-lb. bombs from the racks and drop them out the bomb bay into the Channel. I don't know how they did it, but without hesitation and with superhuman effort they managed to get rid of our load to everyone's relief.
>
> Our next little problem arose when the Engineer told me we had no braking power. The only thing left was to head towards an emergency base called Woodbridge. There, the runway was of such a length that it was possible to land without brakes, but the question now was "could we make it?" with very little fuel left. I had gained some altitude and everyone was set to bail out if necessary. Woodbridge came into sight, and with a wing and a prayer we landed, hoping our tires were OK. We took every foot of the runway and, when reaching the end, we were slow enough that I could do a one-eighty turn. We counted over 200 flak holes in that B-24 that day. The aircraft underwent major repairs, and after its return to Rackheath, it next flew on a combat mission on 21 March 1945, and on a further four missions before cessation of combat missions in the ETO.
>
> To everyone's surprise, the only one to receive the Purple Heart was the Copilot, a Capt. on his first mission. He had received a small piece of shrapnel in his right arm.

Mission 117 –22 February 1945 to Hildesheim, Germany
Group Mission #176 – Target – Railway Marshalling Yards

Witchcraft, flown by Lt. C.D. Barker and Crew #69, was one of thirty-eight B-24s and crews assigned to attack the railway marshalling yards at Hildesheim. The 467th Group's planes, each carrying 12 x 500-lb. GP bombs and led by Maj. John J. Taylor (788th Squadron Commanding Officer), commenced take-off at 0830. Three planes returned to base early for various reasons.

The weather was very good en route to and over the target. Bombs were dropped visually from the unusually low altitude of 8,000ft. The results were rated very good. Intelligence learned later that at the time of the strike, there was a stationary ammunition train on a siding in the marshalling yard and it was destroyed.

Flak over the target area was moderate but very accurate, causing damage to some of the Group planes and injuries to two of the flight crew; however, no planes were lost.

Group records show a flight time of seven hours seven minutes for Lt. Barker and Crew #69 in the "Witch." Records also show that a total of 2,030 gallons were used to fill the fuel tanks.

Mission 118 – 23 February 1945 to Gera, Germany
Group Mission #177 – Target – Railway Marshalling Yards

The 467th put up twenty-nine planes—including *Witchcraft*, flown by Lt. J.W. Rice and Crew #52—for the long-haul mission to Gera. Each plane was loaded with 10 x 500-lb. GPs, or a mixture of GPs and IBs. Two of the B-24s made an early return to base soon after take-off.

Very little flak was encountered over the target area, which was covered by 10/10 undercast. Initially, the bombing was planned to be visual from 10,000ft, but due to the undercast, bombs were dropped by PFF; being unobserved, the results are unknown.

Another good day for the 467th, as it did not incur any crew casualties or aircraft losses.

Group records show the flight time for Lt. Rice and Crew #52 in *Witchcraft* was eight hours three minutes. The records also show that 2,300 gallons were used to top up the "Witch's" tanks.

Mission 119 – 24 February 1945 to Bielefeld, Germany
Group Mission #178 – Target – Railway Marshalling Yards

To attack the railway marshalling yards at Bielefeld, the Group assigned twenty-nine planes, including *Witchcraft* flown by Lt. J. W. Rice and Crew #52. The B-24s, each

Witchcraft participating in the attack on Nurnburg, Germany; flying alongside is B-24H-25 FO 42-95201 Stinker, flown that day by Lt. Robert Willis and Crew #64.

carrying 12 x 500-lb. GPs, commenced take-off at 0900 and were led by 790th Squadron Commanding Officer Maj. Fred E. Holdrege.

The target was covered by clouds, but broke clear just long enough to change the bombing method from PFF to visual and the target was bombed from 22,500ft. Results achieved were rated very good. The crews could see several trains in the marshalling yards.

No flak was encountered and no fighters were seen. Excellent fighter support was provided by several P-47s and P-51s.

A good mission for the Group, as no aircraft losses or crew casualties were incurred.

A flight time of six hours eight minutes is shown in Group records for *Witchcraft*, Lt. Rice, and Crew #52. Records also reveal that 2,050 gallons were used to top up the fuel tanks on *Witchcraft*.

Mission 120 –25 February 1945 to Schwabisch-Halle, Germany
Group Mission #179 – Target – Luftwaffe Jet Fighter Airfield
Twenty-nine planes—including *Witchcraft*, flown by Lt. J.W. Rice and Crew #52—were assigned for this mission. The B-24s, some loaded with 12 x 500-lb. GPs and some with 12 x 500-lb. M17 incendiary bombs, commenced take-off at 0830.

Due to bad weather, assembly of the formations at "Splasher Beacon 9," near Beachy Head, took much longer than scheduled.

The skies were clear over the target area and bombs were dropped visually from 19,000ft; the results were rated excellent. Only the occasional flak burst was encountered over the target, and a few German fighter aircraft made an unsuccessful attack on the 467th Group formations. P-51s provided good escort support.

Witchcraft on hardstand #32.

Another good mission for the 467th, as it did not incur any crew casualties or aircraft losses.

Group records reveal a flight time of eight hours for Lt. J. W. Rice and his crew members in *Witchcraft*. The records also reveal that following the mission, a total of 2,100 gallons filled the fuel tanks in *Witchcraft*.

Mission 121 – 1 March 1945 to Ingolstadt, Germany
Group Mission #183 – Target – Railroad Junction
Thirty-seven aircraft, each loaded with 10 x 500-lb. GP bombs, were assigned to fly to Ingolstadt. This included *Witchcraft*, flown by Lt. J.W. Rice and Crew #52.

For most of the long-haul flight across France and into southern Germany the weather was good, but there was quite a lot of undercast. On the way out, for some particular but unknown reason, the Group aircraft circled Munich.

The target was bombed by PFF from 17,500ft and the results are unknown, as the bombing was unobserved.

No flak was encountered and no enemy fighters were seen, but the crews had a good look at the tops of the Alps as they flew to the south of Munich.

The 467th did not incur any crew casualties or aircraft losses on this nine-hour mission, but one ship—42-51289, flown by Lt. Robert E. Jacobsen and Crew #49—was forced to make an emergency landing at the airfield at Merville, France, to refuel before completing the return flight to Rackheath.

Group records show a flight time of nine hours four minutes for *Witchcraft* and Lt. Rice and his crew; they also show the plane had 2,175 gallons pumped into its fuel tanks.

Mission 122 – 2 March 1945 to Magdeburg, Germany
Group Mission #184 – Target – Military Tank Production Factory
For this seventh mission to Magdeburg, the 467th assigned twenty-nine B-24s and crew, including *Witchcraft* flown by Lt. John G. Phillips and Crew #63.

Each of the planes was loaded with 12 x 500-lb. GPs. The target was alongside the railroad marshalling yards that were attacked some sixteen days previously.

Flak over the target was intense and accurate, and enemy fighter aircraft attacked the Group planes.

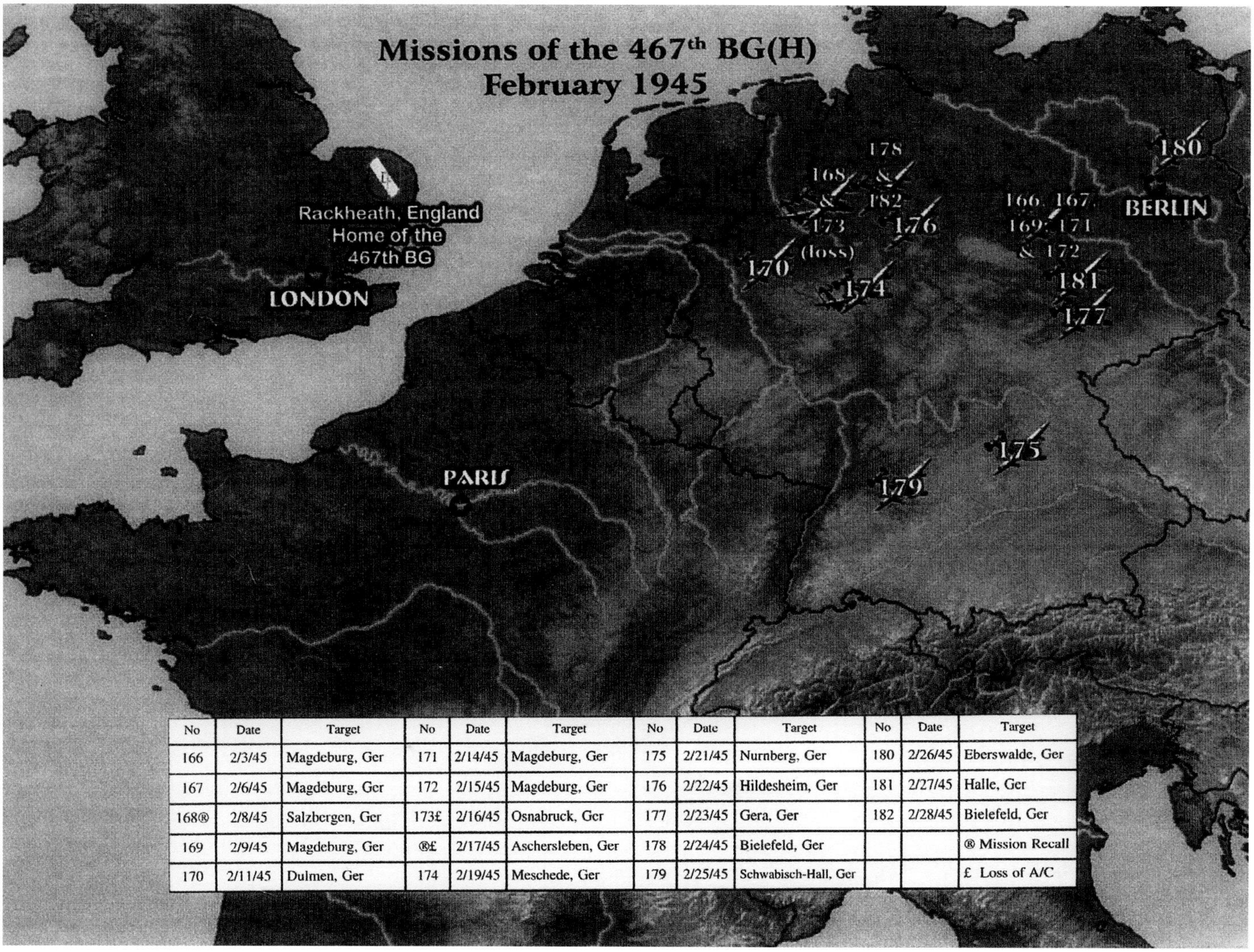

No	Date	Target	No	Date	Target	No	Date	Target	No	Date	Target
166	2/3/45	Magdeburg, Ger	171	2/14/45	Magdeburg, Ger	175	2/21/45	Nurnberg, Ger	180	2/26/45	Eberswalde, Ger
167	2/6/45	Magdeburg, Ger	172	2/15/45	Magdeburg, Ger	176	2/22/45	Hildesheim, Ger	181	2/27/45	Halle, Ger
168®	2/8/45	Salzbergen, Ger	173£	2/16/45	Osnabruck, Ger	177	2/23/45	Gera, Ger	182	2/28/45	Bielefeld, Ger
169	2/9/45	Magdeburg, Ger	®£	2/17/45	Aschersleben, Ger	178	2/24/45	Bielefeld, Ger			® Mission Recall
170	2/11/45	Dulmen, Ger	174	2/19/45	Meschede, Ger	179	2/25/45	Schwabisch-Hall, Ger			£ Loss of A/C

467th Bombardment Group Combat Missions, February 1945.

Fortunately, good fighter protection for the B-24s was provided by P-51s.

The target was bombed by PFF with some visual assistance from 23,000ft, and the results appeared successful.

Unfortunately, one of the Group aircraft—42-51171 *Eli Swof Jr*, flown by Lt. Alvah D. Reid and Crew #59 from the 790th Squadron—lost an engine over the target and a further engine was knocked out by enemy fighter attacks. *Eli Swof Jr* dropped back from the formation and was hit by flak that resulted in the ship catching fire. Three of the four crew members that bailed out were taken POW; unfortunately, the fourth was KIA due to parachute failure. The pilot and the remaining four crewmembers on board were KIA when it crashed near Dorsten, Germany.

The records show a flight time of seven hours four minutes for Lt. Phillips and his fellow crew members in *Witchcraft*. Records also reveal that 2,200 gallons were pumped into the fuel tanks of the "Witch."

Mission 123 – 3 March 1945 to Nienburg- Bielefeld, Germany

Group Mission #185 – Target – Primary: River Bridge at Nienburg; Secondary: Railroad Station at Bielefeld

Thirty-seven B-24s were assigned this mission—including *Witchcraft*, flown by Lt. J.W. Rice and Crew #52. Thirty-three planes, each loaded with 6 x 1,000-lb. GP bombs, and each of the four lead ships loaded with 4 x 1,000-lb. GP bombs and two smoke markers commenced take-off at 0610.

The mission was given special priority and the 467th Group led the 96th Combat Wing. Col. Albert J. Shower flew as Command Pilot with Lt. Ralph H. Elliott and Crew #95 in JSH 42-50950 (791st Squadron), leading the

Second Air Division formations and the first Squadron. Lt. Russell E. Scott and Crew #90 led the second Squadron; Capt. William B. Ridgway flew with Lt. Billy Williams and Crew #80, leading the third; and the fourth squadron was led by Lt. William R. Chapman and Crew #92.

Orders were given that the planes were to circle the area until the target was clear, despite the fact that the target site was just below Dummer Lake and Bremen, an area where enemy fighter planes were most likely to be encountered.

The crews found that when they arrived over the target area at 0930, it was covered by scattered clouds with occasional breaks, but despite making four bomb runs on the primary target, only one Squadron, plus the Deputy Lead ship from the second Squadron—flown by Lt. Edward W. King and Crew #46—were able to bomb the bridge visually from 17,600ft. Strike photographs revealed the results were excellent, with fourteen direct hits on the bridge. The clouds over the bridge prevented a further strike and the formations flew to the secondary target at Bielefeld, where the three Squadrons dropped their bombs by PFF-H2X on the railroad station and marshalling yards. This was the third time in two weeks the Group had bombed it, and it was the sixth time that Bielefeld was an assigned target for the 467th.

No flak was encountered over the Nienburg Bridge area, but the crews faced heavy flak over Bielefeld; no enemy aircraft were seen. Moderate fighter escort was provided by P-47s. All thirty-seven ships and their crewss made it safely back to Rackheath.

Aerial photo taken of *Witchcraft* on hardstand #32; note the Dakenham Farm buildings in the background.

Lt. John G. Phillips and Crew #63. Standing (L to R): Joe Appleby (R/O), Fred Walkey (C/P), John Phillips (P), David Swiss (N), and Reuben Eaton (E). Kneeling (L to R): David Bliss (R/O), Julius Summa (G), Manuel Alzfan (G), and Jose Solorzano (G).

An aerial photo of Magdeburg, Germany, taken 2 March 1945, showing bomb damage.

Former Copilot 2/Lt. John B. Brinson remembers flying that day with Lt. Leo L. Jones and Crew #71 in 41-29378 from the 790th Squadron, and that they were low on fuel. They had to make an emergency landing on an airfield in Belgium to refuel before continuing the flight back to Rackheath.

General Kepner was at the hardstand, awaiting the return of Col. Shower and Capt. Elliott's plane 50950, specifically to get the film that would show what had been achieved by the strike on the Nienburg Bridge. When he got back with the pictures, he placed his arm around Col. Shower's shoulders and said, "Well, Colonel, excellent, we did it again."

The well-earned Oak Leaf Cluster to the Distinguished Flying Cross that he already held was awarded to Col. Albert Shower following the excellent results on this mission. DFCs were also awarded to two crew members who flew on the Lead ship with the Colonel: Lt. James R. Andrews (Bombardier) and Lt. Natale F. Parodi (Pilotage/Navigator). Lt. Ralph Elliott's Crew #95 received the second of only two special 467th Bomb Group commendations awarded during WWII for their outstanding performance of duty.

Following the mission, *Witchcraft*'s fuel tanks were topped up with 2,050 gallons after Lt. Rice and his crew members had flown her for some seven hours sixteen minutes.

Mission 124 – 4 March 1945 to Stuttgart, Germany
Group Mission #186 – Target – Railway Marshalling Yards
Twenty-nine planes and their crews—including *Witchcraft*, flown by Lt. John W. McFarland and Crew #73—were assigned the mission to Stuttgart. Each B-24 was loaded with 10 x 500-lb. GP bombs. Three of the aircraft made an early return to base due to various reasons.

The weather over mainland Europe and the target area was bad, and the target could not be located. Bombs were dropped by PFF from 23,000ft on nearby targets of opportunity in Stuttgart. The bombing was unobserved and the results are unknown. Flak over the target area was moderate and inaccurate, and no enemy aircraft were encountered.

On the return flight, 41-28981 *Wolves Inc*, flown by Lt. George W. Mills and Crew #42 from the 789th Squadron, ditched in the North Sea about ten miles from Cromer, Norfolk, and only about forty miles from base. The eight crew members on board perished and were listed as KIA.

Group records show a flight time of eight hours nine minutes for *Witchcraft* and Lt. J.W. McFarland and his crew. They also show a total of 2,075 gallons filled the fuel tanks in the "Witch."

Mission 125 – 11 March 1945 to Kiel, Germany
Group Mission #191 – Target – U-Boat Pens and Shipyards
For the mission to Kiel, the Group assigned thirty-six aircraft, each loaded with 52 x M17 100-lb. IBs. *Witchcraft* was flown by Lt. Donald M. Rosenthal and Crew #54. Soon after take-off, one of the assigned B-24s developed a mechanical malfunction and had to make an early return to base.

The crews flew over the North Sea on a course that took them nearly to Denmark before heading south to Kiel.

The target was bombed from 21,000ft via PFF, and as the bombing was unobserved, the results are unknown. Flak over the target area was heavy, but the heavy screen of aluminum foil that was dropped countered the accuracy of the gun tracking. No German aircraft were seen.

Another good day for the Group, as it did not incur any crew casualties or aircraft losses.

Group records show a flight time of five hours fifty-three minutes for Lt. Rosenthal and Crew #54 in *Witchcraft*. The records also reveal that 1,650 gallons were used when the fuel tanks were topped up.

Mission 126 – 12 March 1945 to Swinemunde, Germany
Group Mission #192 – Target – Railway Marshalling Yards
Witchcraft, flown by Lt. John G. Phillips and Crew #63, was one of thirty-six B-24s the Group assigned this mission to Swinemunde. The Lead ships were each loaded with 3 x 1,000-lb. GP bombs and each of the wing planes with 5 x 1,000-lb. GPs.

Bombs were dropped by PFF from 21,000ft; the bombing was unobserved, so the results are unknown. Moderate to heavy flak was encountered over the target area, but no enemy fighters were seen. Good fighter protection was provided by P-51s.

No crew casualties or aircraft losses were incurred.

The records reveal a flight time of seven hours thirty minutes for Lt. Phillips and crew in *Witchcraft*. The records also show 2,035 gallons were used to top up the fuel tanks.

Lt. James W. McFarland's Crew #73. Standing (L to R): ?, Robert Held (R/O), ?, ? (?), Robert Trantor (TG), and Howard Lyon (E). Kneeling (L to R): James McFarland (P), Steve Maznio (C/P), Joseph Dzenowagis (N), and ? (?).

Mission 127 –14 March 1945 to Giessen, Germany
Group Mission #193 – Target – Railway Marshalling Yards
Twenty-nine planes—including *Witchcraft*, flown by Lt. Robert H. Willis and Crew #64—were assigned this mission to Giessen. Each B-24—except for the Lead ships—was loaded with 44 x 100-lb. GPs and 2 x 500-lb. IBs and commenced take-off at 1115. One B-24 made an early return to base for some unknown reason.

The target was bombed visually, and the results were rated fair. Flak over the target area was moderate and fairly accurate.

Another good mission for the Group, as no crew casualties or aircraft losses occurred.

Group records show a flight time of six hours fifty-two minutes for *Witchcraft* and Lt. Willis and crew. The records also indicate 1,950 gallons filled the fuel tanks.

Mission 128 – 15 March 1945 to Zossen, Germany
Group Mission #194 – Target – German Army Headquarters
The Group assigned twenty-nine B-24s and crew—including *Witchcraft*, flown by Lt. Joseph C. Wilson and Crew #60—to attack the German Army HQ at Zossen, about twenty miles from Berlin. The B-24s, loaded with 10 x 300-lb. GPs and 4 x 500-lb. IBs, commenced take-off at 0730.

As the weather over the target area was good, the bombing was visual from 20,000ft and the results were rated good. It was really remarkable the German Army HQ was not better protected against an aerial attack, but that was fortunate for the Group, as they did not encounter any flak nor saw any enemy fighters.

A good mission for the Group, as it did not incur any crew casualties or loss of aircraft.

The flight time for Lt. Wilson and Crew #60 in *Witchcraft* is shown in Group records as six hours fifty-two minutes, and 2,170 gallons were used to top up the fuel tanks of the "Witch."

Mission 129 – 24 March 1945 to Kirtorf, Germany
Group Mission #203 – Target – Luftwaffe Airfield
Witchcraft, flown by Lt. Marvin R. Davis and Crew #57, was one of twenty-nine B-24s the 467th assigned to strike the airfield at Kirtorf. The four lead planes, each loaded with 10 x 100-lb. GPs, and the twenty-five wing ships,

each loaded with 52 x 100-lb. GPs, were led by Capt. Earl S. Jensen and commenced take-off at 1315.

Good weather over Germany held and the target was bombed visually from 22,000ft; the results were rated excellent.

Fak was only meager as they flew over the battle lines, and no enemy aircraft were seen. P-51s provided very good fighter cover.

Another good mission for the Group, as no losses, damage, or casualties were incurred.

A flight time of five hours fifty-six minutes is shown for Lt. Davis and Crew #57 in *Witchcraft*. Records also show that 1,750 gallons topped the fuel tanks.

To mark the achievement of 200 credited combat missions by the 467th Group, Col. Shower authorized the printing of a celebratory "special note" in the form of a bank note, and a copy was given to each member of the Group on the base at that time as a "keep-sake."

The occasion was also celebrated on 21 and 22 April 1945, with extensive and well-organized programs for all personnel. The front page of the programs carried the following greeting to members of the 467th Group and all Allied Units from the Group Commanding Officer:

> Each and every member of the 467th Group and Allied Units may well view with pride and satisfaction the enviable record established in carrying out in less than a year, two hundred bombing attacks against enemy installations, as well as numerous efficiently run "Trucking" missions – hauling supplies to rapidly moving ground forces during September 1944. The record has been outstanding because of the unfailing interest, untiring devotion to duty, and wholehearted co-operation of all officers and men on this station,

Lt. Marvin Ralph Davis and Crew #57. Rear (L to R): Walter Robinson (B), Walter Weaver (N), Robert Rush (C/P), and Ralph Davis (P). Front (L to R): Russell Ely (E), Ronald Neisse (R/O), Eugene Honea (AEG), Paul Bridges (WG), Richard Ash (TG), and Max Hoffbauer (WG).

both on the ground and in the air. Your co-ordinated efforts have resulted in relentless attrition upon the enemy's resources and fighting facilities, and you may feel rightfully conscious that yours was a tangible contribution toward the impending final triumph of Allied Arms.

While giving thanks for past success, let us be mindful of the sacrifice of those who have not returned from these missions. Their only request would undoubtedly be that we continue during the ensuing months of the war to display that same zeal and enthusiasm which have during the past year achieved such splendid results, to the end that we may see chatisement of the last aggressors and the establishment of a just and lasting peace.

Signed: ALBERT J. SHOWER – Colonel, Air Corps Commanding

Mission 130 – 30 March 1945 to Wilhelmshaven, Germany
Group Mission #205 – Target – German Navy Dockyard
For the mission to Wilhelmshaven, the Group assigned twenty-nine B-24s and crews, including *Witchcraft* flown by Lt. R.H. Willis and Crew #64. Each plane was loaded with 6 x 1,000-lb. GP bombs, whereas the lead ships were each loaded with 2 x 1,000-lb. GPs and 2 x Smoke Markers. One of the B-24s made an early return to base for unknown reasons.

Most of the flight to the target was over water and reasonably clear, but over the target area there was 5 to 7/10 cloud cover.

The target was bombed by H2X with some visual assistance. The bombing was unobserved and the results are unknown.

Flak was moderate and inaccurate until the planes reached the target area. It was then that the crews faced intense flak, but no enemy fighters were seen.

Lt. Robert H. Willis and Crew #64. No information is available relating to the names of any of the crewmembers.

Brunswick, Germany, taken during the attack on 31 March 1944.

Face of the "200 Mission Note."

Back of the "200 Mission" Note.

The crews encountered bad weather over the North Sea as they made their homebound flight.

Another good mission for the Group, as it had no losses of any kind.

The flight time for Lt. Willis and Crew #64 in *Witchcraft* is shown in Group records as five hours forty-five minutes, and when the fuel tanks on the "Witch" were topped up, a total of 1,600 gallons was used.

Mission 131 – 31 March 1945 to Brunswick, Germany
Group Mission #206 – Target – Railway Marshalling Yards

Twenty-nine B-24s and crew—including *Witchcraft*, flown by Lt. Frederick J. Jansen and Crew #61—were assigned for this mission to Brunswick. Each Lead ship was loaded with 4 x 500-lb. GP bombs and 2 x Smoke Markers; each of the wing planes was loaded with 12 x 500-lb. GPs. The Group commenced take-off from Rackheath at 0545. One plane made an early return to base for unknown reasons.

Lt. Col. Smith flew as Command Pilot with Capt. Ralph H. Elliott and Crew #95 in MSH 44-50325 from the 791st Squadron, leading the Second Air Division formations.

The target was bombed from 22,500ft through 10/10 undercast using PFF; the bombing was unobserved and the results are unknown. Flak was moderate and inaccurate, although the crews had been briefed that the flak would be intense for some four and a half minutes.

No damage was caused to the 467th's planes and no crew casualties were incurred.

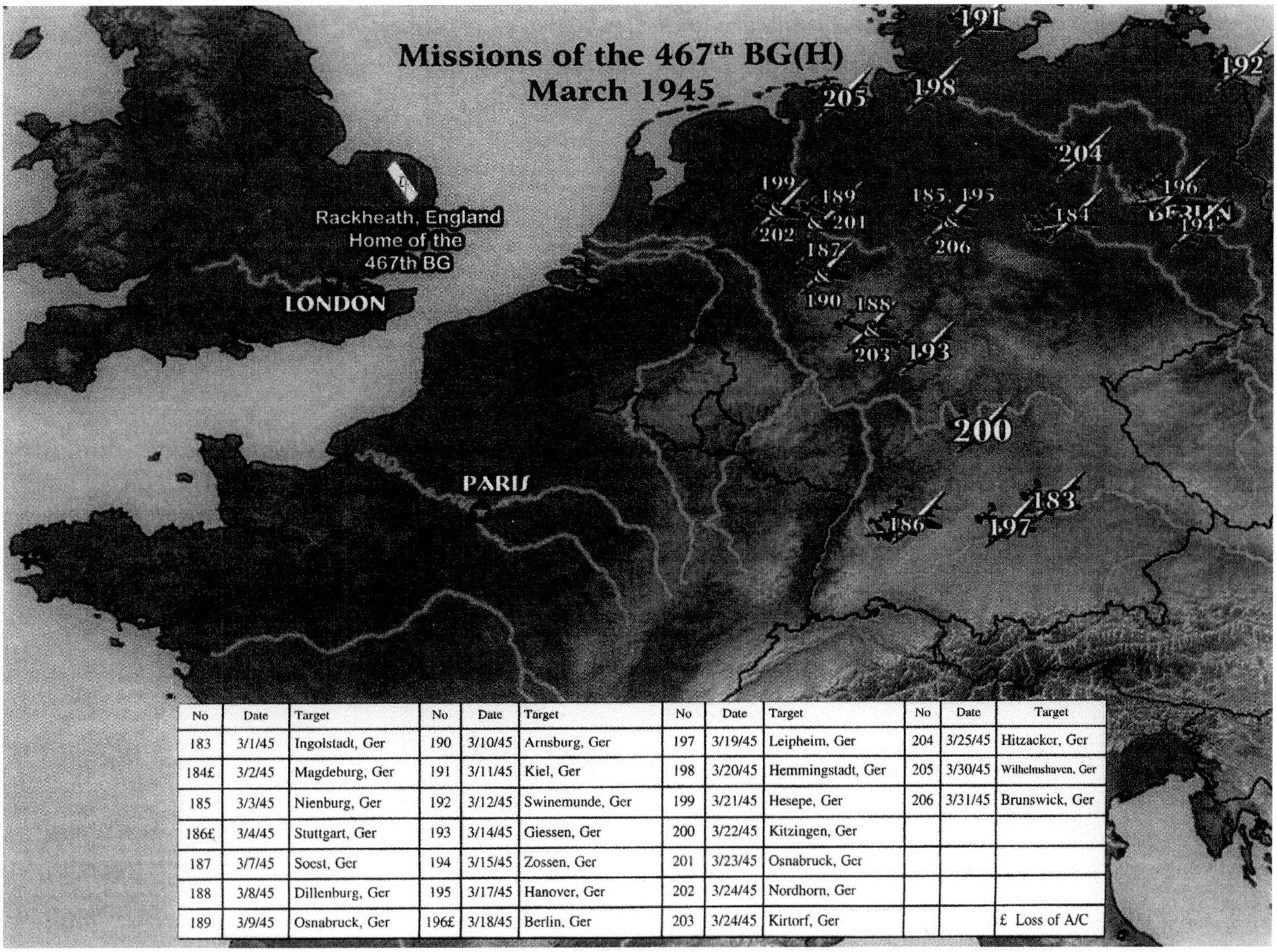

No	Date	Target	No	Date	Target	No	Date	Target	No	Date	Target
183	3/1/45	Ingolstadt, Ger	190	3/10/45	Arnsburg, Ger	197	3/19/45	Leipheim, Ger	204	3/25/45	Hitzacker, Ger
184£	3/2/45	Magdeburg, Ger	191	3/11/45	Kiel, Ger	198	3/20/45	Hemmingstadt, Ger	205	3/30/45	Wilhelmshaven, Ger
185	3/3/45	Nienburg, Ger	192	3/12/45	Swinemunde, Ger	199	3/21/45	Hesepe, Ger	206	3/31/45	Brunswick, Ger
186£	3/4/45	Stuttgart, Ger	193	3/14/45	Giessen, Ger	200	3/22/45	Kitzingen, Ger			
187	3/7/45	Soest, Ger	194	3/15/45	Zossen, Ger	201	3/23/45	Osnabruck, Ger			
188	3/8/45	Dillenburg, Ger	195	3/17/45	Hanover, Ger	202	3/24/45	Nordhorn, Ger			
189	3/9/45	Osnabruck, Ger	196£	3/18/45	Berlin, Ger	203	3/24/45	Kirtorf, Ger			£ Loss of A/C

467th Bombardment Group Combat Missions, March 1945.

Group records show the flight time for Lt. Jansen and crew in *Witchcraft* was six hours two minutes, and that 1,950 gallons were used to fill the tanks.

Mission 132 – 4 April 1945 to Perleberg, Germany
Group Mission #207 – Target – Luftwaffe Airfield
Twenty-nine planes—including *Witchcraft*, flown by Lt. Donald M. Rosenthal and Crew #54—were assigned this mission to Perleberg. The wing airplanes were each loaded with either 36 x 150-lb. GP or 52 x 100-lb. GP bombs and the Lead ships each carried 10 x 100-lb. GPs and 1 x Smoke Marker.

The crews encountered light flak en route to the target and fairly heavy flak was put up near Lubeck, but over the target, there appeared to be only two to four anti-aircraft batteries operating. A German Me-262 jet fighter passed through one of the Group's Squadrons and was fired at by several of the waist gunners. One of the escorting P-51s also chased after it.

One Squadron bombed the target, although it was covered with 9/10 undercast, but the other two Squadrons brought their bombs back to base, as the drop was supposed to be visual. The results were rated poor.

No losses of any kind were incurred.

Group records show a flight time of seven hours twenty-nine minutes for *Witchcraft* and Lt. Rosenthal and crew; they also reveal that 1,875 gallons were used to top up the "Witch's" fuel tanks.

Mission 133 – 7 April 1945 to Krummel, Germany
Group Mission #210 – Target – Ordnance Depot
The 467th assigned thirty-seven B-24s and crews—including

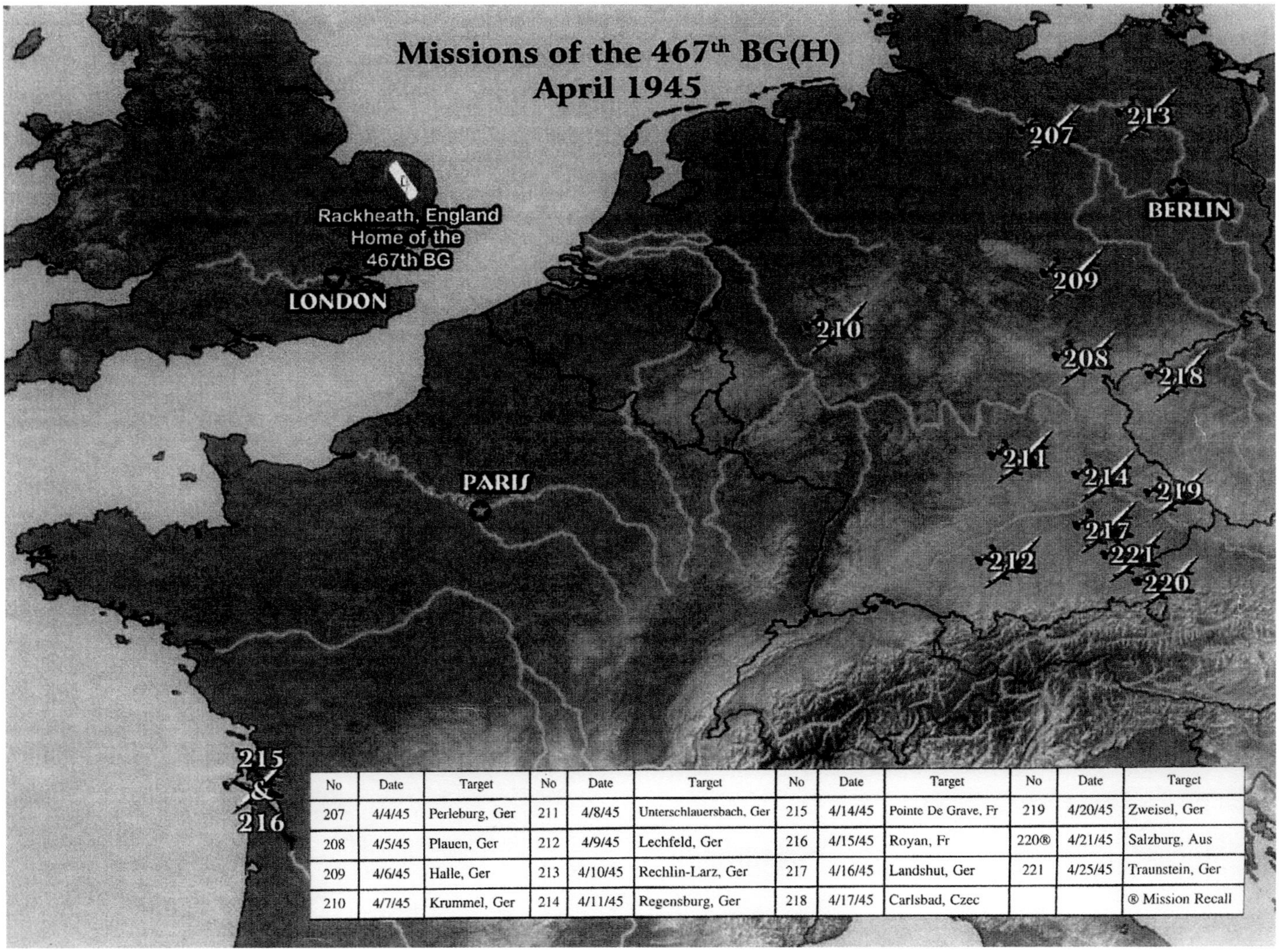

No	Date	Target	No	Date	Target	No	Date	Target	No	Date	Target
207	4/4/45	Perleburg, Ger	211	4/8/45	Unterschlauersbach, Ger	215	4/14/45	Pointe De Grave, Fr	219	4/20/45	Zweisel, Ger
208	4/5/45	Plauen, Ger	212	4/9/45	Lechfeld, Ger	216	4/15/45	Royan, Fr	220®	4/21/45	Salzburg, Aus
209	4/6/45	Halle, Ger	213	4/10/45	Rechlin-Larz, Ger	217	4/16/45	Landshut, Ger	221	4/25/45	Traunstein, Ger
210	4/7/45	Krummel, Ger	214	4/11/45	Regensburg, Ger	218	4/17/45	Carlsbad, Czec			® Mission Recall

467th Bombardment Group Combat Missions, April 1945

Witchcraft, flown by Lt. R.H. Willis and Crew #64—to strike the ordnance depot at Krummel.

The Lead ships were loaded with 4 x 1,000-lb. GP bombs and each of the thirty-four wing aircraft were loaded with 6 x 1,000-lb. GPs. The bombing results were rated good.

Flak was only very moderate, but that day, the Luftwaffe launched its final effective fighter attack on the B-17s and B-24s flying on the 931st bomber raid by the US 8th Air Force.

The Group lost one plane due to enemy action, but all of the crew members safely returned to base after abandoning their severely damaged B-24 over Belgium. No crew casualties or injuries were incurred.

Group records show a flight time of six hours thirty-two minutes for Lt. Willis and Crew #64 in *Witchcraft*. The records also show that 1,785 gallons filled her tanks.

Mission 134 – 8 April 1945 to Unterschlauersbach, Germany

Group Mission #211 – Target – Luftwaffe Airfield

The Group assigned twenty-nine B-24s—including *Witchcraft*, flown by Lt. J.W. McFarland and Crew #73—for this mission to Unterschlauersbach. The Lead ships were each loaded with 6 x 250-lb. GPs and the wing aircraft were each loaded with 20 x 250-lb. GPs.

Weather was reasonably good; there was some undercast at first on the flight to the target, but it cleared, and the crews had contact with the ground for the remainder of the flight.

The target was bombed from 20,000ft and the result achieved was rated as good. No flak or enemy fighters were encountered, although some jet aircraft were seen on the ground at the targeted airfield.

The Group did not incur any aircraft losses or crew casualties.

The flight time for *Witchcraft* and Lt. McFarland and Crew #73 is shown in Group records as seven hours two minutes; records also show that 2,125 gallons were used to top up the fuel tanks.

Mission 135 – 15 April 1945 to Royan, France
Group Mission #216 – Target – Coastal Gun Batteries
The Group put up thirty B-24s—including *Witchcraft*, flown by Lt. J.W. McFarland and Crew #73—for this eight-hour mission to Royan, just north of Bordeaux. Each B-24 was loaded with 2 x 75 gallon and 6 x 85 gallon napalm bombs (a new type of firebomb that was literally a heavy-gauge cardboard cylinder filled with jellied petroleum ignited by phosphorous).

Maj. Robert S. Seiler flew as Command Pilot with Capt. Ralph H. Elliott and Crew #95 in LSH 44-49340 (791st Squadron) and led the 467th's B-24s, which commenced take-off at 0605.

The napalm bombs were dropped on the target from 15,500ft and the bombing was unobserved. Capt. Elliott reported that at 15,500ft, the smoke caused by the bombing was so thick he could not see his wingmen.

The crews were informed at the briefing that for this mission, due to the hazardous nature of the payload carried by the wing planes, only a minimum crew consisting of Pilot, Copilot, Radio Operator, and Engineer would be flying in each plane, and that the Lead ships would also be carrying one Waist Gunner.

Only a few puffs of flak were seen over the target and no enemy fighter planes were encountered.

No crew casualties or aircraft losses were incurred.

Group records reveal a flight time of eight hours eleven minutes for Lt. McFarland and Crew #73 in *Witchcraft*. Records also show that 2,150 gallons topped up *Witchcraft*'s tanks. Capt. Ralph Elliott wrote:

> There were some 122,000 German troops in the area around Royan, which was one of the German-held pockets, along with St. Nazaire and a few others, and we used a new type of bomb on that mission. The jellied gasoline was contained in a heavy cardboard casing that had no ballistic characteristics whatsoever and measured about 8ft long and about 1½ft in diameter, and on impact with the ground it covered an area of 60 square yards, took oxygen out of the air, and destroyed everything in the vicinity. At altitude, some of the detonators popped out of the containers like loose corks, so the bomb bay smelled of raw gasoline most of the way to the target. We all sort of held our breath and hoped no wayward spark would set the whole thing off. For once, I didn't have to mention "no smoking" to the crew.

Mission 136 – 17 April 1945 to Carlsbad, Czechoslovakia
Group Mission #218 – Target – Railroad Center and Viaduct
The 467th assigned twenty-seven B-24s—including *Witchcraft*, flown by Lt. F.J. Jansen and Crew #61—for the seven and a half hour mission to Carlsbad. Each Lead ship was loaded with 4 x 500-lb. GPs and 1 x Smoke Marker, and the twenty-four wing planes each carried 10 x 500-lb. GPs.

The target was bombed from 17,000ft, and the result achieved was rated very good. No flak or enemy fighters were encountered.

A good mission for the 467th Group, as no crew casualties or aircraft losses were incurred.

Group records show the flight time for Lt. Jansen and Crew #61 was seven hours twenty-one minutes. Records also indicate it took 2,050 gallons to top up the "Witch's" fuel tanks.

Mission 137 – 21 April 1945 to Salzburg, Austria
Group Mission #220 – Target – Railroad Junction
Witchcraft, flown by Lt. J.W. McFarland and Crew #73, was one of twenty-seven B-24s and crews assigned to fly this long-haul mission to Salzburg. Except for the three Lead ships, each of which carried 4 x 500-lb. GPs and 2 x Smoke Markers, the Liberators were each loaded with 5 x 1,000-lb. GPs.

Due to inclement weather over the European continent, the crews were instructed to abort the mission; at that time, they were only 130 miles from the target. Several of the Group B-24s lost their formations due to the intense cloud conditions.

Napalm bombs being made ready for loading by ordnance personnel.

Some flak was encountered, but caused no damage to Group planes or crews.

On the homeward flight, the course took the crews over Remagen and they were able to see the bridge, wrecked tanks and trucks, and several crashed aircraft and gliders.

Because of the rain and fog, the B-24s let down and flew back to Rackheath at about 500ft.

The Group was given credit for this mission because the planes flew over enemy-held territory.

A 788th Squadron B-24 made an emergency landing on the Continent, but the remaining Group aircraft and crew landed safely at Rackheath with their unused bomb loads after flying an average seven hours fifty-three minutes.

The flight time for Lt. J.W. McFarland and Crew #73 in *Witchcraft* is shown as seven hours fifty-four minutes and 2,000 gallons were used to top up the fuel tanks in the "Witch" after flying on its 137th and final combat mission.

9

The Return Flight of *Witchcraft* to the US

About three weeks following the German surrender to Allied forces and the cessation of hostilities in Europe, the United States Army Air Force issued orders to the various Groups relating to return of aircraft and personnel to the US.

On 29 May 1945, the 467th Bombardment Group issued the following instructions:

> OPERATIONS ORDERS 29 May 1945 NUMBER 52
>
> 46. Under authority contained in letter ETUSA, subject: Movement Orders, Shipment 10060. File No:- 370.5 OPGC dated 27 May 45, the following A/C and personnel assigned thereto will proceed o/a June 1945, via Valley A/D by best available air route to Bradley Field, Windsor Locks, Connecticut. Thence to Camp Miles Standish, Boston, POE. Personnel will report to the AAF Base Commander at Bradley Field. AF Personnel are being returned for the purpose of authorized TD for rest and recuperation and for further assignment.
>
> WD Cir 268 and 35, 1944 will apply.
>
> TDN 212/50424 fsa 1942-45 60-114 T431-01
>
> Shipment No: 10060-JZ Type, Model and Series: B-24H
>
> Unit: 790th Bomb Sq (H) or as indicated
>
> Crew No: 10 of 19 A/C Serial No: 42-52534

The orders were numbered 1 to 72; number 46 related to B-24H-15 FO 42-52534 *Witchcraft*.

For the last time, *Witchcraft* lifted off from the main runway at Rackheath the morning of 10 June 1945, and headed west for Valley, Wales.

B-24 "52534" *Witchcraft* was flown back by Lt. Frederick J. Jansen and nine fellow crew members (Crew #61); also on board were ten passengers, including Master Sgt. Joe R. Ramirez and his assistant and "buddy," Staff Sgt. George Dong (Crew Chief and Assistant Crew Chief of *Witchcraft* who, with their three fellow ground crew members, had looked after that plane from the day it was delivered to the 467th Group at Wendover, Utah).

Only one of the three remaining members of Master Sgt. Joe Ramirez's ground crew team (Cpl. Joe Vetter) flew back to the US Joe Vetter was one of ten passengers in DT 42-51204, flown back by Lt. Joseph C. Wilson and Crew #60. Both Sgt. Raymond A. Betcher and Cpl. Walter L. Elliott stayed on at Rackheath until 5 July 1945, and then, after the train journey to Greenock, Scotland, "took a leisurely five day cruise" on the converted troop ship-Cunard Liner *Queen Mary*, arriving in New York on 11 July, before proceeding to the Reception Center at Camp Kilmer, New Jersey.

Witchcraft had a very short stay at Bradley Field—indeed, only two or three days—and was then flown by an ATC team to Ypsilanti, Willow Run Ford plant, where approximately some eighteen months earlier she had rolled off the assembly lines. The "Witch" remained there for about three months and a vast number of the work force at Willow Run viewed the legendary airplane.

On 16 September 1945, *Witchcraft* made her final flight from Ypsilanti to the Reconstruction Finance Corporation site at Altus, California. It was there, along with many other surplus US Air Force planes, that *Witchcraft* was unceremoniously scrapped.

Witchcraft at Willow Run, Ypsilanti, on display from 17 June to 16 September 1945 (one of the last known photographs to be taken of *Witchcraft*).

Vivid memories of her are highlighted by the Collings Foundation B-24 painted in the colors of the good old "Witch." The author still has treasured memories from way back, when, as a 15-16 year-old schoolboy he enjoyed actually seeing *Witchcraft* standing on hardstand 32 on the former WWII airfield at Rackheath, and on a few occasions seeing her flying out on and returning from a combat mission over Europe during 1944-1945. The author was fortunate to enjoy the close friendship of many of the veterans who were flight crew in *Witchcraft*, plus three of the five ground maintenance personnel who did an excellent job taking care of *Witchcraft*.

10

Copy of Flight Orders for the Movement of *Witchcraft* from Wendover, Utah, to the United Kingdom and Copies of Flight Logs of Pilot Lt. George W. Reed and Copilot Lt. John G. Oder

HEADQUARTERS ARMY AIR BASE

SPECIAL ORDER
NO 42

Wendover Fld Utah
11 Feb 1944

R E S T R I C T E D

- E X T R A C T -

* * * * *

1. Following named O, AC, and EM, (pers indicated on List #1 which is atchd hereto and made a part of this order), Flight Echelon, 467th Bomb Gp, WP via mil ap fr this sta to AAF Herington Kansas.in the following manner: 30 Crews WP so as to arrive 12 Feb 44, 27 Crews WP so as to arrive 13 Feb 44, 1 Crew WP so as to arrive 14 Feb 44.

Upon arrival at AAF Herington Kansas the CG 15th Bomb Wg will relinquish control over pers to CG 21st Bomb Wg.

This is a temp change of sta.

Individual equipment and overseas aircraft only will accompany this orgn.

Movement will be accomplished by mil air and/or rail. If it should be impracticabl to accomplish entire movement by air, pers will continue journey by rail.

Travel by private owned conveyance is not auth.

$7.00 per diem in lieu of subs is auth O and EM while traveling by air.

TDN. 1-5250 P 433-01-02-03-04-05-07-08 A 0425-24. Auth Ltr Hq Second AF 18 Jan 44 file 370.5 G and Memo 35-15 Hq Second AF 18 Dec 43.

* * * * *

By order of LT COL CARTER:

MICHAEL J HAND
CAPT AC
Adjutant

OFFICIAL: /s/ Michael J Hand

MICHAEL J HAND
CAPT AC
Adjutant

par 1
SO 42

-1-

Special Movement Order No. 42, dated 11 February 1944.

LIST #1 (cont) 11 Feb 1944

790th Bomb Sq (cont)

Crew W-38

2LT (1024) JACK M SKINNER 0745205 S Sgt (757) K Norris Harshbarger 14119246
" (1024) CHARLES L STUCKMAN 0809063 Sgt (612) Truman S Thompson 38039847
" (1034) AXEL R DAHLIN 0687997 " (748) Phillip J Mastandrea 1218104
" (1035) EMMETT L WILDER 0743802 " (748) Meyer Miller 12158784
S Sgt (748) Raymond J Eaton 14182367 " (612) Russell E Reed 33490867

Crew Y-7

2LT (1024) ROBERT D SHEEHAN 0687710 Sgt (757) Martin L Altenburg 36502864
" (1024) JOSEPH G MULHERAN 0699706 " (612) John R Healy 36641320
" (1034) ROBERT A SMOLAR 0698173 " (612) Robert E Baker 39201187
" (1035) JESSE E BROOKS 0495650 " (612) Donald H Bisbing 37156372
Sgt (748) John J Fornols 18119393 " (748) Clarence E Love 16162372

Crew Y-14

2LT (1024) EDWIN M HELTON 0687592 Sgt (757) Frank Borchick 13171042
" (1024) MAURICE E NELSON 0699712 " (612) Stanley E Brezowski 32862091
" (1034) RICHARD B HIRSCH 0698711 " (612) Thomas A Gensert 35766187
" (1035) RICHARD K LUDKA 0694919 " (748) Charles L Knowles 18189980
Sgt (748) Ernest E Booth 34235335 " (612) Robert M Clark 39412446

CREW MEMBERS OF B24 H LIBERATOR – "WITCHCRAFT".

Crew Y-15

2LT (1024) GEORGE W REED 0688993 Sgt (757) Melvin L Bland 33390918
" (1024) JOHN G ODER 0699767 " (612) Vernon W Bundrock 32839558
" (1034) CHARLES H MINTZLAFF 0698750 " (612) Alexander D McLean 18089637
" (1035) JOHN C KRAEMER 0691897 " (748) Henry W Kubacek 18216290
S Sgt (748) Robert W DeKerf 17126974 " (612) Robert B McEwen 17090371

Crew Y-16

2LT (1024) VINCENT P SIEBERN 0807883 Sgt (757) Roy P Boesch 18151865
" (1024) ROBERT M PIERCE 0699722 " (748) Phillip H Hasselvander 1303531
" (1034) BENNETT M HENDERSON 0698135 S Sgt (612) Patrick J O'Donnell 13115772
" (1035) ROY SESSLER 0691655 " (612) John L Leeth 35549782
S Sgt (748) William J Drapp 37414707 " (612) Charles C Burden 20402152

Crew Y-17

2LT (1024) FRANK P PROKOP 0687345 Sgt (757) James R Boucher 35544768
" (1024) ROBERT J PITTMAN 0699725 " (612) Richard C Peters 36578724
" (1034) GEORGE W MILLIRON 0698135 Pvt (611) Floyd D Williams 18042480
" (1035) RUSSELL L DIMATTIO 0691379 Sgt (612) John H Burglin 32835000
Sgt (748) Edward J Dreksler 16118911 " (748) Leroy M Hill 18168713

Crew Y-161

CAPT (1024) STANLEY J NEITZEL 0417713 S Sgt (757) Roger E Rafford 11118703
2LT (1024) HOWARD W JOHNSON 0686246 " (748) Guenther H Staedicke 16127307
" (1034) DONALD D KAYNOR 0698297 Sgt (612) Harold J Peek 37552860
1LT (1035) ROBERT E DOLAN 0443496 " (748) Robert R Marek 18188926
S Sgt (748) David A Baumhover 37652268 M Sgt (405) Perc F DeTamble 20613072

Crew 4073

2LT (1024) ELROY W BEANEY 0803084 S Sgt (757) Joseph V Perreault 11051138
" (1024) ROBERT T SANDER 0805684 " (612) George W Leeper 37227577
" (1034) MORTON DEUTSCH 0757771 Cpl (748) Robert B Finch 19003201
" (1035) WILLIAM E DAVIS 0752555 Sgt (748) Carl W Kleinert 33180848
~~S Sgt (748) [illegible] 33326964~~ Cpl (612) Benjamin F Meridith 3332564[illegible]

791st Bomb Sq

Crew Y-20

MAJ (1024) ALBERT L WALLACE JR 0413538 S Sgt (748) Gordon S Freiday 39554918
2LT (1024) VERNON J RIGSBEE 0687765 " (757) Champ C Burkholder 38249817
1LT (1034) PAUL TORRETTI 0736047 Sgt (612) James J Verunac 18230733
" (1035) THEODORE G GERRINGER 01301811 " (612) Dennis O Arnold 12052081
2LT (1035) HENRY W WEDAA 0694487 " (748) Dale E Hamilton 17159420

- 5 -
(over)

Part 2 of Special Movement Order No: 42, dated 11 February 1944.

DEPARTMENT FORM NO. 5 [A]PROVED DEC. 7, 1942

[IND]IVIDUAL FLIGHT RECO[RD]

SERIAL NO. 0-688993 (2) NAME REED GEORGE W. (LAST, FIRST, MIDDLE) (3) RANK 2nd LT. (4) AGE 1917

PERS. CLASS 01 (6) BRANCH AC (7) STATION 145 (ATTACHED FOR FLYING)

ORGANIZATION ASSIGNED 8th [AIR FORCE] II DIV. [COMMAND] 96th [WING] 467th [GROUP] 790th [SQUADRON] [DETACHMENT]

ORGANIZATION ATTACHED (AIR FORCE, COMMAND, WING, GROUP, SQUADRON, DETACHMENT)

(10) PRESENT RATING & DATE Pilot Feb-43 (11) ORIGINAL RATING & DATE SAME

(12) TRANSFERRED FROM MORRISON FLD FLA (13) FLIGHT RESTRICTIONS

(15) TRANSFERRED TO STATION 145 (14) TRANSFER DATE

DO NOT WRITE IN THIS SPACE: PERS. CLASS | RANK | RTG. | A. F. | COMMAND | WING | GROUP NO. | GROUP TYPE | SQUADRON NO. | SQUADRON TYPE | STATION | MO. | YR.

(17) MONTH APRIL 1944

Date	Aircraft Type, Model & Series (19)	No. Landings (20)	Flying Inst. (incl. in 1st Pil. Time) S (21)	Commd. Pilot C CA (22)	Co-Pilot CP (23)	Qualified Pilot Dual QD (24)	First Pilot Day P (25)	First Pilot Night N or NI (26)	Rated Pers. Non-Pilot (27–29)	Non-Rated Other Arms & Services (30)	Other Crew & Pass'gr (31)	Instrument I (32)	Night N (33)	Instrument Trainer (34)	Pilot Non-Mil. Aircraft Over 400 H.P. / Under 400 H.P. (35–36)
APRIL [1]	B-24H	1					:45								
7	"	1					4:30								
10	"	1	v				7:00		Bourges						
12	"	1					3:15								
13	"	1	✓				8:10		Lechfeld						
15	"	1					2:00								
18	"	1	✓				7:45		Brandenburg						
21	"	1					4:00		Recalled - Weather			3:00			
22	"	1	✓				6:45		Hamm				1:00		
26	"	1	✓				5:15								Paderborn
27	"	1	✓				6:15 -s		Blainville						
TOTALS	APRIL 44	11					55:40					3:00	1:00		
MAY															
1	B-24H	1	✓				6:00-s						1:00		Ruisseville
5	"	1					5:00								Weather
7	"	1	✓				6:30								Osnabruck
8	"	1	✓				6:15								Brunswick
10	"	1					4:00								Weather
12		1	✓				8:30		CERTIFIED CORRECT:						Pohlem
13	"	1	✓				7:45		[signature]						Tutow
22	"	1					4:10								
23	"	1	✓				6:45		W.R.SMITH,						Bourges
27	"	1	X				7:30		Major, AC						Neunkirchen
28	"	1	✓				7:30		Opns O						Zeitz
29	"	1	✓				8:45								Tutow
31	"	1					2:10								
COLUMN TOTALS		13					80:50						1:00		

	(42) Total Student Pilot Time	(43) Total First Pilot Time	(44) Total Pilot Time
THIS MONTH		80:50	80:50
PREVIOUS MONTHS THIS F. Y.		217:25	228:25
THIS FISCAL YEAR		299:15	309:15
PREVIOUS FISCAL YEARS	263:50	28:05	446:40
TO DATE	263:50	327:20	749:55

Aircraft (19)	NL (20)	Card No. 1: 21	22	23	24	25	26	Card No. 2: 27	28	29	30	31	Card No. 3: 32	33	34	35	36
B-24H	13					81											

Page 1 of Lt. George W. Reed's Flight Log.

CONFIDENTIAL

INDIVIDUAL FLIGHT RECORD

SERIAL NO. 0688993 (2) NAME REED, GEORGE W. (LAST / FIRST / MIDDLE) (3) RANK 2ND LT (4) AGE 1917

PERS. CLASS 01 (6) BRANCH AC (7) STATION 145

ORGANIZATION ASSIGNED 8 (AIR FORCE) II DIV (COMMAND) 96 (WING) 467 (GROUP) 790 (SQUADRON) ATTACHED FOR FLYING / DETACHMENT

ORGANIZATION ATTACHED (AIR FORCE / COMMAND / WING / GROUP / SQUADRON / DETACHMENT)

PRESENT RATING & DATE PILOT 1-29-43 (11) ORIGINAL RATING & DATE SAME

TRANSFERRED FROM (13) FLIGHT RESTRICTIONS

TRANSFERRED TO (14) TRANSFER DATE

DO NOT WRITE IN THIS SPACE

PERS CLASS	RANK	RTG.	A. F.	COMMAND	WING	GROUP NO.	GROUP TYPE	SQUADRON NO.	SQUADRON TYPE	STATION	MO.	YR.	(17) MONTH JUNE 1944

JUNE	AIRCRAFT TYPE, MODEL & SERIES (19)	NO. LANDINGS (20)	FLYING INST. (INCL. IN 1ST PIL. TIME) S (21)	COMMD. PILOT C CA (22)	CO-PILOT CP (23)	QUALIFIED PILOT DUAL QD (24)	FIRST PILOT DAY P (25)	FIRST PILOT NIGHT P N OR NI (26)	RATED PERS. NON-PILOT (27)	(28)	(29)	NON-RATED OTHER ARMS & SERVICES (30)	OTHER CREW & PASS'GR (31)	SPECIAL INFORMATION INSTRUMENT I (32)	NIGHT N (33)	INSTRUMENT TRAINER (34)	PILOT NON-MIL. AIRCRAFT OVER 400 H.P. (35)	UNDER 400 H.P. (36)
2	B-24H	1	✓				5:30									StellaPage		
3	"	1	✓				4:15									Berckesurme		
6	"	1	✓				6:00									Colleville		
6	"	1	✓				7:30								2:00		Portaubault	
8	"	1	✓				7:30							3:00			"	
10	"	1	✓				6:00										Chateaudun	
12	"	1	✓	✓			6:30										Evreaux	
14	"	1	✓				4:15								1:00		Beauvoir	
15	"	1	✓				6:00								1:00		Gyancourt	
18	"	1	✗	✓			7:45										Bremenshaven	
20	"	1	✓				6:30										Ostermoor	
21	"	1	✓				8:45								:15		Berlin	
23	"	1					5:15										Beaumetz	
28	"	1	✓	✓			7:35								:45		Saarbrucken	
29	B-24H	1	✓	✓			6:50							3:00			Ascheraleben	
COLUMN TOTALS		15					96:10							6:00	5:00			

CERTIFIED CORRECT:

W.R. Smith

W.R. SMITH,
Major, AC
Opns O

Date of last Instrument Check 13 December 1943

	(42) TOTAL STUDENT PILOT TIME	(43) TOTAL FIRST PILOT TIME	(44) TOTAL PILOT TIME
THIS MONTH		96:10	96:10
PREVIOUS MONTHS THIS F. Y.		299:15	217:35 303:15
THIS FISCAL YEAR		395:25 11:00	313:45 399:25 20:00
PREVIOUS FISCAL YEARS	263:50	28:05	446:40
TO DATE	263:50	423:30 11:00	79915 846:05 20:00

AIRCRAFT 19	NL 20	CARD NO. 1: 21	22	23	24	25	26	CARD NO. 2: 27	28	29	30	31	CARD NO. 3: 32	33	34	35	36
B-24H	15					96											

Page 2 of Lt. George W. Reed's Flight Log.

No. 12P

Printed in U.S.A.

THE CIVIL AIR REGULATIONS REQUIRE THAT PILOTS AND STUDENTS KEEP AN ACCURATE RECORD OF THEIR FLYING TIME AND THE NATURE OF THE FLIGHT. A PILOT OR STUDENT MUST SHOW IN LOG ANY ACCIDENTS. ALL ENTRIES MUST BE MADE IN INK. NO PAGES CAN BE TORN FROM LOG BOOK. NO ERASURES ARE ALLOWED. REFER TO ENCLOSED SHEET FOR ADDITIONAL INFORMATION ON CIVIL AIR REGULATIONS REGARDING LOG BOOKS.

PUBLISHED BY

AIR ASSOCIATES, INC.

CHICAGO, ILL. MUNICIPAL AIRPORT — BENDIX, N. J. BENDIX AIRPORT — DALLAS, TEX. LOVE FIELD — LOS ANGELES, CALIF. AIRPORT AND CENTURY BLVDS.

IDENTIFICATION

PILOT'S NAME: JOHN G. ODER — CERTIFICATE NUMBER:

ADDRESS: — PILOT RATING:

CITY AND STATE: HASTINGS, NEBRASKA — AIRCRAFT RATING:

PHONE No.: — AIRPORT BASE:

PILOT'S SIGNATURE: John G. Oder

BOOK No.: — DATE: Dec. 24, 1943

DATE 1943	MAKE OF AIRCRAFT	CLASS	TYPE	CERTIFICATE NUMBER	MAKE OF ENGINE	H. P.	REMARKS OR INSPECTOR'S SIGNATURE CERTIFICATION NUMBER AND RATING	FROM	TO	INSTRUMENT RADIO OR HOOD	DUAL AS INSTRUCTOR	DUAL AS STUDENT	SOLO DAY	SOLO NIGHT	DAILY TOTAL TIME
12-25	Consolidated	B	24 D	U.S. Army	4-Pratt-Whitney	1200	[illegible]	Wendover	Local			30			30
12-27	"	"	"D	"	"	"	SEE RECAP	"	"			5 00			5 00
1-1-44	"	"	"E	"	"	"	ON BACK PAGES	"	"				2 00		2 00
1-2	"	"	"E	"	"	"		"	"					3 00	3 00
1-8	"	"	"E	"	"	"		"	"					6 30	6 30
1-15	"	"	"H	"	"	"	1st FLIGHT IN WITCHCRAFT	"	"				1 45		1 45
1-19	"	"	"	"	"	"		"	"				6 00		6 00
1-20	"	"	"	"	"	"		"	"				5 30		5 30
1-21	"	"	"	"	"	"		"	"				6 30		6 30
1-22	"	"	"	"	"	"		"	"				8 00		8 00
1-23	"	"	"	"	"	"		"	"				2 00		2 00
									TOTAL			5 30	31 45	9 30	46 45
									AMT. FORWARD						
									TOTAL TO DATE						

I HEREBY CERTIFY THAT THE FOREGOING ENTRIES ARE TRUE AND CORRECT.

SIGNED John G. Oder

Part 1 of Lt. John G. Oder's Flight Records.

DATE 1944	MAKE OF AIRCRAFT	CLASS	TYPE	CERTIFICATE NUMBER	MAKE OF ENGINE	H. P.	REMARKS OR INSPECTOR'S SIGNATURE CERTIFICATION NUMBER AND RATING	FROM	TO	INSTRUMENT RADIO OR HOOD	DUAL AS INSTRUCTOR	DUAL AS STUDENT	SOLO DAY	SOLO NIGHT	DAILY TOTAL TIME
1-29	Consolidated	B-	24-H	U.S. Army	Pratt & Whitney	1200		Wendover	Local				3 00		3 00
1-31	"	"	"	"	"	"		Wendover	Casper Wyo.				2 50		2 50
2-1	"	"	"	"	"	"		Casper, Wyo.	Local				5 15		5 15
2-2	"	"	"	"	"	"		"	"				5 00		5 00
2-4	"	B-	24-E	"	"	"		"	"	OUT OF WENDOVER 60 35			2 00		2 00
2-5	"	B-	24-H	"	"	"		"	"	" " [illegible] 20 15			4 30		4 30
2-6	"	"	"	"	"	"		Casper, Wyo.	Wendover	" " [illegible] 12 [illegible]			3 30		3 30
2-12	"	"	"	"	"	"		[illegible]	[illegible]	TOTAL [illegible] 73 [illegible]			8 00		8 00
2-19	"	"	"	"	"	"		Herrington	Local				4 00		4 00
2-22	"	"	"	"	"	"		"	"	[illegible]			1 30		1 30
2-27	"	"	"	"	"	"		Herrington Kans	Morrison Fld. Fla.				7 00		7 00
									TOTAL				46 35		46 35
									AMT. FORWARD			5 30	31 45	9 30	46 45
									TOTAL TO DATE			5 30	78 20	9 30	93 20

I HEREBY CERTIFY THAT THE FOREGOING ENTRIES ARE TRUE AND CORRECT.

SIGNED John G. Oder

DATE 1944	MAKE OF AIRCRAFT	CLASS	TYPE	CERTIFICATE NUMBER	MAKE OF ENGINE	H. P.	REMARKS OR INSPECTOR'S SIGNATURE CERTIFICATION NUMBER AND RATING	FROM	TO	INSTRUMENT RADIO OR HOOD	DUAL AS INSTRUCTOR	DUAL AS STUDENT	SOLO DAY	SOLO NIGHT	DAILY TOTAL TIME
2/29	Consolidated	B	24H	U.S. Army	Pratt & Whitney	1200		Morrison Fld. Florida	Waller Fld. Trinidad				6 00	4 00	10 00
3-1 (2/30)	"	"	"	"	"	"		Waller Fld. Trinidad	Belem, Brazil				8 15		8 15
3-2	"	"	"	"	"	"		Belem, Brazil	Natal, Brazil				7 30		7 30
3-9	"	"	"	"	"	"		Natal, Brazil	Dakar, French West Africa				10 15		10 15
3-12	"	"	"	"	"	"		Dakar	Local				3 00		3 00
3-13	"	"	"	"	"	"		Dakar	Marrachek Africa	TIME TO FLY TO UK			7 45		7 45
3-16	"	"	"	"	"	"		Marrachek	Newquay, England	55.15			3 00	5 30	8 30
3-18	"	"	"	"	"	"		Newquay, England	Local				30		30
3-19	"	"	"	"	"	"		"	Rackheath England				2 30		2 30
3-20	"	"	"	"	"	"		Rackheath England	Watton England				1 15		1 15
3-31	"	"	"	"	"	"		Rackheath	Local				2 15		2 15
									TOTAL				52 15	9 30	61 45
									AMT. FORWARD			5 30	78 20	9 30	93 20
									TOTAL TO DATE			5 30	130 35	19 00	155 0[illegible]

I HEREBY CERTIFY THAT THE FOREGOING ENTRIES ARE TRUE AND CORRECT.

SIGNED John G. Oder

Part 2 of Lt. John G. Oder's Flight Records.

Date 1944	Make of Aircraft	Class	Type	Certificate Number	Make of Engine	H.P.	Remarks or Inspector's Signature Certification Number and Rating	Cross Country From	Cross Country To	Instrument Radio or Hood	Dual as Instructor	Dual as Student	Solo Day	Solo Night	Daily Total Time
4/1	Consolidated	B	24 H	U.S. Army	4-Pratt-Whitney	1200		Rackheath	Local	[illegible] Combat 11:45			45		45
4/8	"	"	"	"	"	"		"	"				4 30		4 30
4/10	"	"	"	"	"	"	#1	"	Bourges, France				7 00		7 00
4/12	"	"	"	"	"	"		"	Local				3 15		3 15
4/13	"	"	"	"	"	"	#2	"	Leichfeld Germany				8 10		8 10
4/15	"	"	"	"	"	"		"	Local				2 00		2 00
4/18	"	"	"	"	"	"	#3	"	Oranienburg Germany				7 45		7 45
4/21	"	"	"	"	"	"		"	Local				4 00		4 00
4/22	"	"	"	"	"	"	#4	"	~~Rackheath~~ Hamm Ger.				6 45		6 45
4/26	"	"	"	"	"	"	#5	"	Minden Germany				5 15		5 15
4/27	"	"	"	"	"	"	#6	"	Blainville France				6 15		6 15
									TOTAL				55 40		55 40
									AMT. FORWARD			5 30	130 35	19 00	155 05
									TOTAL TO DATE			5 30	186 15	19 00	210 45

I HEREBY CERTIFY THAT THE FOREGOING ENTRIES ARE TRUE AND CORRECT.

SIGNED John G. Oder

Date 1944	Make of Aircraft	Class	Type	Certificate Number	Make of Engine	H.P.	Remarks or Inspector's Signature Certification Number and Rating	Cross Country From	Cross Country To	Instrument Radio or Hood	Dual as Instructor	Dual as Student	Solo Day	Solo Night	Daily Total Time
5-1	Consolidated	B	24	U.S. Army	4-Pratt-Whitney	1200	#7	Rackheath	Noball France				6 00		6 00
5-5	"	"	"	"	"	"		Rackheath	over Channel				5 00		5 00
5-6	"	"	"	"	"	"	Left Seat	"	Local			1 20	20		1 40
5-7	"	"	"	"	"	"	#8	Rackheath	Osnabrock Germany				6 30		6 30
5-8	"	"	"	"	"	"	#9	"	Brunswick Germany				6 15		6 15
5-12	"	"	"	"	"	"	#10	"	Boehlen Germany				8 30		8 30
5-13	"	"	"	"	"	"	#11	"	Tutow Germany				7 45		7 45
5-22	"	"	"	"	"	"	Left Seat	"	Local			4 10			4 10
5-23	"	"	"	"	"	"	#12	"	Bourges France				6 45		6 45
5-28	"	"	"	"	"	"	#13	"	~~Zeost~~ Zeitz Germany				7 30		7 30
5-29	"	"	"	"	"	"	#14	"	Tutow Germany				8 45		8 45
									TOTAL			5 30	63 20		68 50
									AMT. FORWARD			5 30	186 35	19 00	210 45
									TOTAL TO DATE			11 00	249 35	19 00	279 35

I HEREBY CERTIFY THAT THE FOREGOING ENTRIES ARE TRUE AND CORRECT.

SIGNED John G. Oder

Part 3 of Lt. John G. Oder's Flight Records.

Date 1944	Make of Aircraft	Class	Type	Certificate Number	Make of Engine	H.P.	Remarks or Inspector's Signature Certification Number and Rating	Cross Country From	Cross Country To	Instrument Radio or Hood	Dual as Instructor	Dual as Student	Solo Day	Solo Night	Daily Total Time
5/31	Consolidated	B	24	U.S. Army	4-Pratt-Whitney	1200		Rackheath	Local				2 10		2 10
6/2	"	"	"	"	"	"	#15	"	Coast of France				5 30		5 30
6/3	"	"	"	"	"	"	#16	"	"				4 15		4 15
6/6	"	"	"	"	"	"	#17	"	North Coast of France				6 00		6 00
6/6	"	"	"	"	"	"	#18	"	"				7 30		7 30
6/8	"	"	"	"	"	"	#19	"	France				7 30		7 30
6/10	"	"	"	"	"	"	#20	"	Chateaudun France				6 00		6 00
6/12	"	"	"	"	"	"	#21	"	Buraux France				6 30		6 30
6/14	"	"	"	"	"	"	#22	"	Noball France				4 15		4 15
6/15	"	"	"	"	"	"	#23	"	Paris				6 00		6 00
6/18	"	"	"	"	"	"	#24	"	Hamberg				7 40		7 40
									TOTAL				63 20		63 20
									AMT. FORWARD			11 00	249 35	19 00	279 35
									TOTAL TO DATE			11 00	312 55	19 00	342 55

I HEREBY CERTIFY THAT THE FOREGOING ENTRIES ARE TRUE AND CORRECT.

SIGNED John G. Oder

Date 1944	Make of Aircraft	Class	Type	Certificate Number	Make of Engine	H.P.	Remarks or Inspector's Signature Certification Number and Rating	Cross Country From	Cross Country To	Instrument Radio or Hood	Dual as Instructor	Dual as Student	Solo Day	Solo Night	Daily Total Time
6/20	Consolidated	B	24 H	U.S. Army	4-Pratt-Whitney	1200	#25	Rackheath	Ostermoor Germany (Kiel)				6 30		6 30
6/21	"	"	"	"	"	"	#26	"	BERLIN				8 45		8 45
6/23	"	"	"	"	"	"	#27 Observer time 5:15	"	Noball France						
6/28	"	"	"	"	"	"	#28	"	Saarbrucken Germany				7 35		7 35
6/29	"	"	"	"	"	"	#29	"	Aschersleben Germany				6 50		6 50
6/30	"	"	"	"	"	"		"	Local	55		55	1 00		1 55
7/5	"	"	"	"	"	"		"	Local	40		1 00	1 20		2 20
7/7	"	"	"	"	"	"	#30	"	Lutzkendorf Germany				6 45		6 45
7/8	"	"	"	"	"	"	#31	"	Coast of Belgium				3 55		3 55
	"	"	"	"	"	"		"	Local	1 00		1 40	1 55		3 35
7/9	"	"	"	"	"	"		"	Local				x 2 15		2 15
									TOTAL	2 35		3 35	46 50		50 25
									AMT. FORWARD			11 00	312 55	19 00	342 55
									TOTAL TO DATE	2 35		14 35	359 45	19 00	393 20

I HEREBY CERTIFY THAT THE FOREGOING ENTRIES ARE TRUE AND CORRECT.

SIGNED John G. Oder

Part 4 of Lt. John G. Oder's Flight Records.

DATE	MAKE OF AIRCRAFT	CLASS	TYPE	CERTIFICATE NUMBER	MAKE OF ENGINE	H. P.	REMARKS OR INSPECTOR'S SIGNATURE CERTIFICATION NUMBER AND RATING	CROSS COUNTRY FROM	CROSS COUNTRY TO	INSTRUMENT RADIO OR HOOD	DUAL AS INSTRUCTOR	DUAL AS STUDENT	SOLO DAY	SOLO NIGHT	DAILY TOTAL TIME
7/11	Consolidated	B	24	U.S. Army	4-Pratt Whitney	1200		Rockheath	Local				1 50		1 50
7/13	"	"	"	"	"	"		Rockheath	"				3 50		3 50
7/14	"	"	"	"	"	"		"	"	30			4 15		4 15
7/15	"	"	"	"	"	"		"	"	25			3 50		3 50
7/18	"	"	"	"	"	"		"	"		4 00				4 00
7/20	"	"	"	"	"	"	#32	"	Eisenach Germany				6 40		6 40
7/21	"	"	"	"	"	"	#33	"	MUNICH				8 00		8 00
7/24	"	"	"	"	"	"	#34	"	St. Lo, France	1 45			5 45		5 45
7/25	"	"	"	"	"	"	#35	"	St. Lo, France	1 00			5 40		5 40
7/26	"	"	"	"	"	"		"	Local				40		40
8/15	"	"	"	"	"	"		"					4 10		4 10
									TOTAL	3 40	4 00		44 40		48 40
									AMT. FORWARD	2 35		14 35	359 45	19 00	393 20
									TOTAL TO DATE	6 15	4 00	14 35	404 25	19 00	442 00

I HEREBY CERTIFY THAT THE FOREGOING ENTRIES ARE TRUE AND CORRECT.

SIGNED

DATE 1944	MAKE OF AIRCRAFT	CLASS	TYPE	CERTIFICATE NUMBER	MAKE OF ENGINE	H. P.	REMARKS OR INSPECTOR'S SIGNATURE CERTIFICATION NUMBER AND RATING	CROSS COUNTRY FROM	CROSS COUNTRY TO	INSTRUMENT RADIO OR HOOD	DUAL AS INSTRUCTOR	DUAL AS STUDENT	SOLO DAY	SOLO NIGHT	DAILY TOTAL TIME
8/24	Consolidated	B	24 d	U.S. Army	4 Pratt & Whitney	1200		Rackheath-Watton-Rackheath					4 00		4 00
								COMBAT HRS -		226 45		26.05 as P/C			
								UK LOCAL		57 10					
													(CERT — NEXT PAGE →)		
								TOTAL TIME	TOTAL						
								WITH 467th	AMT. FORWARD	6 15	4 00	14 35	404 25	19 00	442 00
								Gb Group →	~~TOTAL TO DATE~~	6 15	4 00	14 35	408 25	19 00	446 00

I HEREBY CERTIFY THAT THE FOREGOING ENTRIES ARE TRUE AND CORRECT.

SIGNED

Part 5 of Lt. John G. Oder's Flight Records.

DATE	MAKE OF AIRCRAFT	CLASS	TYPE	CERTIFICATE NUMBER	MAKE OF ENGINE	H. P.	REMARKS OR INSPECTOR'S SIGNATURE CERTIFICATION NUMBER AND RATING	CROSS COUNTRY FROM	CROSS COUNTRY TO	INSTRUMENT RADIO OR HOOD	DUAL AS INSTRUCTOR	DUAL AS STUDENT	SOLO DAY	SOLO NIGHT	DAILY TOTAL TIME
									RECAP - HOURS WITH [illegible]						
				TRAINING [illegible]			389.45		TRAINING OUT OF WENDOVER, UTAH						60 35
				TOTAL [illegible]			[illegible]		" " " CASPER, WYO						26 15
									" " " HERRINGTON, KANSAS						12 [illegible]
									FLIGHT HOURS TO UNITED KINGDOM						55 15
									PRE-COMBAT TRAINING OUT OF RACKHEATH						11 45
									COMBAT HOURS AS CO-PILOT						200 40
									COMBAT HOURS AS PILOT						26 05
									UK LOCAL AS CO-PILOT						27 10
									UK LOCAL AS PILOT						30 10
									TOTAL						
									AMT. FORWARD						
									TOTAL TO DATE						

I HEREBY CERTIFY THAT THE FOREGOING ENTRIES ARE TRUE AND CORRECT.

SIGNED

MEMORANDUM DATE

4-10-44 - Mission #1 - Engine Factory - Results Good - No Opposition
4-13-44 - Mission #2 - Training Field - Results Poor - Heavy Flak over target
Two holes in airplane
4-18-44 - Mission #3 - Aircraft Factory - Results Poor - Little Opposition
4-22-44 - Mission #4 - R.R. Yards - Results Good - Heavy Flak - Ten holes in ship -
Jerry followed us home - Hectic night landing
4-26-44 - Mission #5 - Bombed thru clouds - Little Flak - Two holes
4-27-44 - Mission #6 - R.R. Yards - Results Fair - Little Flak - No Damage
5-1-44 - Mission #7 - Noball - Recalled due to weather over target - Hectic
early take off.
5-7-44 - Mission #8 - PFF Bombing of town - Flak heavy over target - Two
holes in ship.
5-8-44 - Mission #9 - PFF Bombing - Moderate Flak - First fighters -
5-109's attacked low Sqd. - Murphy's crash-landing - Two holes
5-12-44 - Mission #10 - Synthetic Oil Plant - Results Good - Heavy Flak
over Target - One Hole in ship

MEMORANDUM DATE

5-13-44 - Mission #11 - Aircraft Field & Factory - Results Fair - No Damage
5-23-44 - Mission #12 - Airfield - Results Excellent - No Opposition
5-28-44 - Mission #13 - Synthetic Oil Plant - Results Good - No Opposition - Some Fl[ak]
Lost #3 engine over target - Came Home alone
X 5-29-44 - Mission #14 - Aircraft Field & Factory - Results Fair - Heavy Flak at
bombs away - No Damage - 1st mission without Witchcraft
6-2-44 - Mission #15 - Coastal Defences - No Flak, No Opposition - Target
250 Yards inside enemy coast - PFF.
6-3-44 - Mission #16 - Coastal Defences - Ditto of 6-2-44
T 6-6-44 - Mission #17 - D-Day - Pre-Dawn T.O. - PFF bombing of Invasion Coast
just ahead of ground forces - No Opposition
T 6-6-44 - Mission #18 - 2nd time out on D-Day - Missed target, a bridge
in invasion area - Bad weather on night return - landed at Eng. field -
No Damage
T 6-8-44 - Mission #19 - Hiway bridge - Unable to find our own group - No Opposit[ion]
T 6-10-44 - Mission #20 - Airfield - Bombed thru clouds - Flak over target - No Damage

Part 6 of Lt. John G. Oder's Flight Records.

MEMORANDUM

DATE

X 6-12-44 - Mission #21 - Airfield - Excellent Results - Flak at target & on coast
No Damage - 2nd mission without Witchcraft. - Hung Bombs
6-14-44 - Mission #22 - Military Installations - Results Poor - Flak over Target - No Damage
6-15-44 - Mission #23 - Bombed secondary target - Results Fair - Flak over Paris
& Evreux (ST) - One hole.
6-18-44 - Mission #24 - Bombed LRT at Wesermund - Results Good - Flak over Target
X No Damage - With new crew - 1st without crew - 3rd without Witchcraft.
6-20-44 - Mission #25 - Synthetic Oil Plant - Results Excellent - Flak over Target.
No Damage
6-21-44 - Mission #26 - City of Berlin - Results O.K. - Heavy Flak - 6 holes -
Enemy fighters but escort kept them off. - 467th lend 8th AF.
6-23-44 - Mission #27 - PFF on Pilotless Aircraft - Results Unobserved - Some
Flak - No Damage - Rode in Waist.
X 6-28-44 - Mission #28 - RR Yards - Out of gas on two engines just before
Bombs away - Landed at fighter base. - 4th without Witchcraft
X 6-29-44 - Mission #29 - Aircraft Plant - Heavy Flak over target - No Damage
5th without Witchcraft - Rest of crew finished

X 7-7-44 - Mission #30 - Oil Plant - Results Good - Flak over
target - two holes - CP for Dickinson in #559.
X 7-8-44 - Mission #31 - Recall Weather - Flak on coast - No Damage
CP for Granfeld.
X 7-20-44 - Mission #32 - Engine Plant - Results Good - Inaccurate Flak
en route & at target - No Damage - 1st Mission as Pilot - Low on gas.
X 7-21-44 - Mission #33 - Aircraft Plant - Intense Flak over target - Hit in right
arm - Two Holes in ship - Enemy Fighters, but little friends helped - 2nd as pilot
X 7-24-44 - Mission #34 - No Bombs dropped - Weather - No Damage -
Led High Flight - 3rd as Pilot
X 7-25-44 - Mission #35 - Frags on Troops - Flak at Target - No Damage -
Led High Flight - 4th as Pilot - THE END

PARTICIPATION IN SORTIES

JOHN G. ODER (1092) has participated in a Heavy Bombardment Sortie on the following dates:

(See Back)

DATE				DATE			
4-10-44	1	Bourges, France	1	6-6-44	18	Pontaubault, France	44
4-13-44	2	Lechfeld, Germany	4	6-8-44	19	Pontaubault, France	46
4-18-44	3	Brandenburg, Germany	6	6-10-44	20	Chateudon, France	47
4-22-44	4	Hamm, Germany	10	6-12-44	21	Evreux, France	50
4-26-44	5	Paderborn, Germany	13	6-14-44	22	Beauvoir, France	51
4-27-44	6	Blainville, France	15	6-15-44	23	Guyancourt, France	52
5-1-44	7	Russeauville, France	17	6-18-44	24	Luneberg/Fossberg, Germany	53/56
5-7-44	8	Osnabruck, Germany	21	6-20-44	25	Ostermoor, Germany	58
5-8-44	9	Brunswick, Germany	22	6-21-44	26	Berlin, Germany	60
5-12-44	10	Bohlen, Germany	26	6-23-44	27	Beaumetz, France	61
5-13-44	11	Tutow, Germany	27	6-28-44	28	Saarbrucken, Germany	66
5-23-44	12	Bourges, France	31	6-29-44	29	Oschersleben, Germany	67
5-28-44	13	Zeitz, Germany	35	7-7-44	30	Lutzkendorf, Germany	72
5-29-44	14	Tutow, Germany	36	7-8-44	31	Fismes, France RECALLED	73
6-2-44	15	Stella Place, France	37	7-20-44	32	Eisenack, Germany	81
6-3-44	16	Berck, France	40	7-21-44	33	Munich, Germany	82 XX
6-6-44	17	Port-En-Bessin, France	43	7-24-44	34	Montrevil, France	83
				7-25-44	35	Montrevil, France	84

Part 7 of Lt. John G. Oder's Flight Records.

HEADQUARTERS
FOUR HUNDRED SIXTY SEVENTH BOMBARDMENT GROUP (H)
Office of the Operations Officer
AAF 145 APO 558

OPERATIONS ORDERS)
: 29 May 1945
NUMBER.........52)

46. Under authority contained in letter ETOUSA, SUBJECT: Movement Orders, Shipment 10060 , File No.-370.5 OPGC dated 27 May 45 , the following A/C and personnel assigned thereto will proceed o/a June 1945, via Valley A/D by best available air route to Bradley Field, Windsor Locks, Connecticut, thence to Camp Miles Standish, Boston, POE. Personnel will report to the AAF Base Commander at Bradley Field. AAF Personnel are being returned for the purpose of authorized TD for rest and recuperation and for further assignment.
WD Cir 260 and 356, 1944 will apply.
TDN 212/50424 FSA 1942-45 60-114 T431-01

Shipment No: 10060-JZ
Unit: 790th Bomb Sq (H) or as indicated.
Crew No: 10 of 19

Type, Model & Series: B-24H
A/C Serial No: 42-52534

NAME AND ADDRESS	GRADE	ARM OR SERV.	ASN	CREW SPEC	MCS
Jansen, Frederick J. 516 Third Ave., West Bend, Wisc.	1st Lt	AC	0-825391	Pilot	1092
Knierieman, Lorin C. Sycamore, Ohio.	1st Lt	AC	0-768123	Co-Pilot	1092
Buchmiller, Gordon A. 189 Lake Avenue, Saratoga Springs, N.Y.	F/O	AC	T-134635	Navigator	1034
McDannald, Clyde E, Jr 116 East 63rd St., New York City, N.Y.	1st Lt	AC	0-498587	Bombardier	1035
Bryan, Terry J. Brantley, Ala.	T/Sgt		14201638	Engineer	748
Burton, Louis, 1228 West 65th St., Los Angeles, Calif.	T/Sgt		39549305	Radio Opr.	757
Hayes, Howard J. 4230 S. Van Buren, Los Angeles, Calif.	S/Sgt		19175572	Gunner	611
Pilgram, Jack J. 4040 27th Ave, So. Minneapolis, Minn.	Sgt		37579887	Gunner	611
Harper, William I. Route #3, Box 23 Columbus, Miss.	Sgt		14177142	Gunner	611
Busby, Paul D. 210 North Forest Ave., Indiannapolis, Ind.	Sgt		35891966	Gunner	611

Operations/Movement Order No. 52 dated 29 May 1945, for the return of B-24 42-52534 *Witchcraft* and crewmembers to the US.

CONFIDENTIAL

467th Bomb Gp (H), Operations Orders No. 52 dated 29 May 45 Cont'd.

PASSENGERS

Name / Address	Grade	Serial No.		
Ramirez, Joe R. 871 No. Figueroa Terrace Los Angeles, Calif.	M/Sgt	19128274	X	750
Dong, George Y. 832 "C" Ave Coronado, Calif.	S/Sgt	39538285	X	747
Rhodes, James S. 55 Arch St Athens, Ga.	Cpl	34767230	X	345
Palmer, Ralph J. 700½ Cherokee St Leavenworth, Kan.	T/Sgt	6864698	X	505
Porter, Frederick R. 600 S. Edgeworth Royal Oak, Mich.	Cpl	36857304	X	901
Pattillo, John E. P.O. Box 581 So. San Antonio, Tex.	M/Sgt	6258732	X	750
Brown, Merle H. 622 Exchange St., Keokuk, Iowa.	1st Lt AC	0-1549899	X	4532
Tormey, Leonard J. Rosenberg, Tex., P.O. Box 301	Pfc	38239544	X	941
Clifton, M. G. 519 S.W. 31st. St., Oklahoma City, Okla.	S/Sgt	38022190	X	014
Sayers, Franklin, W. 400 Argyle Road Brooklyn, N.Y.	Cpl	32437121	X	754

By order of Colonel SHOWER:

WALTER R. SMITH,
Lt Col., Air Corps,
Operations Officer.

OFFICIAL:

J. E. Griggs

J. E. GRIGGS,
Capt., Air Corps,
Asst Adjutant.

Operations/Movement Order No. 52 dated 29 May 1945, listing the passengers flying in *Witchcraft* on its return to the US.

11

Additional Photographs of *Witchcraft*, the Original Flight Crew, and the Ground Maintenance Crew

Witchcraft and the original crewmembers (photograph taken at Rackheath). Rear (L to R): Sgt. Henry Kubacek (G), Sgt. Alex McClean (BTG), Sgt. Melvin Bland (RO), Sgt. Vernon Bundrock (G), Sgt. Robert McEwen (TG), and Tech Sgt. Robert DeKerf (Eng-Top Turret). Front (L to R): Lt. John Oder (CP), Lt. George Reed (P), and Lt. John Kramer (B). Lt. Charles Mintzlaff (N) is not in this photo. Also, the final nose art was not completed at the time the photograph was taken.

Staff Sgt. Henry Kubacek (original *Witchcraft* crew waist gunner).

Members of the maintenance team working on *Witchcraft* pause to pay their respects on Remembrance Day.

Witchcraft and four members of her maintenance team (L to R): Cpl. Walter Elliott, Staff Sgt. George Dong, Master Sgt. Joe Ramirez, and Sgt. Ray Betcher.

Witchcraft after the completion of 130 credited combat missions.

The cattle continue to enjoy grazing, despite having noisy planes as their neighbors.

Thursday, March 15, 1945

This Witchcraft is No Jinx

By Andy Watts
Stars and Stripes Staff Writer

Out of the shadow of the Liberator Witchcraft which they crewed to an 8th Air Force heavy bomber maintenance record—117 consecutive missions without a turnback for mechanical reasons—came M/Sgt. Jose R. Ramirez, ground-crew chief from Los Angeles, and his four crewmen, to take the spotlight at a London press conference recently for newsmen to interview a few of the war's many unsung heroes—the GIs who keep 'em flying.

One of the original planes of the 467th Bomb Group, Witchcraft has logged 735 combat hours in 11 months, carrying 35 complete separate crews and unloading 290 tons of bombs on enemy targets, while its ground crew made 17 engine changes and replaced battered tail sections four times.

Although the bomber has been riddled with more than 300 flak holes, none of the airmen has been killed or injured.

A heterogeneous group, the five crewmen represent five nationalities. Ramirez is of Mexican stock and the assistant crew chief, S/Sgt. George Y. Dong, of Coronado, Cal., is of Chinese descent.

Sgt. Raymond A. Betcher, of Mt. Clemens, Mich., and Cpl. Joseph J. Vetter, of Merrick, N.Y., are of Dutch and German parentage, respectively, while Cpl. Walter L. Elliott, of St. Louis, claims only American ancestry.

During the interview, Ramirez spoke

M/Sgt. Jose R. Ramirez

Spanish fluently with a Madrid journalist, and Dong chatted easily in Mandarin with a Chinese writer. Twice a recipient of the Bronze Star, Ramirez has also been commended by Lt. Gen. Carl A. Spaatz, USSTAF commander.

An interesting article by Andy Watts printed in the Thursday, 15 March 1945 edition of *The Stars and Stripes*.

790th Bombardment Squadron Insignia. Over and through a white disc edged black. A caricatured "flak happy" combat crewmember in a brown high-altitude flight suit, holding a basket of yellow/orange colored bombs with his left arm. A caricature with his face to the front, but with his body turned to the left, balancing on the right foot at back of three yellow/orange aerial bombs resting on the base line, while hurling a yellow/orange aerial bomb with his upraised right hand. The insignia was approved 24 July 1944.

Photo taken inside the 467*th* Group Operations Room just prior to the demolition.

Witchcraft in flight following the completion of 130 credited combat missions.

In Sicherheit!

Tausende Aachener wurden von der Partei unter falschen Vorspiegelungen verschleppt und dann auf den Landstrassen ausgesetzt. Tausende Aachener haben durch die Plünderungen der Partei, der SS, der Gestapo und verzweifelter deutscher Soldaten all ihr Hab und Gut verloren. Tausende Aachener wurden von ihren Familien versprengt und werden von ihren Lieben auf lange Zeit getrennt sein. ABER:

Tausende Aachener haben nicht den Lügen der Partei und des Nazi-Kommandeurs der Stadt geglaubt. Sie haben sich der Zwangsevakuierung widersetzt. Sie haben vom Kommandeur mutig die Übergabe der Stadt gefordert. Tausende von Aachenern suchten Zuflucht in amerikanischen Auffangs-Quartieren, die nur wenige Kilometer von Aachen entfernt waren. Sie sind von dort in ihre Heimatstadt zurückgekehrt, um am Wiederaufbau zu arbeiten. Sie sind in Sicherheit.

In Sicherheit vor Zwangsevakuierung.
In Sicherheit vor der Gestapo.
In Sicherheit vor Schanzen unter Feuer.
In Sicherheit vor Bombenangriffen.

In Sicherheit!

WG 26
12.G.21

Verteidiger von Aachen!

Der Führer hat befohlen, Aachen zu halten.

Wir werden diesen Befehl durchführen, komme, was da wolle.

Nichts kann unsere Standfestigkeit erschüttern.

Jeder Versuch des Feindes, uns von diesem Befehl abzubringen, ist einfach lächerlich. Wir wissen ganz genau, daß er nur Angst vor dem Kampf um die Stadt hat und uns auf diese billige Tour herumbringen will, nachdem ihm seine Angriffe bisher mißlungen sind. Nicht unser Blut [illegible] sein Blut will er sparen.

[illegible]shalb schlagt ihn, wo ihr ihn treffen könnt, wie bi[illegible] Starke Kräfte sind im Begriff, euch zu entlasten.

Die [illegible] auf Aachen — Deutschland [illegible] vertraut auf euch! [illegible]

Ein Todesurteil!

Nach dem 10. Oktober, als sich die Garnison von Aachen in einem hoffnungslosen Zustand befand, liess der Nazi-Kommandeur der Stadt, Oberst Wilck, unter seinen Soldaten das abgebildete Flugblatt verteilen. Darin hiess es: „Der Führer hat befohlen, Aachen zu halten." Darin hiess es: „Starke Kräfte sind im Begriffe, Euch zu entlasten." Der Kommandeur wusste, dass Aachen abgeschnitten und kein Entsatz möglich war. Aber er vollzog dennoch das Todesurteil an seinen Soldaten. Genau so sind jetzt andere Kommandeure im Begriffe, ihren Soldaten zu sagen: „Der Führer hat befohlen . . ." Genau so sagen jetzt andere Kommandeure: „Starke Kräfte sind im Begriffe, Euch zu entlasten." Wer diesen Parteifanatikern glaubt, der unterschreibt sein eigenes Todesurteil. Wer ehrenhafte Kriegsgefangenschaft wählt, der rettet sich für ein besseres Deutschland.

Wer auf Entsatz wartet, unterschreibt sein eigenes
Todesurteil.

Copy of the front and back of a leaflet as dropped over German Occupied Europe by the 467th.

Photo taken by the author of the front part of a painting of *Witchcraft* by aviation artist Mike Bailey. Note the intense detail of the fuselage panels and rivets, the pilot, top turret gunner, and nose gunner wearing flight helmets, goggles, Mae West, oxygen masks, and parachute harness.

Photo taken by Perry Watts at the 467th Group Reunion in October 1995. Col. Albert J. Shower is standing on the extreme left and Joe Ramirez is seated on a chair. On the extreme right are Joseph Famme (Consolidated Project Engineer) and standing next to him (on his right) is Bill Chana (Consolidated Flight Test Engineer).

Part of the Consolidated Aircraft Company factory at San Diego in 1995.

Left to Right: Col. Albert J. Shower, Joe Ramirez, Jill Watts, and George Dong, taken in San Diego in October 1995.

Joe Ramirez (center) and his friend Pete Petris (right) attending a US Veterans Day function. Pete Petris also served with the 467th as radio operator in the control tower at Rackheath. Joe and Pete were close friends from the time they were based at Rackheath and during the postwar years until Joe's death.

12

Interesting Articles and Correspondence From 467th Group Veterans

Perry Watts

From: "Perry Watts"
To: "jim bates"
Sent: Sunday, January 30, 2011 11:33 AM
Subject: Re: Ray Betcher

Dear Janice,

I know you sent me an email regarding your Dad's response regarding the question of the color of the engine cowlings on 'Witchcraft and well remember that he told you that when the cowlings had to be replaced they used whatever was available and were some were painted Olive Drab, Neutral Gray or unpainted and in Natural Aluminum Finish BUT NEVER EVER IN RED OR WHITE. Would you please write and confirm that as unfortunately my external hard drive 'crashed' and I lost such information as you sent me. I certainly do not like bothering you at such a time as this as your Dear Dad's health is much more important and quite rightly you have that to attend to, but when you happen to just have a spare couple of minutes sure would like to hear from you.

In the meantime both Jill and James (he is here visiting us just for the wee-end) and I send Our Very Best Wishes to Your Dad and also to both you and Jim. We will pray for Dear Ray and hope that all goes well for him.

Our Love and best wishes,

Perry

Information received from Ray Betcher via his daughter Janice, confirming the engine cowlings on *Witchcraft* were never red. Ray was a member of Joe Ramirez's ground crew team that was responsible for the maintenance of that particular B-24 from 15 January 1944, when it was delivered to the Group at Wendover, Utah, through 10 June 1945, when it lifted off from Rackheath, England, on its homebound flight to the US.

Perry Watts

From: "Perry Watts"
To: "Perry Watts"
Sent: 22 June 2012 11:32
Subject: Fw: Witchcraft Cowlings

----- Original Message -----
From: "jim bates" <janicebates
To: "Perry Watts"
Sent: Sunday, January 30, 2011 1:34 PM
Subject: Fw: Witchcraft Cowlings

--- On Thu, 11/4/10, jim bates <janicebates wrote:

> From: jim bates
> Subject: Witchcraft Cowlings
> To: "Perry Watts"
> Date: Thursday, November 4, 2010, 2:40 PM
> The Official Answer is: The
> cowlings on Witchcraft were olive drab to start, but later
> on they were getting unpainted ones. At no time were they
> EVER red, according to Dad (Ray Betcher). He also said
> that by the 100th mission, 12 engines had been changed.
> But by the 130th mission, there had been 25 engines changes
> because they were getting rebuilt ones that were not lasting
> as long.
>

Jeff Malet/Staff Photographer

HAVING HIS CAKE: Bob McEwen receives a cake with a Witchcraft bomber symbol on it during a dedication at Yanks Museum at Chino Airport on Thursday. McEwen donated many items related to the B-24 aircraft. McEwen was a tail gunner on the plane during World War II.

Witchcraft continues to cast its spell

B-24 memorabilia to be displayed at Chino Airport

By Joe Florkowski
Staff Writer

Bob McEwen still has no idea why he and his crew mates decided to call their B-24 bomber Witchcraft before flying to England during World War II.

When they flew the ship across the Atlantic in April 1944, the crew also had no idea that the name would cause some fear among the superstitious English.

"A lot of the English were afraid to go near the airplane because of its name," McEwen said. "That was a no-no to them."

"We tried to think of a name that would scare the Germans but it ended up scaring the English," he said.

Despite the fears of the English, Witchcraft proved to be luckier than many other American planes during the

is proud to say his plane never turned back because of mechanical problems.

"It had a great life," McEwen said.

He served 26 missions aboard Witchcraft from April and June 1944 as a tail gunner. After his tour ended, McEwen collected many items and artifacts from the plane and donated them to nine museums across the country. He recently donated a large number of his photographs and paintings to the Yanks Air Museum at Chino Airport, which arranged a separate room to store McEwen's memories. The room will soon be open to the public.

The museum arranged the room after McEwen, a former Ontario resident, called and asked if he could donate the items, said Yanks historian Tom Schroeter.

The Yanks staff was impressed by the amount of detailed information McEwen

had developed between McEwen, his crew and a 16-year-old English boy, Perry Watts, during the war, Schroeter said.

Many of the photographs in the exhibit show McEwen and the crew but also include some of Watts. There are also several paintings created by Watts.

Watts, 72, has remained friends with McEwen and the other crew members since the war and is currently working on a book about their time in England.

Growing up near the Witchcraft's air base, Watts was fascinated with the planes and pilots during the war.

"We saw history being made," Watts said from his home in England.

Since nobody was killed or injured on Witchcraft, it was a pity that the U.S. government did not retain the aircraft, Watts said.

"I think Witchcraft was the most famous of the lot," he said.

Bob McEwen has a very enjoyable day when donating his memorabilia to the "Yanks Air Museum" in Chino, California.

Tail gunner on B-24 Liberator donates mementos to museum

By JOE FLORKOWSKI
Staff Writer

CHINO — Bob McEwen still has no idea why he and his crewmates decided to call their B-24 bomber Witchcraft before flying to England during World War II.

When they flew the ship across the Atlantic in April 1944, the crew also had no idea that the name would cause some fear among the superstitious English.

"A lot of the English were afraid to go near the airplane because of its name," McEwen said. "That was a no-no to them."

"We tried to think of a name that would scare the Germans, but it ended up scaring the English," he said.

Despite the fears of the English, Witchcraft proved to be luckier than many other American planes during the war. The plane survived 130 missions into Germany and more than 300 bullet holes from enemy aircraft. McEwen, 78, is proud to say his plane never turned back because of mechanical problems.

"It had a great life," McEwen said.

Bob McEwen talks with friends Thursday before a ceremony at Yanks Air Museum at Chino Airport.

He served 26 missions aboard Witchcraft from April and June 1944 as a tail gunner. After his tour ended, McEwen collected many items and artifacts from the plane and donated them to nine museums across the country. He recently donated a large number of his photographs and paintings to the Yanks Air Museum at Chino Airport, which arranged a separate room to store McEwen's memories.

The room will soon be open to the public.

The museum arranged the room after McEwen, a former Ontario resident, called and asked if he could donate the items, said Yanks historian Tom Schroeter.

The Yanks staff was impressed by the amount of detailed information McEwen had about Witchcraft, Schroeter said. But when designing the room, museum staff wanted to show the friendship that had developed between McEwen, his crew and a 16-year-old English boy, Perry Watts, during the war, Schroeter said.

Many of the photographs in the exhibit show McEwen and the crew but also include some of Watts. There are also several paintings created by Watts.

Watts, 72, has remained friends with McEwen and the other crew members since the war and is working on a book about their time in England.

Growing up near Witchcraft's air base, Watts was fascinated with the planes and pilots during the war, he said.

"We saw history being made," Watts said from his home in England.

Since nobody was killed or injured on Witchcraft, it was a pity that the U.S. government did not retain the aircraft, Watts said.

"I think Witchcraft was the most famous of the lot," he said.

TOM WAS HERE TODAY WITH THIS ARTICAL
FROM THE SAN BERNARDINO SUN, IN SAN BERNARDINO, CA
WILL ALSO SEND YOU COPIES IF YOU CAN GET THEM
ON YOUR COMPUTER.
IF NOT LET TOM KNOW AND HE WILL MAIL THEM
TO YOU.
HOPE YOU HAD FUN IN LONDON —
5-24-2001

Bob McEwen has a very enjoyable day when donating his memorabilia to the "Yanks Air Museum" in Chino, California.

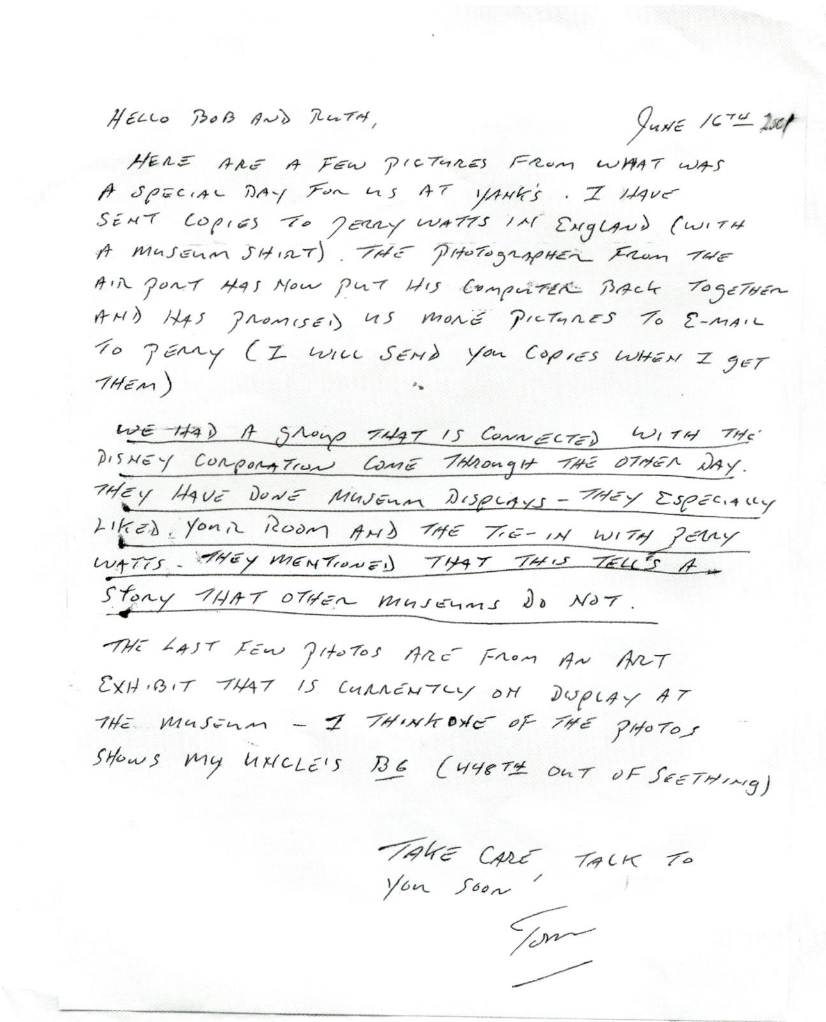

HELLO BOB AND RUTH, JUNE 16TH 2001

HERE ARE A FEW PICTURES FROM WHAT WAS A SPECIAL DAY FOR US AT YANK'S. I HAVE SENT COPIES TO JERRY WATTS IN ENGLAND (WITH A MUSEUM SHIRT). THE PHOTOGRAPHER FROM THE AIR PORT HAS NOW PUT HIS COMPUTER BACK TOGETHER AND HAS PROMISED US MORE PICTURES TO E-MAIL TO JERRY (I WILL SEND YOU COPIES WHEN I GET THEM)

WE HAD A GROUP THAT IS CONNECTED WITH THE DISNEY CORPORATION COME THROUGH THE OTHER DAY. THEY HAVE DONE MUSEUM DISPLAYS - THEY ESPECIALLY LIKED YOUR ROOM AND THE TIE-IN WITH JERRY WATTS. THEY MENTIONED THAT THIS TELL'S A STORY THAT OTHER MUSEUMS DO NOT.

THE LAST FEW PHOTOS ARE FROM AN ART EXHIBIT THAT IS CURRENTLY ON DISPLAY AT THE MUSEUM - I THINK ONE OF THE PHOTOS SHOWS MY UNCLE'S B6 (448TH OUT OF SEETHING)

TAKE CARE, TALK TO YOU SOON'

TOM

Copy of a letter dated 16 June 2001 received by Bob McEwen from his friend Tom.

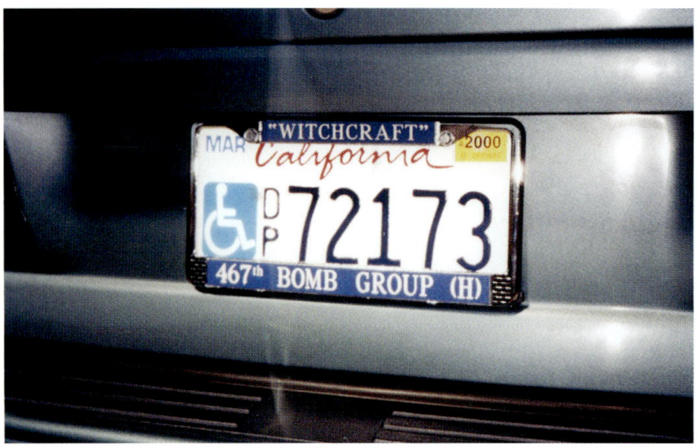

Photograph of Bob McEwen's license plate.

Photograph of the *Witchcraft* patch that Bob McEwen painted on his flight jacket.

8 March 02

Dear Jill & Perry

Received your most welcomed letter of 7 Feb. As always we are very pleased to hear from you and to read that both of you are still able to get around and enjoy a few of lifes pleasures. We are pleased to report that both of us are doing quite well despite our old age and ailments. We are looking forward to see both of you at the next reunion in Savannah, Ga. It will be wonderful to see both of you again.

We have been enjoying a wonderful mild winter until to day. It is snowing cats and dogs to day. 12" to 15" due to day ☹. I'll have to dust off the snow blower.

Now about the five questions you are concerned about.

Note? Myra said she had a teacher by that name + he was German.

#1 I cannot remember what nationality Joe Vetter claimed to be. I shall try to find out.

#2 I don't remember if the word "Witchcraft" was decided upon or who painted the word Witchcraft on our aircraft. Somebody from the paint shop at Rackheath did it shortly after we arrived there. If Joe were around, I'm sure he would know.

#3 I do not believe that the "Witch" went on any tour of the USA. The only photo I have of her after her return to the states

(OVER)

2.

is the enclosed picture of a woman in coveralls pointing up to the number of bombs that Joe Ramirez painted on the pilot side of the A/C.

#4. Enclosed is a article about the Ford plant in Ypsilanti, Michigan.

#5. I was not the Flight Engineer on the mission that John Oder mentioned in the A/C's log book "Out of gas on two engines" just before bombs away. I cannot dispute John's entry in the A/C's log book since I wasn't there. Usually I assisted the co pilot in the write up of A/C's problems after each mission. I doubt a B24 could fly that distance on two engines at full power. I beleive that entry was incorrect. I wonder if we could find out who the flight engineer was on that mission? I have my theory about this entry made by John Oder. I had completed my 30th mission as a substitue flight engineer on either "Super Wolf" or "Tangerine". I was the 1st airman to complete 30 missions in the 467th Gp. Lt Col. Smith, the C.O. of the 790th informed me that I could not fly my 31st mission with my regular crew on their 30th mission. I really had mixed emotions about that decision. As I stood near the main runway watching the "Witch" take off on their last mission. I spent the afternoon at the hard stand with Joe & some of the ground crew sweating out their return. When the "Witch" failed to return, we all became very

3.

upset, thinking that they may have been shot down. We learned later that they had to land at another airfield near the coast of southern England due to fuel shortage. No need to tell you how releived we all were. I don't remember who the flight engineer on that mission. Would you be able to acquire that data?

#6 Regarding Tokyo fuel tanks. The 250 gal. wing tip tanks were refered to as Tokyo tanks. The flight engineer was required to transfer the fuel from both wing tip tanks (a total of 500 gals) into the main fuel cells as soon as possible. All fuel cells were self sealing type fuel cells. In flight the 4 Pratt & Whitney 1200 HP engines consumed approx. 250 gals/hr. It seems that the tanks got that name from the Asian theater, so I was told.

I hope that the enclosed info. will satisfy some of your questions. It's been a long time since they occured. We can discuss them further when we get together at the next reunion.

I wonder if you have heard about the book written by Stephen E. Ambrose: The Wild Blue – The men & boys who flew the B24's over Germany. I enjoyed it very much.

Take care of each other & write if you can find the time to do so dear friend. Your Dear Friends

Bob + Myra

Copy of a letter dated 8 March 2002 that Bob DeKerf wrote to the author.

13

Statistical Data and Relative Information Plus Photographs

1. Number of combat missions flown including the seven recalled and not credited -- 137
2. Number of combat missions credited including the six recalled -- 130
3. Group combat mission numbers relating to the seven missions recalled and not credited
- missions #9, 17, 19, 24, 68, 145 and "X" (mission on 17 February 1945)
4. Group combat mission numbers relating to the six missions recalled and given a credit rating - missions #3, 63, 73, 83, 106 and 220
5. *Witchcraft* was allocated to 790th Squadron of the 467th Bombardment Group and flew all combat missions with the 790th except on one occasion when it was loaned to the 788th Squadron on 19 April 1944 and flown on Group mission #7 by Lt. James A. Roden and Crew #9.
6. The number of pilots and crews that flew *Witchcraft* on combat missions on one or more occasions was 40.
7. No flight crew personnel were KIA or injured while flying missions on *Witchcraft*.
8. Total time of flight to cover the seven "legs" on the flight from Morrison Field, Florida, to Rackheath (depart 29 February and arrive 20 March 1944) was 54 hours 45 minutes.
9. Total flight for the 130 credited combat missions flown, including the six recalled (467th Group mission #3, 63,73, 83, 106, and 220) was 837 hours 15 minutes and total gallonage used for those 130 combat missions was 238,683 gallons
10. Total number of flight for the seven missions flown that were not given a credit rating (467th Group mission #9, 17, 19, 24, 68, 145 and "X" mission on 17 February 1945) was 29 hours 23 minutes. Total gallonage used was 9,225 gallons.
11. Number of engines replaced up to 100th combat mission on 14 January 1945 was twelve and the total number of engines replaced for all missions was twenty-five.
12. Total tonnage of bombs dropped on targets on the 124 combat missions was 304 tons. The figure includes both explosive GP bombs and Incendiaries and also the 660 gallons of Napalm (approximately three tons) bombs on the Group mission #216 to Royan, France, on 15 April 1945. (Note: 124 combat missions relate to when the targets were bombed, plus six missions recalled and credited, plus the seven recalled missions not credited = 137 missions flown.)
13. During the latter part of 1944 the original open waist gun windows were modified by using a field kit comprising of a three-piece window that was fitted over the waist opening and that modification to *Witchcraft* was carried out on the base at Rackheath.
14. The RCM - Radar Counter Measure – referred to as the "Carpet Blinker Antenna" device was fitted to *Witchcraft* in the latter part of 1944 (probably in October or November 1944).
15. Thanks to the thoughtfulness and kind generosity of Mr. Nick Hovey and his company, Tilia Properties, which own a sizeable number of the remaining

buildings related to the 467th in Rackheath, a number of local roads have been named and maintained in honor of and as a tribute to the Bombardment Group: Albert Shower Road in memory of the former Base Commanding Officer; the road named *Witchcraft* Way leading to the beautifully restored control tower; and Ramirez Way in memory of *Witchcraft*'s Crew Chief and Master Sergeant Joe Ramirez.

"Witchcraft Way" road sign on the former Rackheath airfield. On the left is Ray Betcher (Mechanic on Joe Ramirez's team), while on the right is Norman Felbinger (former pilot of Crew #20, 788th Squadron).

Albert Shower Road at Rackheath, with Norman Felbinger and author Perry Watts.

Presentation of the painting of *Witchcraft* displayed in the restored control tower at Rackheath (L to R): Ray Betcher, Nick Hovey (Chairman of Tilia Properties), and Norman Felbinger, 2008.

Bob McEwen looking at the interior of the rear gun turret on a B-24.

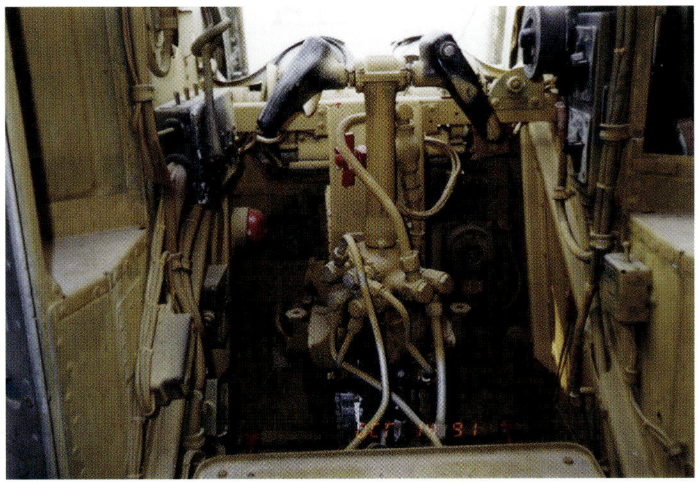

A view of the interior of the rear gun turret on a B-24; note the abandon airplane warning bell at center left.

14

Witchcraft Reminders

There are paintings, photographs, and models; the room dedicated to Bob McEwen at "The Yanks Air Museum" in Chino, California; and of course we are fortunate to have the Collings Foundation B-24 painted in *Witchcraft* colors—all are a reminder of this famous plane.

Photo taken by Perry Watts of the room at "The Yanks Air Museum," Chino, California, which is dedicated to Bob McEwen (tail gunner on the original crew of *Witchcraft*).

Bob McEwen presenting Perry Watts with a .50-caliber shell and a firing pin that came from one of the guns in the tail turret of *Witchcraft*.

The 50 caliber shell and firing pin from *Witchcraft*, plus Bob McEwen's Air Gunner's Badge (Wings).

B24-H-15 FO 42-52534 *Witchcraft*
As it was at the end.